D0003632

Lori McWilliams

Psychotherapy of the
Brain-Injured Patient

A NORTON PROFESSIONAL BOOK

Psychotherapy of the Brain-Injured Patient

RECLAIMING THE SHATTERED SELF

Laurence Miller, Ph.D.

W. W. NORTON & COMPANY · *NEW YORK* · LONDON

Line drawings from *Structure of the Human Brain: A Photographic Atlas*, 2nd ed., by Stephen J. DeArmond, Madeline M. Fusco, & Maynard M. Dewey. Copyright © 1976 by Oxford University Press, Inc. Reprinted by permission.

Copyright © 1993 by Laurence Miller

All rights reserved.

Printed in the United States of America.

The text of this book was composed in English Times. Composition by Bytheway Typesetting Services, Inc.

Library of Congress Cataloging-in-Publication Data
Miller, Laurence, 1951–
    Psychotherapy of the brain-injured patient : reclaiming the shattered self / Laurence Miller.
        p.   cm.
    Includes bibliographical references and index.
    ISBN 0-393-70158-1
    1. Brain damage — Patients — Mental health.   2. Brain damage — Patients — Rehabilitation.   3. Psychotherapy.   I. Title.
II. Title: Psychotherapy of the brain injured patient.
    [DNLM: 1. Brain Injuries — therapy.   2. Cognition.
3. Psychotherapy.   WL 354 M648p]
RC451.4.B73M55   1993
617.4'81044 — dc20   DNLM/DLC
for Library of Congress   92-48297   CIP

W. W. Norton & Company, Inc., 500 Fifth Avenue, New York, N.Y. 10110

W. W. Norton & Company, Ltd., 10 Coptic Street, London WC1A 1PU

2   3   4   5   6   7   8   9   0

P9-DHL-379

For those men and women,
boys and girls,
past and present,
whose extraordinary courage
is a beacon in the night:
You know who you are.

And for
Gerry and Melissa.

Contents

IV. SPECIAL POPULATIONS

V. THE ROAD AHEAD

VI. BROADER IMPLICATIONS

Preface

EVEN IN THIS SO-CALLED "Decade of the Brain," there exists within clinical psychology and psychiatry an unfortunate tradition of dichotomizing mental disorders into "organic" vs. "functional." Patients with psychological disorders are said to be amenable to psychotherapy, perhaps supplemented by medication for symptom control, while organic patients — well, they need something else, right? But what?

Sadly, most brain-injured patients are treated by the mental health care system as if they somehow lacked individual personalities before their injuries, and are now expected to behave in accordance with textbook descriptions of "organic brain syndrome" — a unitary syndromic monolith with a single clinical presentation, calling for a single treatment approach. If anything, most discussions of intervention after brain injury are framed in terms of cognitive rehabilitation — retraining language, memory, attention, and other functions — with rather less focus on the emotional, personal, psychodynamic, and existential aspects of recovery from brain damage that psychotherapy should properly address.

Over the years of working with brain-injured patients, it became clear to me that these so-called "organics" need psychotherapy at least as much as, if not more than, the traditional clinical groups that psychotherapists are used to working with. Moreover, to have a truly positive and enduring effect, therapy should go beyond the passive, hand-holding type of counseling that many clinicians mistakenly believe is sufficient for this group to help them "adjust" to their disability. In many cases, the types of personal psychological changes produced in these patients through psychotherapy can be profound and long-lasting—if the clinician knows how to deal with them.

In this spirit, *Psychotherapy of the Brain-Injured Patient* offers both a theoretical rationale and a practical clinical guide for doing psychotherapy with this challenging group of patients. One aim is to demystify and explicate organic brain impairment for the psychotherapist, because—let's admit it—many traditionally trained therapists may be spooked by brain-injured patients, firstly, because of the strange presentation they often make, and secondly, because the clinician may feel unknowledgeable and therefore incompetent to help these patients.

But good psychotherapy is good psychotherapy, and, indeed, the broad fundamentals of effective intervention apply to virtually all patient populations—brain injury patients are no exception. However, as good clinicians recognize, it is equally true that we must adapt our therapeutic approaches, techniques, and processes to the particular type of patient being treated, whether psychotic or depressed patients, alcohol and drug abusers, patients with psychosomatic disorders, or culturally different patients—again, the same applies to brain-injured patients.

Thus, if the skilled psychotherapist can understand the basics of brain injury and its effects on the patient's personality and larger psychosocial world, he or she can bring to bear the knowledge, training, clinical intuition, and other therapeutic skills that have made him or her an effective healer with other patients. As a result, more brain-injured patients may feel encouraged to seek out the help they need.

In this book, I've tried to integrate and summarize the diverse literatures tying together neuropsychology, personality, and psychotherapy. The design is for each chapter to review the neuropsychodynamic and biopsychosocial factors surrounding the particular clinical topic, and then offer practical guidelines for implementing effective therapeutic approaches. In addition to dealing with such traditional aspects of individual psychotherapy as support, interpretation, insight, behavioral change, and the therapeutic relationship, this volume covers the special problems and issues that arise with the brain-injured population, such as aggression and impulsivity, alcohol and drug abuse, chronic pain and somatization, sex and relationships, vocational and forensic issues, and the role of the family and significant others. This book should not be seen as a substitute for actual on-line clinical experience with these patients, but I hope it can smooth the way for competent therapists to work with these individuals.

Finally, consistent with my philosophy that there is no hard line between "organic" and "functional" psychopathology, one further purpose of this book is to show how the lessons learned from effective psychotherapy with brain-injured patients can be generalized and applied to the treatment of virtually all patients—the more traditional, workaday psychotherapy cases—who come to us for help. In this sense, the present volume is an extension of my previous and ongoing work at elaborating a comprehensive neuropsychodynamic model of personality and psychotherapy.

This book owes both its substance and its spirit to a number of personal as well as more academic efforts and influences. The work of the late Leonard Small is an inspiration to anyone attempting to present a model of brain injury psychotherapy that is at once clinically rigorous and trenchantly humane. My thanks and appreciation to Odie Bracy III, Sandy Owens, and the editorial faculty of the *Journal of Cognitive Rehabilitation* in whose pages many of this book's ideas were first developed. Once again, the tireless energy of literary agent John Ware in securing appropriate outlets for my ideas is gratefully acknowledged. The editorial support of Norton Professional Books Editor Susan Barrows Munro and Associate Editor Margaret Farley has made the writing and refining of this book a pleasure. The moral support of my family, Joan and Halle, has made possible the opportunity to devote the necessary hours to this task, and my gratitude to them transcends the printed word.

My affiliation with various local and national support and advocacy groups, including head injury, stroke, brain tumor, epilepsy, multiple sclerosis, Alzheimer's disease, Tourette syndrome, and attention deficit disorder, has been a source of great understanding about the effects of different types of brain syndromes on the nitty-gritty aspects of everyday life. In particular, the growth, in less than two years, of the South Florida Brain Tumor Association from a handful of strangers to a nationally-recognized organization is a tribute to the awesome dedication of its members.

Finally, although it may have become trite for clinicians to explicitly acknowledge the influence of their patients in books of this type, many of my own patients have provided me with insight, both practical and philosophical, that no textbook or teacher could possibly convey. It takes real guts to pick yourself up after a brain injury or similar blow to the self; this book salutes that effort.

Psychotherapy of the Brain-Injured Patient

PART I

The Syndrome

CHAPTER 1

Traumatic Events: Causes and Mechanisms of Brain Injury

IN THE UNITED STATES ALONE, traumatic brain injuries account for an estimated 400,000 new hospital admissions a year, with approximately one million people suffering from their effects at any given time (Slagle, 1990). This chapter will provide an overview of brain functioning and discuss those aspects of the pathophysiology and neuropsychology of brain injury that psychotherapists who work with these patients should understand.

THE BRAIN: AN OVERVIEW

Although this is not primarily a textbook of neuropsychology, understanding the clinical phenomenology of brain injury necessarily involves some familiarity with the fundamental principles of brain functioning. This section will provide a review of basic functional neuroanatomy relevant to the understanding of brain injury and its effects (see Figure). More comprehensive accounts of neuropsychology may be found in Dimond (1980), Hecaen and Albert (1978), Heilman and Valenstein (1985), Joseph (1990), Kolb and Whishaw (1985), Luria (1980), and Walsh (1978).

The Brainstem:
Consciousness and General Life Maintenance

The brainstem consists of a "stalk" of nerve cells and nerve tracts, which begins at the junction of the upper spinal cord and extends upward into the

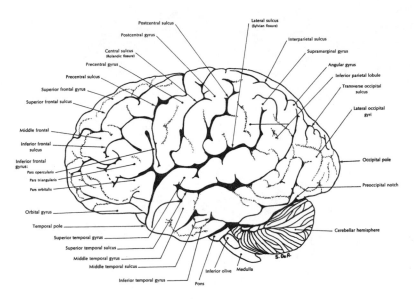

FIGURE 1:   Lateral surface of the brain

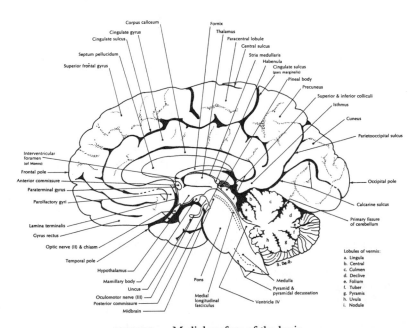

FIGURE 2:   Medial surface of the brain

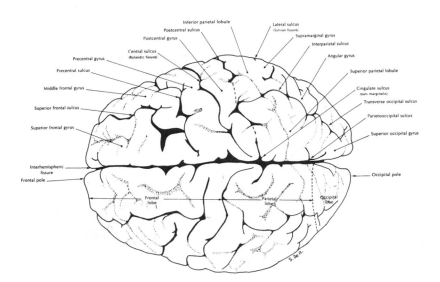

FIGURE 3:   Superior surface of the brain

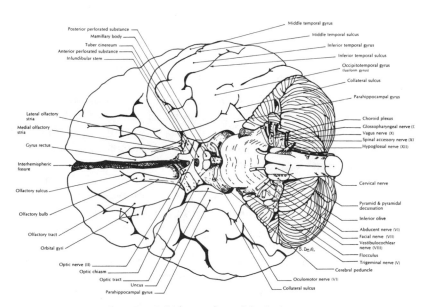

FIGURE 4:   Inferior surface of the brain

core of the brain itself. The brainstem is mainly responsible for the basic life-sustaining functions of breathing, heart rate, sleep, and wakefulness. Extensive damage to the lower brainstem usually causes death. Mystery and crime novel buffs may be interested to learn that shooting oneself in the mouth is a particularly effective form of suicide because a gun barrel at jaw level directs the bullet through the brainstem. Similarly, a bullet to the lower back of the head—what the tabloids refer to as an "execution-style" slaying—is so precisely lethal for the same reason.

The brainstem is also important for maintaining normal states of consciousness. Being "knocked out" by a blow to the head typically results from the sudden compression and shearing effects exerted on the brainstem by the force of the blow being transmitted centripetally through the brain substance and/or the sudden bending, turning, or twisting of the neck. If the disturbance causes no serious physical damage to the brainstem, consciousness soon returns. With more extensive physical injury, the period of unconsciousness can be much longer.

Events elsewhere in the brain can affect the brainstem's regulation of consciousness, as when pressure in the cranial cavity from a blood clot or fluid build-up causes secondary pressure on the brainstem. In addition, the brainstem contributes to the processes of attention while awake and the intact processing of incoming sensory information. Effects on these attentional processes may be seen long after consciousness per se has apparently returned to normal. In these cases the person is "awake," but may seem dazed or confused.

The Subcortex: Motivation and Emotion

Here, we're mainly concerned with the brain's *limbic system*, a collection of neuron clusters and fiber tracts that regulate a person's ability to experience and express emotional states in a normal way. Damage to these structures may produce a marked propensity for emotional outbursts, such as rage attacks or crying jags. Mood swings may occur, along with fluctuating episodes of increased and decreased drive and motivation. Extreme apathy may alternate with bouts of frenetic, if aimless, activity. Disorders of sexual drive and expression are sometimes seen. In addition, certain limbic structures are important in memory, especially the initial processing and registration of information in the memory store.

The structures of the limbic system are among the most electrophysiologically excitable in the brain, and many posttraumatic seizures have their origin here. Since a number of important limbic structures lie at the tips of the brain's frontal and temporal lobes (see below), they are particularly prone to injury in head trauma. This may be why memory problems and emotional/behavioral changes are among the most commonly reported complaints even years after brain injury.

Other parts of the subcortex include the *basal ganglia*, a system of structures involved in the regulation of movement and drive to action. The *cerebellum*, while not strictly regarded as a subcortical structure, lies at the base of the brain and is primarily responsible for the coordination of precision voluntary movements. Other subcortical structures include the *thalamus*, which is a major subcortical sensory-motor-affective relay station, and the *hypothalamus*, which regulates basic functions such as hunger, thirst, sex drive, sleep, and emotionality, and which also controls the body's endocrine hormone system via the pituitary gland (see Parker, 1990, for an account of the possible neuroendocrine effects of traumatic brain injury). Damage to any of these structures by brain injury may produce symptoms that range from subtle to dramatic and must be properly diagnosed by the evaluating team.

The Cortex:
Thinking and Perceiving, Planning and Acting

The human cerebral cortex allows us to fine-tune our perceptions and actions, to use spoken and written language, and to think, reason, plan, evaluate, act, and remember in an adaptive way. Any one or a combination of these abilities may be affected by generalized cerebral impairment after brain injury, but in many cases, focal damage to a particular lobe or hemisphere of the brain may produce specific patterns of deficit. As a rule, more focal deficits are seen in cases of stroke or brain tumor (see Chapter 9), while the effects of traumatic brain injury tend to be more diffuse; however, exceptions occur.

Left Hemisphere   This is the more analytic, more "rational," more verbal side of the brain. In most people, the language systems of the brain are on this side. Damage to the left hemisphere may result in difficulties in speaking, comprehending, reading, writing, arithmetic calculation, verbal reasoning, verbal memory, and any task that requires the rapid analysis of many details over short spaces of time. Emotionality, irritability, and an agitated type of depression may be seen.

Right Hemisphere   Spatial thinking, integration of parts into wholes, recognition of faces, musical appreciation and perception, spatial memory, and the analysis of the emotional and inflective aspects of language—called *prosody*—are the tasks of this hemisphere. Damage may result in the person getting lost easily, in an inability to remember people's faces or other visually-oriented material, or to produce or appreciate drawings or musical pieces, and sometimes in a lack of attention to the left side of space. Emotional blandness and unawareness of, or denial of, physical and cognitive deficits—called *anosognosia*—may also occur, sometimes as part of a "flat" depressive syndrome.

The cerebral cortex of each hemisphere is divided into four lobes. Focal damage to any of these may produce characteristic symptoms and syndromes of impairment:

Frontal Lobe

Abstract reasoning, planning, judgment, evaluation, volition, control of complex movement, expressive language (speech and writing), goal-directedness of actions, flexibility in thinking and behavior, and social appropriateness.

Parietal Lobe

Appreciation of bodily sensation, sensory-motor integration, body image, arithmetic (left hemisphere) and spatial (right hemisphere) reasoning, integration and interpretation of input from the different senses.

Temporal Lobe

Hearing and higher-order auditory processing, oral language comprehension (left hemisphere), musical appreciation (right hemisphere), verbal memory (left hemisphere) and visuospatial memory (right hemisphere), emotional experience and expression.

Occipital Lobe

Vision and higher-order visual processing, reading (left hemisphere), recognition of faces (right hemisphere).

The Brain as a Dynamic, Interactive System

Although we speak of the brain anatomically as being divided into hemispheres, lobes, systems, and so on, all parts of the brain ordinarily interact closely with one another to produce the ongoing complex range of activities we each engage in at any given moment. For example, being able to understand and utilize the information in this chapter depends on your ability to sustain (brainstem) and direct (frontal lobes) attention; to understand the verbally (left temporal) and pictorially (right occipital) presented material; to encode and retain this material in memory (right and left temporal lobes, limbic system); to appreciate both the literal, informational content (left hemisphere) and suggestive, metaphorical innuendo (right hemisphere) of the text; to be able to call up from memory whatever pieces of information from this chapter you may need and productively apply them to your particular clinical cases (frontal, temporal, and parietal lobes), and so on. This interactive complexity is why brain injuries — which rarely obey the localizational maps of the neuroanatomists — can and do produce a wide range of symptoms. Each case of brain injury is likely to be somewhat unique, and each requires careful individual evaluation.

PATHOPHYSIOLOGICAL MECHANISMS IN BRAIN INJURY

This section will deal mainly with traumatic brain injury. (Note: In most modern usages the terms "traumatic brain injury" and "head injury" are used interchangeably, and this will be the practice of the present book, except where stated otherwise.) Discussions of stroke and brain tumor pathophysiology can be found in Chapter 9. The basics of brain injury pathophysiology will be reviewed here. More comprehensive coverages may be found in Adams and Victor (1977), Binder (1986), Friedman (1983), Grubb and Coxe (1978), Leestma (1991), Lishman (1978), Slagle (1990), Teasdale and Mendelow (1984), Wood (1987), and the present section is adapted mainly from these sources.

Open vs. Closed Head Injury

In an *open head injury* the skull has been penetrated and there is contact between brain tissue and the outside environment. Typical examples include gunshots and stab wounds or blows from other sharp objects. In such cases, the physical force of the trauma may be deflected through the brain tissue to the outside, as in a bullet passing through the head. In a *closed head injury* there has been no such penetration; the force of the trauma is transferred almost directly to the brain within the closed, bony space of the skull. Consequently, there may actually be more damage with a closed head injury than with an open one, depending on other aspects of the injury.

Unconsciousness is actually more common with closed than with open head injuries, again, depending on overall severity and other factors. Typical examples include crashing against a windshield or dashboard, or being struck on the head with a blunt weapon. As a general rule, focal damage is more likely to result from open head injuries, more diffuse impairment from closed. In practice, many brain traumas represent combinations of open and closed head injuries: for example, a hammer falls on a worker's head fracturing the skull, sending bone fragments into the brain, but not causing a gaping, "open," wound.

The most common sites of brain damage in closed head injury are the anterior portions of the temporal lobe and the inferior portion of the frontal lobe due to the close proximity of these areas to the inwardly projecting portions of the inner table of the skull. Contusions and hematomas are most likely to occur in these areas, and scarring and cerebral atrophy may result from these lesions. Microscopically, rotational acceleration and deceleration injuries create shear strain, which pulls apart axons and disrupts cell bodies. Further injury may occur secondarily from hypoxia, systemic complications, or intracranial hemorrhage.

Concussions and Contusions

A *concussion* refers to the temporary loss or diminution of consciousness or other function due to a blow to the head; there need not be any macroscopically observable damage to the gross structure of the brain, although microscopic nerve and blood vessel damage may occur. A *contusion* refers to actual bruising of the brain, usually involving some combination of swelling, laceration, and hemorrhage that can be clearly observed. In some usages, a concussion refers to the altered state of behavior and consciousness that the injury produces, while a contusion is its observable pathophysiological correlate. In closed head injuries, contusions are most likely to occur in brain regions that lie near bony prominences within the cranial cavity, particularly the frontal and temporal poles.

Coup lesions result from trauma at the impact site; *contrecoup* lesions at the opposite pole may occur either from rebound trauma or from a cavitating pressure wave at the pole opposite the impact site. *Gliding contusions* occur when the force of the blow causes the brain to slide over bony landmarks on the inner table of the skull, usually at the base of the skull or in inferior frontotemporal regions.

In closed head injury, a blow to a movable head produces a much more severe brain injury than one to a rigidly fixed head, which is one reason for head supports on automobile seats. Nearly all head injuries have some rotational component to the trauma due to the various motions and forces on the brain via the head's suspension on the flexible neck. The effects of the rotational components of accelerative trauma tend to begin at the brain's surface and extend inward, or centripetally.

According to Leestma (1991), this type of injury, called *inner cerebral trauma*, or *intermediary coup lesion*, produces perhaps the most complex and serious clinical consequences. The injury is caused by movements of the brain against itself (rotational or shear forces) that may damage midline brainstem structures, focally or diffusely damaging long axons of passage and other brain structures. According to this account, some degree of inner cerebral trauma occurs in virtually every significant head injury, probably as a result of axonal injury. Even mild head injuries may cause aberrations of functioning that are made worse by repeated head trauma; this has become part of the debate over the medical effects of boxing (see below) and also is relevant to litigation over head trauma damages (see Chapter 10).

Physical Effects of Closed Head Trauma

In addition to contusions, traumatic effects can be many and varied, and may occur within seconds, minutes, hours, or days of the actual impact. Neurons may be killed, or the long axonal fibers that send their messages severed. The white matter, or *myelin*, that sheaths the nerve tracts may be damaged. Damage to blood vessels may deprive portions of the brain of oxygen. Ruptured blood vessels may result in a blood clot, or *hematoma*, forming within the cranial cavity, which exerts pressure on the brain tissue around it. Further pressure may occur as the brain swells in response to the trauma due to fluid retention. Secondary pressure on the brainstem can cause unconsciousness or cardiorespiratory failure. Pressure and fluid imbalances may also cause seizures. The supportive glial cells in the brain may proliferate and produce scars that later form the sites of origin for seizures.

Brain Surgery and Its Consequences

The most common reason for brain surgery after closed head trauma is to remove a blood clot that has formed in the brain. This entails the risks involved in any brain surgery—the deeper the clot, the greater the risk. Diuretic drugs may be administered to reduce brain swelling, and coma may be deliberately induced by barbiturates to slow down the brain's metabolism in an attempt to forestall some of the adverse physiological reactions to the brain injury.

Posttraumatic Epilepsy

Recovery from head trauma may be complicated by the development of seizures. According to Slagle (1990), posttraumatic seizures within seven days after injury will occur in two to five percent of civilian closed head injuries over all ages, with the incidence significantly higher in children. There are great individual differences in the susceptibility to seizures after head injury. Risk factors include increased duration of impaired consciousness and focal brain injury associated with a mass lesion or depressed skull fracture. Early seizures are less likely to be associated with lifetime epilepsy than those commencing more than one week after injury, but early seizures have been strongly correlated with psychiatric disability.

CLINICAL INVESTIGATIONS OF BRAIN INJURY

The brain-injured patient is likely to be subjected to a wide array of investigative procedures from brain scans to EEGs to neuropsychological testing. Some of the major evaluative procedures are described below.

Radiology

This encompasses a group of procedures that are all basically ways of viewing the structure of the brain. Depending on the technique, they are useful for detecting blood clots, atrophy of brain tissue, degenerated myelin, and other lesions big enough to actually see. However, they may miss very small lesions, such as tiny hemorrhages scattered throughout the brain, as well as pathological processes that have no gross structural correlates, such as seizures or biochemical disturbances. The following are the major types of radiological techniques used in the evaluation of the brain-injured patient.

Computerized Tomography   Conventional X-rays project a two-dimensional visualization of the skull and its contents. Since the head is a three-dimensional structure, overlapping images may be difficult to distinguish. The *computerized tomography*, or CT, scan produces a series of X-ray "slices" of the brain from which a three-dimensional image of the brain can be reconstructed. This allows much more precise localization of normal and abnormal structures than the conventional X-ray, which it has replaced at virtually all major medical centers—indeed, the CT scan itself is rapidly being supplanted by newer technologies (see below). With regard to traumatic brain injury, the CT scan has yielded some valuable data with respect to brain variables, clinical findings, and functional outcome.

Rao et al. (1984) studied a group of brain trauma patients within ten days of injury. The sample seemed to divide naturally into normal scan, single hemisphere involvement, and bilateral involvement subgroups, and these categories had distinct implications for later outcome. Patients with normal scans achieved independent functioning in all areas assessed. Most of those with one hemisphere affected achieved functional independence, while half had residual intellectual deficits. A little over half of the patients with bilateral lesions achieved functional and language independence, while most had persisting intellectual deficits. Apparently, the more of the brain that is injured, the poorer the outcome.

In a study that directly compared CT scan results and neuropsychological test data in brain-injured patients, Cullum and Bigler (1986) found that Wechsler Performance IQ, but not Verbal IQ, was negatively correlated with ventricle-brain ratios and cortical atrophy, particularly in terms of right hemisphere measures. That is, there appeared to be a greater association between structural change in the right hemisphere and deficient performance on nonverbal, spatial-perceptual tasks than between verbal-oriented tasks and left hemisphere measures. The Wechsler Memory Quotient was also negatively correlated with ventricle-brain ratio and cortical atrophy, with no observable lateralizing pattern. Significant relationships were found between enlarged ventricles and poor performance on the Wechsler Memory Scale's Paired-Associate Learning subtest and the Halstead-Reitan Category Test, particularly with left frontal cortical atrophy (see section below on neuropsychological testing).

Magnetic Resonance Imagery   *Magnetic resonance imagery*, or MRI, is gradually replacing the CT scan as the diagnostic imagery technique of choice for many neurological and other medical conditions — where it can be afforded. Briefly, the MRI uses a powerful magnet to align the atoms in the subject's brain tissue, then sends a radio wave across the field to cause the atoms to spin synchronously. When the radio waves are turned off, the synchrony induces a voltage in the magnetic field that is picked up by a conducting coil. The data is computer-analyzed to produce an image of the brain. The MRI shows certain brain structures and pathologies much more clearly than does the CT scan, although the latter still retains some useful diagnostic functions. CT is of value in demonstrating large acute hematomas after head injury, and MRI is more sensitive in showing smaller traumatic lesions. During early recovery, MRI may be more sensitive in demonstrating cerebral lesions than CT.

MRI results were compared with neuropsychological findings in a study by Wilson et al. (1988). Results showed a clear relationship between depth of abnormality on MRI and neuropsychological test performance. The Wechsler Performance IQ subscales of Digit Symbol, Block Design, and Object Assembly showed particularly strong correlations with MRI abnormalities, consistent with previous findings of greater brain injury impact on Wechsler Performance subscales than Verbal subscales (Mandelberg & Brooks, 1975). Inasmuch as the Performance subscales are all timed tests, the present authors suggest that MRI abnormalities may be reflecting slower information processing in traumatically brain-injured patients.

Positron Emission Tomography   CT and MRI imaging methods demonstrate anatomical abnormalities produced by brain injury. While they may have some predictive value, imaging techniques that reflect changes in cerebral function in addition to structure might assess a patient's clinical status and progress yet more accurately. *Positron emission tomography* (PET) provides an effective measure of cerebral metabolism and tissue function.

In this technique, the subject is given a radioactively labeled glucose compound that is easily metabolized by the brain. As the glucose is used up, the PET scanner records the radioactivity given off. The more active a particular brain area is, the more fuel it will need, and so the more radiation will be released from the radioactively tagged glucose as it's metabolized. The PET scanner then transforms this profile of energy utilization into a colored visual display of brain activity. This, in effect, provides a glimpse of living brain-behavior activity in which the particular subject's patterns of metabolic functioning in different brain regions can be examined. PET has actually been used more in psychiatry (e.g., in the study of schizophrenia) than neurology, and its application to brain injury is just beginning to be explored.

Single Photon Emission Computer Tomography   The logistic constraints and expense of PET scanning may make it unavailable to many centers. *Single photon emission computer tomography* (SPECT), using a easily obtainable and convenient lipophilic tracer compound, has made the assessment of *regional cerebral blood flow* (rCBF) readily available. Since patterns of rCBF frequently match the metabolic requirements, and thus the functional status, of cerebral tissue, alterations of rCBF may be useful in defining underfunctioning areas of the brain in many cerebral disorders, including brain injury.

In a study by Newton et al. (1992), a group of patients with closed head injury underwent SPECT to compare the defects shown by CT and MRI. SPECT showed more focal cerebral lesions than either CT or MRI alone or in combination. Most lesions shown by SPECT were not shown by CT or

MRI in the corresponding anatomical regions. The most severely disabled patients showed the highest number of SPECT lesions compared with less disabled patients. Thus, the perfusion defects may correlate with clinical signs that were not explained by CT or MRI findings.

Electrophysiology

Still another way of assessing the function of the brain is by analyzing its patterns of electrophysiological activity; indeed, this is one of the oldest diagnostic technologies in neurology, dating back to the 1930's.

Electroencephalogram   The *electroencephalogram*, or EEG, measures the electrical activity of different parts of the brain. By analyzing the "brain waves" of a particular patient, the location and nature of various types of cerebral pathology may be identified. A series of recording electrodes are placed at standard sites on the skull surface, or in some surgical cases, on the brain substance itself. The pattern of results is typically portrayed on a strip-graph and "read" by the neurologist much in the same way an electrocardiogram (EKG) is "read" by a cardiologist. In brain injury, the EEG is useful for identifying areas of slowed activity that may indicate focal brain damage, or to detect sites of seizure activity.

Quantitative EEG   Just as computers have been applied to radiological imagery, so have they recently been pressed into service to analyze the brain's electrical activity. In the *quantitative EEG* (QEEG), a sensory stimulus is presented repeatedly, and the brain's electrical activity associated with each stimulation is recorded. These electrophysiological responses are computer-averaged to cancel out background activity, and the resulting waveform represents the brain's response to the stimulus. Different activity in different areas may be represented on a colored chart, thus "mapping" the different brain areas. The QEEG is finding application in both neurology and psychiatry (Kahn, 1992).

The Neurologic Examination

This includes a physical exam of the patient's sensory, motor, and basic mental status functioning as it relates to the nervous system, as well as any laboratory tests and ancillary procedures that the neurologist considers useful. However, the clinical skill of today's neurologist typically plays a minor role.

Long before CTs, MRIs, QEEGs, or PETs, expert neurologists of the late nineteenth and early twentieth centuries were able to make astonishingly accurate clinicoanatomical diagnoses using a combination of extensive interview and examination of the patient and their own encyclopedic scholarship with regard to the structure and function of the nervous system. Read the case histories of Hughlings Jackson, Henry Head, even Sigmund Freud (whose early neuropsychological studies are described in Miller, 1991f), and you can't fail to be impressed with what they were able to do with their eyes, ears, hands, and minds.

Today's dazzling technologies have relegated the skillful neurologic exam to the status of a lost art (other fields of medicine may have their own, similar laments). Part of the reason is probably bottom-line. Long, careful, extensive clinical examinations are not cost-effective from a medical-economics point of view: compare the billing rate for a clinical exam with that for an MRI scan. Abetting this trend is the growing idea that these technologies are supposed to replace, rather than supplement, the clinical evaluation, that somehow they are more "scientific" and therefore more reliable. Interestingly, in many settings, the role of the careful clinical examination of cognitive functions has been taken over by the neuropsychologist who now often functions as the "above-the-neck" clinical expert in brain function.

Neuropsychological Assessment

The neuropsychological assessment involves a more comprehensive and detailed evaluation of cognitive functioning by means of specialized tests and assessment procedures. Ideally, neuropsychological reassessment occurs at a number of points in time after the head injury in order to objectively document the course of recovery. This will be discussed further below. As this is not a textbook of neuropsychology, the details of neuropsychological assessment will not be covered (see, for example, Lezak, 1983). However, a number of comments are warranted.

Many neuropsychologists seem determined to repeat the sins of their neurologist colleagues by relying almost exclusively on standardized tests to make the diagnoses for them—once again, emphasizing the tools instead of the craftsman. One result is the all-too frequent overtesting of brain-injured patients. The use of extensive megabatteries taking six, eight, twelve, or more hours to administer typically serves less a clinical function than a way of generating billable hours for the neuropsychologist. It, not inconsequentially, also puts the patient through hell. In case after case I've interviewed after such lengthy test ordeals by other neuropsychologists, the patient has told me that, by the fourth or fifth hour of testing, even with frequent breaks to "control for" fatigue, the main goal was simply to get the damn thing over with. From a methodological standpoint, therefore, motivation is affected and test validity is suspect.

What makes this practice all the more questionable is that many of the commonly used lengthy neuropsychological batteries have not, to my knowledge, shown their superiority in assessing brain injury over other measures that take shorter times to administer. Interestingly, the practice of lengthy testing seems to take place far more frequently in circumstances where it is financially compensated, such as forensic cases, while in circumstances where test fees are constrained by limited patient or third-party resources, the same neuropsychologists often seem to be able to assert equally confident clinical judgments with far fewer tests.

Not that I am advocating a uniformly "less is more" approach to neuropsychological assessment. Nor am I necessarily criticizing the tests themselves, any more than I am promulgating a retrogressive, antitechnological attitude toward diagnostic neurologic techniques; MRIs and psychometric tests have their place. But testing — any testing — must be guided by clinical skill and wisdom toward a reasonably clear purpose. With regard to neuropsychological testing, my own preference is to use a shorter, basic screening battery, composed of tests that have acceptable normative data and adequate clinical interpretability, as a first step. This basic battery takes about three hours to administer and samples the fundamental functions of attention, concentration, verbal and visuospatial reasoning, language, memory, sensory-motor functioning, higher-order problem solving, intellectual level, and basic personality functioning. Based on the findings of this initial assessment, a decision-tree approach is taken toward further testing. That is, if impairment is detected or suspected in a particular function, further measures in those areas are chosen to follow up the diagnostic impression. A similar approach is starting to be utilized in the neuropsychological assessment of toxic exposure (Bowler et al., 1986; Ryan et al., 1987; see Miller, 1993a for a review).

There are literally thousands of psychological tests and subtests in existence. Hurling test after test at patients without concern for the clinical questions being asked amounts to nothing more than trawling for organicity. Everybody's got at least one area of relative weakness and if I throw enough tests at you, sooner or later you'll bomb on one or two of them. But this is a fishing expedition, not clinical assessment. Remember, tests don't make the evaluation — the *clinician* makes the evaluation, using the test results as one part of a whole array of data which includes history and records, clinical interview, observation of test-taking and other behavior, and adequate knowledge of brain mechanisms and of the functions and limitations of the measures employed. The goal should be to arrive at a picture of the patient that will translate into the best level of clinical care. And good, comprehensive care can only be provided by knowledgeable clinicians, not rote technicians.

Cognitive Rehabilitation

In the last decade, a veritable cottage industry has sprung up based largely on the idea that, as injured or atrophied muscles and joints can be strengthened by specialized exercises, similarly "exercising" mental functions can rehabilitate cognitive functions lost or damaged by brain injury. Unfortunately, the brain is not a muscle, and general "strengthening" exercises don't seem to automatically foster the reacquisition of specific skills. Even authorities who recommend and teach cognitive rehabilitation are forced to acknowledge its limitations (e.g., Harrell et al., 1992; Meier et al., 1987; Wilson, 1987).

This is not a text on cognitive rehab, but some observations are pertinent. The main issue seems to be generalizability or transfer of training. The analogy with physical rehab is simply not an accurate one. Doing general exercises with a leg strengthens that leg for all or most of the functions a leg can perform: running, kicking, swimming, etc. But training memory on a computerized memory program is likely to foster skill development in that particular computer game only—transfer to other, real-life memory tasks is typically insignificant. The problem is that muscle contraction as a "function" and memory (or attention or self-monitoring) as a "function" are two different things. One is simple and general, the other complex and specific.

The major basis for the failure to observe generalization may be the assumption that it will occur automatically from skill-specific training, sometimes referred to as the "train-and-hope" method (Cicerone & Tupper, 1991). The assumption of automatic generalization is clearly not supported by clinical or empirical evidence. People do not automatically transfer solutions to logically isomorphic problems that differ in content unless they first detect the underlying similarities between the problems. This may be especially the case with generalization to real-life tasks from computer programs (Pipitone, 1992). Also, rehabilitation becomes confounded with natural recovery when the training takes place within the first two years or so after brain injury (Benedict, 1989; Cicerone & Tupper, 1991).

Yet, individual cases of remarkable recovery from profound cognitive impairment can occasionally be seen (e.g., some of the cases in Wilson, 1987), so let's not throw out the proverbial baby with the bathwater. To maximize the benefits of cognitive rehabilitation, Cicerone and Tupper

(1991) suggest the following strategies: (1) train identical elements; (2) train in the natural environment; (3) train general principles; (4) train sufficient examples; (5) train mediation; (6) train generalization. In other words, as many different ways as you can teach the patient to do a task in as many different situations, will foster the acquisition, use, and maintenance of that skill. Of course, general adaptive skill-training is also related to appropriate interpersonal functioning and emotional stability, and Chapters 3 and 12 will discuss the areas where cognitive rehabilitation overlaps with psychotherapy.

TRAUMATIC BRAIN INJURY AND OTHER NEUROLOGIC SYNDROMES

Head trauma has been reported to be a risk factor for such neurologic syndromes as brain tumors, Parkinson's disease, Alzheimer's disease, multiple sclerosis, amyotrophic lateral sclerosis, and mental retardation (Kurtzke & Kurland, 1985). This section will discuss some of the more notable areas of controversy in this field.

Brain Tumor

In general, although they occur almost anywhere along the surface or within the deep structure of the brain, *astrocytomas*, a common type of malignant brain tumor arising from the supportive glial cells of the brain, occur most frequently along the frontal-temporal convexity—areas that are most susceptible to contusion caused by traumatic brain injury. Moreover, both structurally and metabolically, grade 1 astrocytomas resemble a normal astrocytic reaction to an injury in which there is rapid proliferation of glial cells in and around the injury site (Salcman & Kaplan, 1986). From a few published reports, it appears that some patients develop these tumors after a head injury, although there is of course no way of determining if the tumors would have occurred anyway. Theoretically, at least, the injury could act as a precipitating event interacting with a genetic predisposition to trigger tumor formation (Joseph, 1990)—much like cigarette smoking in lung cancer or sun exposure in skin cancer. More on the clinical and neuropsychological aspects of brain tumors can be found in Chapter 9.

Alzheimer's Disease

Anecdotal reports have suggested a connection between head trauma and the development of an Alzheimer-like dementia later in life, sometimes many decades later. With regard to controlled studies, some have found a statistical association between head trauma and later Alzheimer's disease (Heyman et al., 1984; Mortimer et al., 1985), while other studies have not (Amaducci et al., 1986; Chandra et al., 1987; Sulkava et al., 1985). Recently, Chandra et al. (1989) found that, even with a rather large sample size, the frequency of occurrence of head trauma in a study population of Alzheimer's patients was low. According to these results, there is no association between head trauma with loss of consciousness, followed by complete recovery, and later development of Alzheimer's disease. The authors speculate that recall bias may have accounted for the positive findings of previous studies. That is, where data concerning head trauma are obtained by questioning the patients, individuals with a chronic neurologic disease and their relatives or friends who serve as informants may report even minor events — such as mild head injury — which they feel may have predisposed them to the illness.

Dementia Pugilistica

In the movie *Requiem for a Heavyweight*, Anthony Quinn portrays an affable, spaced-out, veteran boxer who has apparently suffered too many blows to the head and now lumbers about, slurring his words, forgetting things, and showing generally lousy judgment. If there is one area where traumatic brain injury is known to occur and could potentially be avoided, it is professional boxing. In no other professional sport is the object specifically to inflict maximal pain and physical damage on one's opponent. Moreover, while hitting below the belt is strictly against the rules, pummeling the head is enthusiastically encouraged — which ought to tell us something about the values and priorities of those who practice, promote, and patronize this form of modern-day gladiatorial entertainment.

Martland (1928) provided the first systematic description of experienced and retired boxers' tendencies to develop unsteadiness on their feet, to become forgetful, and to think and move more slowly than in their pre-boxing days. This condition was apparently quite familiar to promoters, trainers, and fight fans as being "slug nutty," "punch drunk," "cutting paper dolls," or becoming, as the Germans quaintly put it, a "soft pear." Millspaugh (1937) subsequently introduced the term *dementia pugilistica*, or boxer's dementia, to describe the syndrome that is also known as *chronic traumatic encephalopathy*. The symptoms described by modern researchers are quite consistent with earlier reports: slowed motor performance, clumsiness, dysarthria, ataxia of gait, tremors, rigidity, spasticity, memory impairment, slowness of thought, and personality change (Ross et al., 1983).

The neuropathological findings in dementia pugilistica typically include

(1) septal and hypothalamic abnormalities, particularly a rupture of the septal membrane, or "cavum septum pellucidum"; (2) damage to the cerebellum, including small contusions, or "plaques jaunes," and Purkinje cell loss; (3) degeneration of the substantia nigra; and (4) regional occurrence of neurofibrillary tangles similar to those found in the brains of Alzheimer patients (Corsellis, 1978; Ross et al., 1983). According to Corsellis (1978), it is this pattern of four main types of structural change that seems to make them explicable only as being the result of the repeated blows to the head sustained in boxing; there is no other known condition that has this same specific cluster of neuropathological findings.

Unlike the controversy surrounding the role of head trauma in Alzheimer's disease and brain tumor, the cumulative effect of repeated boxing blows in the development of dementia pugilistica seems clear. Ross et al. (1983) examined a sizable sample of professional fighters over three years to determine the effects of boxing on their neurological status and CT appearances of the brain. Results demonstrated a significant relationship between the number of bouts fought and CT changes indicating cerebral atrophy. Positive neurologic findings were not significantly correlated with number of bouts fought, but EEG abnormalities were significantly correlated with number of bouts.

Both former and active boxers underwent neurologic examination, EEG, CT, and neuropsychological testing in a study by Casson et al. (1984). The majority of the professional boxers had definite evidence of brain damage. All boxers had abnormal results on at least one of the neuropsychological tests. Subjects performed particularly poorly on measures of short-term memory, consistent with pathological reports implicating deep medial brain structures in this syndrome. Results also suggested that the longer one's boxing career, the greater is the likelihood of brain damage, probably due to the cumulative effect of multiple subconcussive blows to the head.

Nor is it just the old-time, burnt-out pugs who show ill effects. A study of boxers that employed neuropsychological testing was carried out by Drew et al. (1986). Young, active, licensed, professional fighters were found to display a pattern of neuropsychological deficits consistent with the more severe punch-drunk syndrome of years past. Neuropsychological test scores were significantly poorer than that of control athletes in other, noninjury-related sports matched for age, race, and level of education. The boxers' deficits included dysarthria, memory impairment, coordination problems, and sensory-motor deficits.

Apparently, these active boxers who were fighting in the modern era of ostensibly improved safety regulations, still suffered from basically the same pattern of symptoms as the original punch-drunk syndrome, albeit at somewhat lower levels of severity. Unfortunately, these impaired abilities are the very ones needed for effective academic, vocational, and social functioning. One wonders about all the other amateur pugs and big-ticket wannabes who batter each other for years without being "discovered," and so end up not just with wasted time, but also having had the cognitive skills needed to pursue other gainful occupations literally knocked out of them.

Other Sports Injuries

Not that other athletes are immune. While head injuries can occur in virtually any form of athletic activity, they understandably occur most frequently in contact sports, such as football or boxing, or from high-velocity collisions or falls in basketball, soccer, and ice hockey. Traumatic brain injury is in fact quite common in such contact sports, with an estimated 250,000 concussions and an average of eight deaths due to head injuries occurring every year in football alone. Twenty percent of high school football players suffer concussion (defined as a traumatically induced alteration in mental status, not necessarily with loss of consciousness) during a single football season, some more than once (Kelly et al., 1991). Repeated concussions can lead to brain atrophy and cumulative neuropsychological deficits. A study of American football injuries reported four cases of marked posttraumatic short-term memory impairment that occurred without any apparent alteration in consciousness while others had delayed retrograde amnesia without losing consciousness (Yarnell & Lynch, 1973). Despite this, concussion as a sports-related injury is too often dismissed as trivial by physicians, coaches, sports reporters, and athletes themselves (Kelly et al., 1991).

The outcome of repeated concussions occurring within a short period can be fatal. Kelly et al. (1991) describe the case of a 17-year-old male high school football player who suffered a concussion without loss of consciousness in a varsity football game and complained of headache during the next week of school and practice. No further injuries occurred during practice, and he did not seek medical attention. In the next game a week later, as a halfback carrying the ball, the player was struck on the left side of his helmet by the helmet of his tackler. He was obviously stunned, but mental functions appeared to clear quickly during a brief time-out. He continued to play for several minutes until, after rising from a pile of players after a tackle, he collapsed unconscious into the arms of a teammate. He became progressively less responsive and was taken to the hospital where efforts to revive him failed. He died 15 hours later, and the cause of death was stated as diffuse, severe brain swelling due to the cumulative effect of the present and week-earlier injuries.

Few sportsmen die during games; indeed, even the boxer who is killed in the ring is the rare exception. We don't see the injury happen, so we generally ignore the later, cumulative effects. But think about the cultural priorities of a society that sanctions and glorifies violent combat as a form of entertainment and — recalling the earlier comment about boxing rules — seems far more concerned about the long-term effects of football on its players' knees than on their brains.

ACUTE EFFECTS OF BRAIN INJURY

The acute effects of traumatic brain injury most closely relate to the pathophysiological events that occur in the first hours to days to weeks after injury. Therefore a discussion of these effects will be included in this chapter. More long-term effects that relate to a combination of brain damage and psychological adjustment reactions to injury will be considered in the next chapter.

Coma, Confusion, and Consciousness

In the mildest cases of brain injury, there may be no disturbance of consciousness, or only a period of temporary confusion. More commonly, some period of unconsciousness deep enough to be called coma occurs. Following the period of unconsciousness, there is usually an interval of confusion, disorientation, and sometimes delirium, with full consciousness gradually returning over a period of minutes to hours to days, depending on severity. Behavioral agitation during the early recovery period has been associated with increased incidence of later anxiety, depression, and thought disturbance (Levin & Grossman, 1978). Approximately 10% of brain-injured patients with prolonged coma develop some degree of hydrocephalus, which may present as progressive mental deterioration after a period of apparent recovery. In addition, inadequate pain relief may contribute to agitation during the confusional period (Slagle, 1990).

Memory and Posttraumatic Amnesia

Typically, if unconsciousness has occurred, the patient doesn't remember the actual incident itself, which is surrounded by varying periods of memory loss. *Retrograde amnesia* refers to a loss of memory for events immediately preceding the trauma and is usually measured in seconds to minutes to hours. *Anterograde amnesia* refers to a disturbance in forming new memories after the impact and this may be affected for hours to days to weeks, overlapping with the period of posttraumatic confusion and continuing on through a subsequent period of apparently normal consciousness. This kind of memory-forming ability tends to return gradually. Amnesia can occur without loss of consciousness (see the section on "mild" head injury in the following chapter), sometimes accompanied by MRI findings of cortical contusion (Jenkins et al., 1986).

Focal vs. Generalized Deficits

As noted above, focal deficits are more common in penetrating or open head injuries, but can also occur in closed head injuries, due to localized contusions, loss of blood supply to certain brain areas, and other factors. In such cases, the focal deficits are likely to appear on the background of more generalized impairment. For example, a speech disturbance or blind spot in the visual field may be observed along with more generalized problems in attention, orientation, etc. As recovery occurs, the generalized impairment may resolve and the focal deficits remain, albeit in milder form. Or both the generalized and focal deficits may improve together. Or sometimes, the focal deficits may resolve, seeming to "blend into" a residual generalized pattern of impairment.

Typically, maximal recovery from the acute neurological effects of a head trauma occurs within six months to a year following the injury. Problems arise where the level of functional recovery is not up to a level "expected" by doctors and textbooks, and long-term problems — particularly in psychosocial adjustment — arise. It is to these that we now turn.

CHAPTER 2

The Shattered Self:
Effects of Brain Injury
on the Personality

SOME PATIENTS, even with relatively serious brain injuries, make a satisfactory recovery and adjustment, pull together the pieces of their lives, and get back to the business of living. However, many don't get better, and some appear to get worse. This chapter will examine the interaction of physical and psychological effects of brain injury producing the clinical patterns of long-term psychosocial maladjustment that confront the psychotherapist.

PHYSICAL DISABILITY

Traumatic brain injuries usually occur along with injuries to other parts of the body. Limitations of activity may be due either to the effects of brain damage on the motor system or to injuries unrelated to the brain injury itself, but co-occurring with it, such as a spinal cord transection, bone fractures, etc. In general, studies have found that physical disability itself is less likely to be a cause of post-head trauma adjustment than cognitive and behavioral dysfunction.

Stambrook et al. (1991) studied samples of ambulatory moderate and severe closed head injury patients and wheelchair-dependent spinal cord injury patients. While the moderate head injury and spinal cord groups were equivalent on many indicators of psychosocial outcome, the severe head injury group was more depressed, angry, hostile, confused, and bewildered. In addition, wives of the severe head injury group rated their husbands as more belligerent, negative, helpless, suspicious, withdrawn, and retarded, and with more general mental disorder than did wives of moderate head injury patients or wives of spinal cord patients.

The authors suggest that, as a result of differential advocacy, spinal cord patients and their families have been able to access greater community resources than head injury patients and their families. A factor I think is important is that spinal cord patients are more visibly "disabled," crutches and wheelchairs getting more attention than cognitive deficits in the walking brain-injured. Compounding the problems is the tendency of many brain-injured patients to have behavioral sequelae that render them apathetic, irritable, confused, impulsive, immature, childish, or otherwise unsympathetic. Thus, they can speak and get about, but may not be able to convey the requisite aura of pathos that appeals to telethon audiences.

Moreover, the ability to sustain goal-directed motivation toward a cause — vital for, say, organizing and participating in political advocacy action — is often damaged by brain injury or may have been impaired premorbidly as part of the predisposing personality and cognitive style pattern associated with traumatic brain injury (see Chapters 5 and 6). Many spinal cord injury patients rise above their paraplegia by dint of courage, determination, and — importantly — intact cognitive functioning; they stage "wheelchair marches" and other active, mediagenic events. Brain-injured patients, by contrast, often just can't seem to pull it all together.

THE POSTCONCUSSION SYNDROME

"Imagine waking up every day with a pounding headache, always feeling like you're suffering from a hangover plus a bad flu after being up the last three nights in a row, having trouble concentrating, remembering, and getting your thoughts together, losing your temper and snapping at people for no reason, walking around jumpy and afraid of your own shadow, and on top of that nobody believes you or thinks you're crazy, and maybe you'll understand what I've been going through since my accident." This is how one patient described his situation approximately one year after a closed head injury in which he sustained no serious physical injuries, was momentarily dazed, but not unconscious, and was kept in the hospital for observation for one night with a diagnosis of "concussion."

Despite the transient nature of the period of unconsciousness caused by even a relatively minor head injury and the rapid immediate recovery, a substantial proportion of patients develop a cluster of persistent and troublesome symptoms. The nature of the syndrome—how much is due to organic brain injury and how much to "hysterical" factors—has been debated at least since the last century by such luminaries of neurology and psychiatry as Dupuytren, Strumpell, Oppenheim, and Charcot (see Levin, 1990 for a review). The malady was officially dubbed the *postconcussion syndrome* by Strauss and Savitsky (1934), and much of the symptomatology was described in that original report as being psychological in nature: irritability, poor concentration, loss of confidence, anxiety, depression, intolerance of noise and bright lights. Somatic components include fatigue, headache, dizziness, vertigo, and intolerance of alcohol.

Today, the postconcussion, or postconcussive syndrome (PCS) describes a cluster of symptoms that often persist "inappropriately"—that is, beyond the point where the patient is supposed to have gotten better. The term is sometimes used pejoratively, but I will employ it descriptively in this chapter and throughout this book as is the practice of most modern neuropsychologists. Commonly reported symptoms include headache, dizziness, fatigue, slowness and inefficiency of thought and action, diminished concentration, memory problems, irritability, anxiety, insomnia or poor sleep patterns, nightmares, hypochondriacal concern, hypersensitivity to noise, hypersensitivity to light (photophobia), blurred or double vision, problems in judgment, anxiety, depression, and altered sex drive (Gouvier et al., 1992; Parker, 1990; Slagle, 1990). The remainder of this section will consider these phenomena in more detail.

Cognitive Deficits

These include residual deficits in any of the cognitive functions that were impaired acutely, such as sensation, perception, attention, concentration, language, memory, visuospatial integration, thinking, and planning. If there has been focal damage to the brain, the deficits may be somewhat circumscribed, e.g., a specific verbal memory deficit due to left temporal lobe damage. In most cases there has been some combination of focal and diffuse damage, so that the specific deficits tend to "blend into" the more general pattern of impairment. Residual problems that occur most commonly in brain-injured patients include the following.

Difficulties in Attention and Concentration

These involve having trouble following the train of conversations, keeping on track with reading material, not being "as sharp as I used to be."

Learning and Memory Problems

These include difficulty retaining material, forgetting people's names or faces, confusing one person with another, experiencing trouble recalling old information "that I know I used to know," and having to struggle to remember things that used to be learned easily. In general, it is harder for new information to get processed, and what does get in seems to be forgotten more quickly.

Slowness and Inefficiency

Many post-head trauma patients who fail many standard timed cognitive tests may be able to complete the tasks if given as much time as they need. In such cases, the basic ability may be there, but the quickness and efficiency of problem-solving has been affected. The patient may have to go back and repeat steps many times, or take two or three times as long to decide on the next step of a problem to be solved. When slowness is combined with actual loss of skill on a task, performance suffers still more.

Concreteness

Generally, these individuals do better with tasks and in situations that are familiar rather than novel, structured rather than open-ended, and specific rather than ambiguous.

Cognitive Deficits in Psychological Trauma   Inasmuch as anxiety and depression are part of the postconcussive syndrome (see below), it is legitimate to ask how much of the cognitive deficit reflects actual organic brain injury and how much is due to "psychological factors." Another way of looking at this, however, is to ask whether psychological trauma can produce actual cognitive impairment that might sum with impairment produced by actual damage to brain tissue. Indeed, Deitz (1992), Kolb (1987), Parker (1990), and Weiner (1992) have discussed the possible role of psychic stress and trauma in causing long-lasting neurobiological and endocrinological changes in brain functioning that may affect cognitive and emotional functioning, presumably summating with the effects of actual structural damage to the brain (see Miller, 1993b for a review).

The question of psychological stress and cognitive functioning has been studied more directly by Gill et al. (1990), who compared patients suffering from psychologically-defined post-traumatic stress disorder (PTSD), but free of organic brain damage, to normal controls and psychiatric patients on a comprehensive cognitive test battery. The PTSD patients had been involved in traumatic military battle events, terrorist attacks, or car accidents but had not been physically injured. Both the PTSD and psychiatric patient groups felt subjectively more impaired than the normals. Performance on measures of intelligence, organicity, verbal fluency, memory, and attention was significantly poorer in patients than in normals. The performance of the PTSD patients and that of the psychiatric controls was, however, very similar. The premorbid intelligence of both the PTSD patients and the psychiatric controls was average and had deteriorated significantly by the time of the current testing. These cognitive problems were not secondary to alcohol, drug abuse, or head injury.

The authors note that the findings do not support the existence of cognitive impairment that is specific to PTSD. Rather, the deficits observed are likely to be a secondary consequence of general psychiatric symptomatology. The results also support the view that the deficits observed in both patient groups was a result of the respective disorders rather than a premorbid characteristic of the subjects, because other possible sources of deterioration, such as head injury, ECT, or psychosurgery were excluded by the selection criteria for the study. I think it would be fascinating to replicate this study including a group of brain-injured patients—perhaps two such groups, one with reported PTSD due to traumatic brain injury and one without PTSD, e.g., stroke or brain tumor patients with equivalent foci and severity of damage.

A related study by Blanchard et al. (1991) measured heart rate, blood pressure, and electrodermal responses of four individuals with PTSD secondary to car accidents while the subjects imagined two separate scenes related to their accident. Results showed reliable heart rate responses to these images, as well as changes in systolic and diastolic blood pressure; however, skin resistance level changed reliably in only two of the four subjects. The authors suggest that psychophysiological measurement could play a role in the assessment and treatment of PTSD, and I wonder what kind of diagnostic impact combining neuropsychological with psychophysiological assessment would have on the clinical evaluation of brain-injured patients (also see the section below on "cryptotrauma").

Emotional, Behavioral, and Psychosocial Problems

Although many of the topics in this section will be elaborated upon in subsequent chapters, they are summarized here as part of the postconcussion syndrome. Commonly reported changes include excessive tiredness, indifference, attention and concentration problems, inflexibility, a tendency toward perseveration, the absence of an ability to anticipate, behavioral disinhibition, impaired capacity for skill acquisition, irritability, and a change in the quality of relationships, especially in the direction of greater shallowness (Slagle, 1990). Obsessive-compulsive symptoms have also been reported to develop as part of this syndrome (Lishman, 1973).

Brooks et al. (1986) have reported that the ten most frequent patient problems reported by families at both one and five years postinjury are personality change, slowness, poor memory, irritability, bad temper, tiredness, depression, rapid mood change, tension and anxiety, and threats of violence. Families often have the most difficulty dealing with aggression and hypersexuality. Previously subtle maladaptive personality traits may become exaggerated during recovery from head injury (Slagle, 1990), perhaps exacerbated by stress effects (Horowitz, 1986).

The single most significant factor in post-injury job adjustment and overall life satisfaction is the psychosocial or behavioral status of the person, rather than the absolute level of physical or even cognitive disability. Often, one of the most important tasks of the evaluation is to discern to what degree these problems predated the head injury vs. how much is directly due to the effects of the injury itself. Much of the material in this section is adapted from the comprehensive review by Slagle (1990), which the reader should consult for more detail.

Depression and Mood Swings   A lability or instability of emotional responses may be seen. Crying spells may occur with minimal provocation. Periods of manic excitement or "getting hyper" may be seen and may alternate with depressive episodes.

Depression appears to occur more frequently with lesions of the frontal and temporal lobes, with lesions nearer the frontal pole more likely to be associated with more severe depression. It has also been reported that mania following brain injury occurs most often with lesions located in limbic structures and pathways, and is associated with right-sided lesions more commonly than left. In a review of neuropathological studies of secondary affective disorders associated with penetrating head injuries, tumor, trauma, epilepsy, and stroke, Jeste et al. (1988) found a tendency for left frontotemporal and right parietooccipital lesions to be associated with secondary depression, while right frontotemporal and left occipitoparietal lesions were more associated with secondary mania. As many as 50% of posttraumatic manic patients have been reported to show abnormal EEGs.

Brain-injured patients often report depression, anxiety, somatic problems, and unusual subjective experiences soon after injury, but this seems to subside with time. Depression commonly occurs during periods of recovery, as the patient must come to terms with his new physical and mental limitations, and may psychologically mourn those functions impaired or lost. If physically disabled, the patient may suffer many losses, including his occupation, financial and social status, previous level of functioning in recreational activities, many friendships, and possibly sexual functioning and self-respect. Fears of separation and death may emerge (see Chapters 3, 4, and 11 for more on these issues). A variety of neurovegetative symptoms, including both agitated and retarded psychomotor activity, may be observed.

The common symptoms of depression may be less pronounced in brain-injured patients due to the masking effect of overall personality flattening. Erratic or poor recovery, or worsening of a neurological deficit after initial recovery, may be signs of depression. Cognitive clouding secondary to depression may occur and may inhibit rehabilitation. The possibility of suicide should be considered.

Posttraumatic mania may present as euphoria, lack of insight into deficits, irritability, assaultive behavior, impaired judgment, sleeplessness, pressured speech, flight of ideas, hyperreligiosity, grandiosity, distractibility, hyperactivity, or hypersexuality. Irritable mood has been reported to be more common than euphoric mood in posttraumatic manic patients — indeed, in mania associated with psychiatric disorders, euphoria frequently gives way to irritability and paranoia. In brain-injured patients, it may be important to determine what proportion of sudden mood shift symptoms are due to subtle seizure phenomena.

Posttraumatic Psychosis   All forms of schizophrenia-like psychosis have been reported after brain injury — although, again, the chicken-and-egg question must be raised as to whether being schizophrenic might predispose one to brain injury: As far as I'm aware, no one has studied this systematically. However, Slagle (1990) points out that schizophrenic patients are more likely to have a history of childhood head trauma than manic, depressive, or control patients. Posttraumatic schizophrenia-like psychosis may be manifested by disorganization of thought, incoherent speech, tangential associations, inappropriate thought content, hallucinations, and delusions. Left-sided temporal lobe lesions seem to have the most significance, but other areas of focal impairment have been implicated in both posttraumatic and idiopathic psychosis (Flor-Henry, 1983; Miller, 1984b, 1986b).

Agitation, Paranoia, Irritability, and Rage   A pervasive chip-on-the-shoulder edginess may be seen. The "littlest things" may be more aggravating than usual. Constant complaining and hostility may strain family, job, and other interpersonal relationships. At times, this may shade into aggression and rage. Most acts of actual physical violence occur early in recovery during confusional states where the patient may become combative if restrained or feeling threatened, or later if and when a posttraumatic seizure disorder develops, which expresses itself in the form of angry feelings and behaviors. However, even where no active pathological process can be identified, many patients seem to develop a "short fuse" that persists posttraumatically. Some of this may be attributable to the increased suspiciousness and paranoia that sometimes develop after head injury; the latter, in turn, are often related to a restricted ability to make sense of the environment, with a resultant misinterpretation of events.

Slagle (1990) reviews the evidence suggesting that traumatic brain injury accounts for an increasing number of cases of episodic behavioral dyscontrol with aggression (Elliott, 1984). Injury to the temporal lobe may result in inappropriate combativeness (Mark & Ervin, 1970; Pincus & Tucker, 1978). A "rage center" is reported to be located in the ventromedial hypothalamus and is inhibited by projections from the dorsomedial nucleus of the amygdala and facilitated by projections from the ventrolateral nucleus of the amygdala (Davis & Boster, 1988), suggesting that lesions affecting these areas may play a role in the genesis of aggressive behavioral dyscontrol. The aggressive behavior may be preceded by dysphoria or may occur abruptly without warning and may be triggered by the use of alcohol. Aggressive behavior may be reinforcing if it results in special attention or peer status for the patient, or if it enables the avoidance of undesired activities. Patients may meet *DSM-III* criteria for intermittent explosive disorder (see Chapter 5).

Impulsivity and Inertia   This is a problem with motivation. The patient may alternate between sitting and doing nothing for hours or days, and then frenetically running about starting and leaving unfinished all kinds of tasks and projects, going on irresponsible buying sprees, taking dangerous physical and social risks, and generally acting impulsively and with poor judgment. This syndrome may be particularly related to frontal lobe impairment and may be accompanied by manic mood swings.

Malingering and Somatization   Although strict dichotomies are difficult to make, *malingering* generally refers to a deliberate, conscious attempt to deceive an observer into believing a symptom exists when the perpetrator clearly knows it does not. Terms like *hysteria* and *conversion* are generally taken to imply that the person "believes" his or her symptom to be "real," but it is actually produced or exaggerated by unconscious psychodynamic factors. After traumatic head injury, such *somatization* phenomena, as they are collectively known, may be seen, especially where legal action and employment issues are relevant.

Pain is the most common somatization complaint, but cognitive disturbances may also form the basis for somatic preoccupation. The challenge is to discern which types of problems are or are not "legitimate," a task made all the more difficult by the fact that there may be genuine posttraumatic symptoms that form the kernel of more exaggerated somatization syndromes. Careful neuropsychological assessment may be useful in teasing out the various factors. This will be discussed further in Chapters 7 and 10.

Alcohol and Drug Abuse　　　Many families of brain-injured persons report an increase in alcohol and drug abuse after the injury. Whatever deleterious effects these substances may have on an otherwise intact brain, the impact can be far greater on a brain already compromised by a previous injury. In many such cases, careful historical investigation discloses that posttraumatic substance abuse is merely a continuation of a previous lifestyle pattern. This will be discussed further in Chapter 6.

Post-Traumatic Stress Disorder and "Cryptotrauma"　　　The term "posttraumatic" as used here refers to the classic PTSD syndrome as described for victims of catastrophic disasters or psychologically traumatic war experiences. The possible cognitive effects of severe psychological stress were considered above. However, it is also plausible that physical injury sometimes involves an accompanying psychological trauma, and this may be overlooked in the emphasis on treating the physical injury. If a standard postconcussion syndrome develops in the presence of what is judged to be a medically trivial injury (see the section on mild head injury below), the patient may be suspected of malingering or suffering from a longstanding psychiatric disorder. Pilowsky (1985, 1992) has drawn attention to this syndrome, which he terms *cryptotrauma*, and provides several case examples, two of which are relevant to our present topic.

A mining engineer in his 20's was struck on the head by a hopper. He was not unconscious at the time and sustained no lasting impairment apart from a headache and a fractured cheekbone. However, the hopper, weighing many tons, had locked his head against a steel railing, threatening to crush it slowly. He recalled hearing the bones in his head cracking and wondering how much more he could take before his skull burst. He was rescued by a workmate and removed to safety. Another case involved a railway worker in his 40's who fell headfirst into a hole and suffered only some muscle and ligament damage, yet complained of pain and disability many months later. When queried, he recalled lying head down in the dark hole with an excruciating pain in his neck, believing that his neck was broken and that he would die before he was found.

Two cases of my own corroborate Pilowsky's (1985, 1992) observations. One middle-aged woman was brutally mugged, the assailant grinding her head and face into the pavement with his shoe for several minutes while threatening to kill her. He robbed her of her purse and jewelry, but left her otherwise unharmed, and her head injury was designated a mild concussion plus scalp and facial lacerations. She subsequently complains of a chronic headache syndrome with memory impairment, dizziness, and fatigue. Another patient, a man in his 30's, was a passenger in an auto accident in which the car caught fire, and he witnessed a close female relative burn to death while trapped in the vehicle. He suffered a mild bump on the head, moderate back injury, and skin burns on his hands and legs from his vain attempts to rescue the relative. Almost two years post-accident, he is just beginning to emerge from a profound depression with severe work and social disability.

Parker (1990) argues that in most cases of brain injury, the overwhelming traumatic event, accompanied by fright, physical injury, and reduced adaptability, has a substantial effect on later recovery. Kolb (1987) has hypothesized that overwhelming stress can produce physiological changes in the brain that affect cognitive and emotional functioning. The studies reviewed in a previous section of this chapter have noted cognitive changes after severe psychological stress. Pilowsky (1985, 1992) notes that these terrifying experiences may not be volunteered at the time of initial history-taking, and he urges the clinician to ask for a detailed description of the patient's experience of the accident in working up each case. Indeed, psychological trauma is a known vector of continuing disability after brain (or other) injury, and effective psychotherapy must address this factor (Deitz, 1992; Horowitz, 1986; Miller, 1993b; see also Chapters 3 and 7).

"Positive" Personality Change   Although it may seem difficult to imagine how traumatic brain injury could produce any kind of change for the better, Ranseen (1990) has described several cases in which the posttraumatic personality changes were perceived by the family as improvements over what had gone before. All of these patients' premorbid personalities were described as being introverted, inhibited, quiet, and perhaps somewhat obsessive and depressed. They were viewed as unhappy individuals, and one suffered from clinically significant depression. Following brain injury, the patients appeared happier, were more talkative, and generally

seemed more extroverted. They were also viewed as being more content with their lives. Consistent with most reports of negative personality change following head injury, however, there was a tendency for these patients to be slightly more impulsive and irritable. This occasionally translated into inappropriate assertiveness or lack of tact, but was never of a severity that would significantly disrupt interpersonal relationships. It was also a change for which the patients retained some degree of self-awareness.

It seemed evident that the family members had been frustrated in the past by their spouses or sons having been aloof, withdrawn, and constricted. Consequently, the personality changes of talkativeness, mild disinhibition, and a more ebullient affect allowed them to achieve a fuller, more satisfactory relationship with their injured family member than had previously been the case.

Ranseen (1990) points out that the changes in emotional tone involving affect that might be described as euphoric, as well as behavioral changes of talkativeness and mild social disinhibition are quite reminiscent of those changes described as a more severe problem in the frontal lobe personality syndrome (e.g., Stuss & Benson, 1984; Stuss et al., 1992). The two most striking cases in this series did sustain documented damage to the right frontal lobe, which has been implicated in the regulation and display of emotions. Consequently, these moderate injuries causing mild disinhibition and euphoria often described following right hemisphere damage (Heilman et al., 1986), combined with relatively well-preserved cognitive skills and self-awareness, left these individuals more extroverted and seemingly less depressed, but without the more grossly inappropriate social disinhibition commonly displayed following severe head injury. Ranseen (1990) suggests that personality traits and all human behaviors fall on a continuum in terms of frequency, strength, and intensity in which pathology lies on both ends of the spectrum. As a result, these patients moved toward a more normal range in terms of frequency of talking, interest in people, and displays of happiness.

Recovery, Competency, and Long-Term Adjustment

Another very rough, general rule: If there is no history of preexisting personality disorder, significant psychopathology, or substance abuse, adjustment to life after brain injury is often surprisingly good in terms of job and family issues. Crucial here are the efforts of the rehabilitation team and the support systems the patient has available—not to mention the job market and economy as a whole. Often some combination of remediating the deficit, rehabilitating the function, and reconstituting the environment can contribute to optimal posttraumatic adjustment. This will be discussed further in Chapter 11.

Slagle's (1990) review has identified a number of patient factors that seem to be associated with outcome. The duration of unconsciousness and the stability of the patient's family seem to be predictive factors for the recovery of function and resumption of work. Employment after injury is less likely in patients with a long duration of coma, presence of aphasia, motor impairment, or seizures that persist more than 30 days after injury. Longer periods of posttraumatic amnesia are also related to poorer prognosis for recovery of social, vocational, and leisure activity at six months postinjury.

Patient problems associated with decreased likelihood of returning to gainful employment include low energy level, poor locomotion, poor memory, poor attention span, social immaturity, suspiciousness, depression, crudity, general inadequacy, poor motivation, unrealistic goals, and lack of emotional support in the home. Patients with agitation during the course of recovery are more likely to require later psychiatric care and less likely to return to work than appropriately active patients. For those unable to return to work, social isolation has been reported to persist at seven years postinjury. Patient motivation is certainly an important factor in recovery.

Prigatano et al. (1990) asked a group of traumatic brain injury patients and their relatives to complete the Patient Competency Rating Scale (PCRS). As predicted, brain-injured patients consistently underestimated their problems in emotional control and social interaction. While measures of verbal learning and simple finger tapping speed were consistently related to ratings concerning activities of daily living, neuropsychological test scores generally failed to predict ratings on the items sampling social interaction and emotional control. Thus, impaired awareness of certain behavioral limitations may reflect a cognitive/affective disturbance not adequately assessed by traditional neuropsychological test measures alone.

Problem areas for these patients included difficulties in handling arguments, adjusting to unexpected changes, knowing when something they had said has upset others, and control of their temper. These complex interpersonal difficulties reflect what the authors broadly refer to as difficulties in social competence. This variable has been specifically identified in predicting the capacity to maintain work in the face of other neurologic and psychiatric disabilities, and may be especially important for the high rate of unemployment seen in this patient group (see Prigatano et al., 1986).

A sample of community-dwelling adults who had sustained very severe closed head injury more than 18 months previously and required long-term rehabilitative support were compared by Marsh and Knight (1991) with a closely matched control group on a number of behavioral measures of skill during social interaction. Results showed that during such interactions the head-injured patients exhibited impaired communication skills. They appeared disinterested, and their speech was characterized as lacking in fluency and clarity due to their difficulty in finding appropriate words, use of inappropriate expressions, and inability to express ideas clearly. Attempts to find a relationship between the patients' cognitive deficits and their impaired communication skills were unsuccessful.

The authors suggest that the often-reported poor social adjustment and inadequate community reintegration of some head-injured patients are in part related to their inappropriate behavior during social interactions. This is particularly manifest in their poor language skills and speech delivery style. Specifically, their speech is lacking in fluency and clarity and they also fail to respond appropriately in conversations. This suggests that social rehabilitation efforts should focus on speech delivery and language skills. Issues of long-term adjustment are discussed further in Chapter 11.

Risk Factors for the Postconcussion Syndrome

What kinds of brain injury patients develop a postconcussion syndrome? Lishman (1988) has identified a number of factors believed to contribute to excessive psychosocial disability from head trauma. Pretraumatic factors include age, cerebral arteriosclerosis, alcoholism, "mental constitution," preexisting psychosocial difficulties, and recent life events. Peritraumatic factors include the brain damage itself, other physical injury, the emotional impact and meaning of the brain injury, the circumstances of the accident, and the effects of the early medical investigations and management. Posttraumatic factors include intellectual impairment, other impairments, epilepsy, emotional repercussions of the accident, ensuing psychosocial difficulties, and compensation and litigation issues.

In Slagle's (1990) review, it is suggested that postconcussion symptoms lasting more than two months after injury occur more frequently in patients with preexisting neurotic conditions or personality disorders (Levin et al., 1982). Similarly, early symptoms have been felt to be more likely related to organic factors, while those symptoms of longer duration may be perpetuated by secondary neurotic developments (Lishman, 1988). Psychological responses to persistent symptoms may play an important role in how disabling those symptoms actually are (Rimel et al., 1981). When the posttraumatic amnesia has been incomplete, there may be dreams, chronic anxiety, or obsessive rumination regarding the circumstances of the injury (Lishman, 1973; Miller, 1989a, 1993b). Somatic preoccupation may serve to focus anxiety in a manageable sphere so that greater ego integrity may be preserved. Interestingly, disabled patients with no observable psychosocial response to their condition may have a poorer prognosis for recovery.

The term *accident neurosis* was coined by H. Miller (1961) to describe patients who complain of a particular constellation of symptoms following an accident that produces head trauma or other injury to the neck, back, or limbs. Regardless of the nature and site of the injury, the following features are common to all patients: a higher incidence in men and unskilled workers, a tendency to follow industrial accidents, and a high frequency of compensation litigation that correlates poorly with the severity of the injury. The symptomatology is mixed and variable: anxiety, depression, and hysterical conversion being common, with a tendency toward histrionic exaggeration of symptoms. In contrast to H. Miller's assertions, later writers have noted that return to work and complete recovery from disability are uncommon even after settlement of compensation claims (Montgomery et al., 1991).

Levin et al. (1982) have argued that while postconcussive symptoms begin on an organic basis, their persistence is psychologically based. However, Binder (1986) concludes that psychological factors play a contributing role to sequelae initiated by organic injury, and that psychological symptoms may exist alongside organic ones. After all, psychological distress seems only normal when a patient suffers symptoms such as headaches, dizziness, or memory loss that seem to go on and on. Such symptoms, especially if associated with irritability and disability, are likely to cause anxiety and depression.

The mechanisms of persisting symptoms in the postconcussion syndrome, argues Binder (1986), are multiple and include psychogenic factors, injury to the brain, and injury to the head and neck. One of the most common symptoms, headache, is thought to be caused by craniocervical injuries (Jacobson, 1969), while migraine can be caused by traumatically induced intracranial arterial spasm (Greenblatt, 1973; Haas & Souvner, 1969). Another possible mechanism of headache is dysfunction of vasomotor regulation (Raskin & Appenzeller, 1980). Dizziness is often caused by damage to the ear (Toglia et al., 1970) or brainstem (Tuohima, 1978). Possible mechanisms of persisting dysfunction after concussion include undetected infarcts, undetected contusions, focal edema, diffuse axonal injury, and abnormal cerebral blood flow, including hypoxia (see Chapter 7).

"MILD" HEAD INJURY

Mild or *minor head injury* refers to a trauma that causes no unconsciousness, or a very short period of unconsciousness—usually seconds to minutes—and in which, according to some definitions, there is little or no objectifiable neuropathology based on the usual array of diagnostic procedures. With moderate to severe injuries, there is some correlation between length of coma, severity of injury, and outcome (Livingston et al., 1985a, 1985b), while in minor head injury, such a relationship does not appear (Davidoff et al., 1988).

The typical mild head injury patient has a variable posttrauma history of one month to a year or more and presents with persisting subjective symptomatology, including headache, memory problems, fatigue, anxiety, irritability, concentration difficulties, vision problems, word-finding difficulties, depression, and mood swings. Neurologic exam and neurodiagnostics including CT and EEG are often negative for central nervous system abnormalities, and even neuropsychological testing may be mostly in the normal range. Often the patient has not returned to premorbid level for home, school, leisure, and/or employment activities, or is experiencing problems in these settings. Litigation and compensation claims are often involved (Levine, 1988).

In some interpretations, then, mild head injury becomes another pejorative label, similar to the postconcussion syndrome. In a sense, one could say that a mild head injury syndrome refers to a postconcussion syndrome that is observed after what clinicians regard as a "nonserious" injury, based on history and objective neuropathological findings. Hence, as we shall see, the clinical issues surrounding mild head injury are similar to that of the postconcussion syndrome as a whole.

Pathophysiology of Mild Head Injury

In severe head trauma, gross movements of the brain within the skull result in widespread, diffuse damage. In contrast, movement effects during minor head trauma are considerably less significant, resulting in a more circumscribed range of cognitive deficits. These are usually limited to functions mediated by the more anterior portions of the brain—the frontal and temporal poles—e.g., memory, attention/concentration, abstract reasoning, and judgment (Davidoff et al., 1988; Kwentus et al., 1985).

Levin et al. (1987) conclude that a single, uncomplicated minor head injury rarely produces permanent cognitive impairment, and that the optimal recovery window should be approximately one to three months. These authors do, however, recognize that residual deficits may occasionally persist beyond this recovery period. They further acknowledge that the generalization of their findings is limited in patients with prior histories of head trauma, chronic alcohol or drug abuse, or other neuropsychiatric disorders. Less well understood are the longer-term sequelae of minor head injury, when they do appear. A sizable proportion of patients suffer from a wide variety of chronic symptoms, which often seem to be out of proportion to the severity of the initial trauma (Binder, 1986; Davidoff et al., 1988).

Gennarelli (1986) has suggested a mechanism relating mild head injury to the results of sudden acceleration/deceleration of the brain, which causes microscopic stretching and tearing, or shearing, of neuronal axons (see Chapter 1). Indeed, in mild head injury, physical destruction of axons need not occur at all as a direct result of the traumatic impact. Povlishock (1992) has experimentally documented that, other than in the most destructive insults, traumatic brain injury does not typically cause direct mechanical disruption of the axon. Rather, subtle, focal axonal change occurs, and over time such change leads to impaired axoplasmic transport, continued axonal swelling, and in some cases ultimate axonal disconnection perhaps hours later. This latter finding leaves open the intriguing possibility of a therapeutic window that might be potentially exploited to mitigate the effects of the brain injury if some yet-to-be-developed treatment could be applied in that interval.

Actually, much of the data on the pathophysiology of traumatic brain injury discussed in Chapter 1 would seem to suggest that some degree of brain disruption is almost unavoidable even in neurodiagnostically "negative" brain injuries. According to Binder (1986), rotational acceleration — the brain sharply bending and twisting on the brainstem — is more likely to cause concussion and diffuse axonal injury, but is less likely than linear acceleration — which tends to damage the observable surface of the cerebral cortex — to cause focal lesions. Centripetally directed forces may be more likely to damage subcortical, diencephalic structures related to emotion, motivation, and visceral functions (Parker, 1990).

Clinical and Neuropsychological Studies   Some authorities, like Binder (1986), assert that direct impact to the head is unnecessary to cause concussion. A case of severe anterograde amnesia of 72-hours duration occurring after a whiplash injury, an injury that was not caused by an impact to the head, has been described by Fisher (1982). Other studies suggest otherwise. Olsnes (1989) compared a group of patients with persistent symptoms following whiplash injury with a control group reporting similar somatic complaints, but no trauma history. All subjects were given an extensive neuropsychological test battery. The whiplash patients with chronic symptoms showed minimally impaired neuropsychological performance. Their main problems seemed to be headache and other pain complaints. Probably, however, group findings like this obscure individual differences in susceptibility to, and reaction to, nondirect head trauma-induced brain damage.

Radiological Studies   There is evidence that the effects of even mild head injuries may be cumulative. A significant number of patients have CT evidence of contusions, infarction, and/or focal edema after seemingly trivial head injuries (Binder, 1986). And, as we discussed in Chapter 1, boxing injuries not involving actual knockouts would probably qualify as "minor" head trauma in each individual case, but the cumulative effects can be substantial. Also, the football case discussed in that section shows that even seemingly trivial injuries can prove fatal in combination.

Electrophysiological Studies   A group of patients admitted to an accident and emergency unit with minor head injury were studied by Montgomery et al. (1991). Minor head injury was defined as trauma warranting brief inpatient overnight stay but with a posttraumatic amnesia of less than 12 hours. Each patient had a neurological examination, EEG power spectral analysis, brainstem auditory evoked potential recordings, a four-choice reaction-time measurement, and each completed a posttraumatic symptom checklist. These assessments were repeated six weeks later. Six months after the head injury, the symptom checklist was redone and reaction time measured again.

Study of brainstem auditory evoked potentials (a way of measuring how the brain processes sensory stimuli) at, or shortly after the trauma suggested that the postconcussion syndrome may follow at least three different courses: (1) acute recovery within six weeks in over 50% of the patients—in the present study, half of this group had normal evoked potentials shortly after injury; (2) a chronic condition with symptoms persisting over six months—only a minority of patients fell into this category and all had brainstem dysfunction following the trauma; (3) an increase of symptoms over a six-month period—less than a third of patients followed this course and most had no evidence of brainstem dysfunction.

The authors speculate that the acute group may have had transient organic damage with recovery, and the chronic patients had unremitting brainstem dysfunction. In contrast, organic factors did not account for the symptom formation in the symptom- exacerbation group; presumably, psychological and social influences were more important here. There was a trend for depression, anxiety, and irritability to be more common in the latter group. These observations fit the hypothesis presented by Lishman (1988) that organic factors are important in early symptom development, whereas psychogenic factors become dominant in the more chronic stage.

Neuropsychological Assessment of Mild Head Injury

According to Binder (1986), memory and concentration deficits are among the most common postconcussion syndrome complaints, and a temporary amnesia can occur as the result of a blow that fails to produce loss of consciousness, thus qualifying as mild head injury. As noted in Chapter 1, a study of American football injuries (Yarnell & Lynch, 1973) reported four cases of marked posttraumatic short-term memory impairment that occurred without any apparent alteration in consciousness, while others had delayed retrograde amnesia without losing consciousness. Severe anterograde amnesia lasting ten hours after a blow to the head without loss of consciousness has been reported (Fisher, 1966), and a number of studies have found evidence of neuropsychological impairment in persons tested within days of their concussive injury. In the first few days after mild head injury, at least, it appears that cognitive deficits may be clearly observed.

Leininger et al. (1990) examined a group of symptomatic mild head injury patients referred for neuropsychological assessment between one and 22 months after injury. These patients performed significantly more poorly than uninjured controls on four of eight neuropsychological tests. Patients who lost consciousness during injury obtained test scores similar to those who experienced disorientation or confusion but no loss of consciousness. The results indicate that minor head injury patients who report postconcussive symptoms possess measurable neuropsychological deficits, and the severity of these deficits is independent of neurological status immediately following injury.

Symptomatic minor head injury patients in this study displayed significantly poorer performance than uninjured controls on tests of reasoning, information processing, and verbal learning. The patient group also performed significantly worse than controls on a test that required the reproduction of a complex geometric design. Inefficient organization, poor attention to detail, and faulty error recognition contributed to reduced scores more than gross visuospatial or motor integration deficits.

Neuropsychological results revealed no evidence that injuries associated with a brief traumatic loss of consciousness were more debilitating than injuries initially associated with "dazing" but no actual loss of consciousness. Unlike severe head injuries, the occurrence and nonoccurrence of a traumatic loss of consciousness does not seem to distinguish persons at a greater risk or reduced risk for neuropsychological consequence in the case of minor head injury. Patients with postconcussive symptoms tested within three months of injury obtained test scores similar to symptomatic patients tested after three months of injury. This suggests that minor head injuries are not always innocuous, fully reversible conditions that resolve within days or a few weeks of injury. Rather, some patients appear to suffer enduring neuropsychological impairment.

Posthuma and Wild (1988) have observed that many of the difficulties experienced by mild head-injury patients fall into the category of what have been called executive control functions. These are indicators of the capacity for self-control and direction, including planning and organization, mental flexibility and problem-solving skills, initiative, motivation, and regulation of behavior. From a clinical standpoint, they note that mild head injury patients often show more acute distress over their deficits either because they are more aware of them than more severely injured patients or because they have higher expectations of themselves.

Prognostic Factors in Mild Head Injury-Induced Postconcussion Symptoms

Physical Factors   Generally, prognosis for recovery in postconcussion syndrome associated with mild head injury is poorer for individuals who have had multiple head trauma, who abuse drugs or alcohol, or who are over age 40 (Binder, 1986; Davidoff et al., 1988). This, Davidoff et al. (1988) believe, is due to the fact that the neurons that are killed or damaged in concussion are part of the brain's natural reserve capacity. If this reserve has already been depleted by prior encephalopathic factors, the brain has less to "fall back on" after a subsequent injury.

Socioeconomic Factors   The motivation and effort to put one's life back together will understandably be influenced by the type of life there is to go back to. Thus, socioeconomic and employment status is an important factor in recovery (Binder, 1986). Managerial-level patients have been found to make a much better readjustment to work than unskilled laborers (Rimel et al., 1981). While socioeconomic status may be related to the period of disability, it is not related to symptomatology (Binder, 1986). In one series of patients with all grades of severity of head trauma, more than two-thirds of those with professional and managerial occupations developed a postconcussion syndrome (Kelly, 1975). H. Miller (1961) implied that unskilled workers of the so-called "lower classes" have insufficient motivation to work because their jobs are undesirable, but professionals and managers may actually return to work more quickly because they have more control over their workload or are able to shunt responsibility to subordinates more easily.

Premorbid Personality and Psychopathology   Binder (1986) has reviewed the evidence that strongly suggests an association between the postconcussion syndrome and premorbid constitutional differences of personality. Adler (1945) found that posttraumatic anxiety dreams were strongly associated with mental symptoms. Krapnick and Horowitz (1981) found that the most prominent themes in psychotherapy with personal injury stress response syndromes were fear of repetition of the event, feelings of responsibility, rage at the source of the trauma, and discomfort over vulnerability.

Many postconcussive syndrome patients are labeled "hysterics" (Binder, 1986). A study of patients with hysterical conversion symptoms found that about half of them had both conversion symptoms and cerebral disease of various types (Merskey & Trimble, 1979). In another study, almost half of the postconcussive patients with hysterical hypalgesia had abnormal EEGs (Denker & Perry, 1954). These studies suggest that postconcussive syndrome patients with conversion or psychogenic symptoms may also have concurrent organic brain damage. Indeed, the traditional dichotomy between "organic" and "hysterical" symptoms is proving to be a rather loose one (Miller, 1984a, 1986–87, 1990f, 1991f; see Chapter 7).

The ground covered in these last two chapters underscores the complexity of the issues facing the clinician who treats brain-injured patients. Obviously, psychotherapy with this group must be broadly conceived and skillfully applied. The remainder of this book will deal with the issues that are important in helping the brain-injured patient reconstruct — or newly construct — his or her life.

PART II

Principles of
Psychotherapy

CHAPTER 3

Reclaiming the Self: Individual Psychotherapy With the Brain-Injured Patient

As THE LAST TWO CHAPTERS have made clear, the view of this book is that brain injury always impacts on a combination of preexisting psychosocial traits and current circumstances that together determine the kind of clinical picture we ultimately see postinjury. These factors will also influence the individual's response to our efforts at treatment.

TREATING THE WHOLE PERSON: GENERAL CONSIDERATIONS

Models and Methods of Psychotherapy

Recognizing the presence of generalized organic personality changes, but respecting the individual variations that typically present in clinical practice, Small (1980) has delineated two major principles of psychotherapy with brain-injured patients.

First, the patient should not be automatically lumped into a generic "organic" category with all other brain-injured individuals. Rather, his limitations in function and the emotional problems that arise from his efforts to cope should be individually assessed. For example, two individuals with a traumatic head injury may differ with respect to premorbid IQ, personality, educational level, degree of proficiency in certain verbal or mathematical or artistic skills, socioeconomic resources, family and community support systems, brain area of focal or greatest damage, presence of seizures, post-traumatic headaches or other chronic pain syndromes, proneness to aggressive outbursts or substance abuse, and so on. All of these will affect the course and prognosis of psychotherapy, and it is this delicate balance between individuality and generality that must always be kept in mind by the therapist.

The second principle is that treatment of the brain-injured patient requires a truly multimodal—psychotherapists like to say "eclectic"—approach. Psychotherapy, in the broadest sense, may include remedial instruction, specialized training, manipulation and structuring of the environment, medication where appropriate, and supportive, behavioral, cognitive, and psychodynamic approaches to psychotherapy. Therapists wedded to a particular theoretical doctrine of psychotherapy soon find that their brain-injured patients haven't read the textbooks—their problems and coping methods don't fit neatly into doctrinaire clinical paradigms. At the same time, the therapist who expects all brain-injured patients to act in the same, flat, concrete, "organic" way will be surprised at the often rich psychodynamic clinical material that sometimes emerges. Indeed, in some cases brain injury seems to lower the threshold to emergence of "repressed" or "primitive" psychical material.

Similar to Small's (1980) approach, O'Hara (1988) suggests a thorough assessment of both the patient's cognitive dysfunction and his emotional distress. Then, the patient can best be served by psychotherapeutic and rehabilitation efforts that address: (1) *cognition*, with emphasis on cognitive rehabilitation; (2) *emotion*, including attention to adjustment reactions to trauma, posttraumatic changes in personality, and preexisting long-term personality traits; and (3) *behavior*, including management of such physical changes as diminished energy, seizures, and posttraumatic pain, as well as the setting of goals and the development of opportunities for successful progress by the patient.

O'Hara (1988) has found that omission of one of these three treatment components ultimately leads to failure in terms of ameliorating the patient's emotional distress and facilitating adequate community integration. In my experience, it is not always necessary to address all three components simultaneously and with equal intensity in order to achieve an acceptable therapeutic payback. Rather, success in one domain eases the way toward being able to tackle the others, and the result is a mutually reinforcing therapeutic effect—one of the "virtuous cycles" (as opposed to vicious cycles) that therapists strive to cultivate.

For example, steady success at mastering a challenging rehab program or real-life job skill may foster just enough ego strength to allow the patient to begin talking about fears, anxieties, and hostilities that may have been suppressed since the injury. Or emotional ventilation and growing support-ive reassurance, perhaps along with improved control of posttraumatic pain, may lift the patient sufficiently out of his demoralization to enable him to begin thinking about, and training for, the future. The approach here should be practical: Seize upon progress in one area, nurture it to some reasonable degree of stability, and then use it as a springboard for moving forward in other areas.

Cognitive Rehabilitation, Cognitive Therapy, and Psychotherapy

As O'Hara (1988) points out, rehabilitation efforts that concentrate on cognitive skills, to the neglect of emotion and personality, not only inhibit the full range of adaptive coping, but also fail to help the patient redefine and integrate a new identity. Indeed, Carberry and Burd (1985) criticize the simplistic, childlike content of many computerized or workbook cognitive rehab programs intended for adult brain-injured patients. While computer programs may be temporarily diverting or entertaining, there remain seri-ous questions about the generalizability of these game-like skills to other, real-life areas of attention, concentration, language, memory, abstract rea-soning, judgment, and so on (see Chapter 1).

Add to this the saturation effect of enforced continuous and tedious practice, and it is not surprising that "cognitive rehab" may come to be viewed as the least enjoyable — if not outright detested — rehabilitation activ-ity in many institutional or in-home programs. This, in turn, can have a decidedly negative effect on patient morale and willingness to participate in other aspects of therapy. As suggested above, better to begin at the point of least emotional resistance and encourage improved cognitive skill train-ing as one of the eventual goals of therapy, rather than further traumatize the patient by chaining him to a computer console where any already-existing humiliation is compounded by failure even at "kid's games."

In some cases, however, the opposite may occur. Computer work may hold back progress if the patient becomes *too* comfortable with video-game playing to the neglect of real-life adaptive skill practice. In this case, the patient may resist all attempts to pry him from the computer console, claiming endless entitlement to this "cognitive rehab."

Fortunately, the majority of mildly brain-injured patients experience only minor cognitive deficits that often improve to some degree. In such cases, extensive and sophisticated remediation of basic cognitive skills, as practiced with more severely brain-injured patients, is usually unnecessary.

Instead, the focus should be on developing confidence in handling the cognitive and adaptive challenges of everyday life, such as problem-solving in social situations, budgeting monies, and handling multiple tasks simultaneously. Improvement in these areas is often most evident in terms of processing speed and stamina, that is, the ability to maintain consistent performance over sustained periods of time (Novack et al., 1988).

From the other direction, psychotherapy or behavioral interventions in the absence of any kind of cognitive rehabilitation—especially training in the use of compensatory strategies—may be useful for emotional ventilation and stress-management, but will necessarily be limited by its failure to address critical cognitive deficits that compromise the patient's ability for insight. These include diminished self-awareness or memory loss, and impaired judgment that maintains the patient's unproductive habits and social distress (O'Hara, 1988).

In fact, cognitive, emotional, and behavioral issues are rarely separable in the real clinical world of brain injury. Prigatano et al. (1986) point out that when patients are cognitively confused, they are generally not clear about what their feeling states are. When the confusion subsides, feelings of depression and deep sorrow often emerge. Also, many of the interpersonal problems of the brain-injured person are related to faulty thinking and incorrect assumptions he may make about himself in a variety of social situations. Compounding the problem is a tendency to deny and cover up deficits by increased rigidity of thinking. Interpersonal dialogue is thus often accompanied by concreteness, loose associations, circumstantiality, and egocentricity—indeed, some patients may talk and act quite "crazy" and in some cases may be mistaken for schizophrenic.

The opposite also sometimes happens. One of my first brain injury inpatients was a young woman who sustained a moderate-to-severe head injury, allegedly as a result of a suicidal dive into the deep end of an empty swimming pool. Postinjury behavior months after the event included social withdrawal, bizarre posturing, and evidence of auditory hallucinations. Since the family insisted that she had been relatively "calm and normal" before the injury (the circumstances of the injury—accidental or intentional—were never fully clarified), the clinical staff assumed the strange behavior to be injury-related. A neurology resident rotating through the unit, who was concerned only with treating the posturing, ordered a trial of haloperidol. We were all subsequently surprised when the hallucinations appeared to stop and the patient emerged from her withdrawn shell. This prompted further history-taking and family interviewing, and it was eventually learned that this patient had indeed had a long psychiatric history. Needless to say, the problems of missed diagnoses and mixed diagnoses cut both ways.

Cognition and Psychotherapy

Traditional insight-oriented psychotherapy places substantial cognitive demands on even the healthy and intelligent, albeit "neurotic," patient (Bennett, 1989; Blau, 1988; Shapiro, 1989) — we usually expect our "good" patients to "work" at getting better, and we hope they have the cognitive skills to do such work, i.e., an appropriate level of development of what Hartmann (1939) called the adaptive ego functions (see Chapter 12).

As the essence of psychotherapy is communication, the successful patient needs to have well-developed receptive and expressive language skills (Bennett, 1989; Miller, 1990d, 1991a). Not only must he be able to understand the content of the therapist's communications, but he must be sensitive to inflection and other nonsemantic language cues, abilities that may be impaired by organic aphasic or aprosodic disorders (Benson, 1977; Ross, 1981). The patient must also be able to speak his mind clearly and fluently, and must also possess the necessary degree of abstract and interpretive ability to be able to generalize from one situation to another and thereby achieve therapeutic insight. Most important, he must be able to apply general principles covered in therapy to issues and instances in real life. The powers of reflection must be intact at least in a rudimentary way for the patient to profit from interpretation and from the formal aspects of the transference relationship.

On an even more basic level, attention must be adequate to follow a given train of thought for any length of time, to track the patient-therapist dialogue, and to retain the focus or theme of the therapeutic session. Some organic patients may "free-associate" only too readily. Ideas spill forth, tripping over and colliding with one another in an almost Jamesian stream-of-consciousness reverie. What is typically absent in these cases is the ability to go back and make some kind of therapeutic sense of any interpretable material thus produced. Memory is also an important factor, since failure to retain the conclusions, insights, or even the emotional context of one session to the next will necessarily impede any cumulative psychotherapeutic effect (Bennett, 1989; Small, 1980).

In most cases, different kinds of cognitive difficulties occur together (Bennett, 1989). The brain-injured patient may be very concrete in his or her thinking and language skills, interpret everything literally, frequently lose the train of conversation, and miss subtleties of language. The ability to remember events from daily life or from past sessions, or even from the beginning of the present session, may be fragmented, distorted, and compounded by confabulation. Difficulties with reasoning, abstraction, and generalization may preclude insight, raise suspicions of therapeutic resistance, or cause confusion that overwhelms the patient and thereby precipitates an emotional outburst—the so-called *catastrophic reaction* in response to frustration and dashed self-esteem—with the total shunning of all further therapy. Thus, it is apparent that for most brain-injured patients, at least in the initial stages, supportive therapeutic measures must take precedence over interpretive or insight-oriented ones.

SUPPORTIVE MEASURES

The Therapeutic Relationship

One area in which there is no fundamental difference between organically impaired and other kinds of patients is in the importance of the relationship between therapist and patient. Experienced therapists know that the quality of the therapeutic alliance often makes a critical difference in successful progress and outcome. Brain-injured patients may disgorge their full pain and fury onto the therapist because no one else will listen to or tolerate it. They may become clingingly dependent, seeming to surrender every last shred of autonomy to the therapist's idealized omnipotence. They may split and triangulate the therapeutic situation to pit doctor against family, to wheedle medication, or to extort money or special privileges. They may use the therapist as discretionary reality-tester, taking or leaving the therapeutic suggestions as they see fit. And they may engage in virtually all the other types of "game-playing" that psychotherapy patients are known for (Blau, 1988; Kottler, 1992).

Small (1980) recommends that the therapeutic relationship be open and positive from the first contact. The patient has to know early on that the therapist will be on his or her side through failures, rages, anxieties, and depressions. The positive therapeutic alliance helps the patient accept clarification of reality, the gentle challenging of denial, the setting of realistic goals, and the constructive working toward of these goals. Failure of the therapist to understand, tolerate, and ride out the brain-injured patient's ups and downs is likely to precipitate a catastrophic reaction, while failure to actively and directedly help the patient into adaptive and reconstructive efforts risks leaving him adrift with a sense of helplessness and futility.

In sum, the patient has to know that the therapist is *there* for him, will provisionally accept and tolerate at least a little more crap than friends or family who are emotionally enmeshed with the patient are willing or able to, but will set firm and realistic limits with regard to what is expected of the patient in or out of the therapy session.

Information and Education

In many cases, the most important immediate intervention is educational (Bennett, 1987). Simply understanding their symptoms and learning that these are normal consequences of brain injury can be extremely beneficial for patients. If nothing else, it may be the first step toward putting some reality on the situation. I'm frequently struck by how otherwise therapeutically zealous medical and rehab clinicians neglect to provide patients and their families with simple and understandable information about their condition. "Why didn't my doctor tell me that?" is a common response to discussions of topics I took for granted the patient already knew about, such as where in his brain a focal injury is located, or what the physical and cognitive sequelae to head injury or brain surgery are expected to be in his case.

In fairness, many busy clinicians may be forced by their schedules to impart such information quickly and choppily, often in jargony medicalese, to patients and families at just the time, usually soon after injury, when the patient is most disoriented and the family most stressed-out. Also, there may be an assumption that someone else must have already gone over the pertinent details—indeed, that's what I used to think. So, primary and secondary care clinicians who read this, please take note: A few extra minutes spent explaining the nature of your patients' problems and the treatments for it may spare them months or even years of anxiety, confusion, and inappropriate action based on inadequate or misinterpreted information.

But beyond the educational aspect of information is an important existential component. When bad things happen, people need reasons. In the course of psychotherapy, some sort of explanatory model should be provided that helps the brain-injured patient understand what has happened to him (Prigatano et al., 1986). Patients should be helped to make some sense of the brain injury and its meaning in their life, and to try to achieve a certain measure of self-acceptance and forgiveness for themselves and possibly for others who may have caused the accident. Patients should be encouraged to make realistic commitments to work and interpersonal relationships, and be taught how to behave in different social situations. The therapist should foster an attitude of realistic hope and back this up by providing specific cognitive and behavioral strategies to compensate for, and cope with, neuropsychological deficits.

In practical terms, psychotherapists should take a direct, gently confrontive (but not aggressively confrontational) approach with brain-injured patients, providing instruction, guidance, and explanation of options where necessary (Prigatano & Klonoff, 1988). For patients with significant problems in judgment, reasoning, or reality testing, the therapist may act as the "auxiliary ego," helping patients with decisions that they are unable to make independently (Werman, 1984), such as realistic employment choices.

INSIGHT AND INTERPRETATION

Awareness and Structure

A goal for some brain-injured patients, beyond a purely directive approach, may be to increase their capacity for self-observation. Cicerone (1989) reports that specific, concrete feedback is the most effective means of dealing with resistance to treatment. This involves the use of formal checklists, self-monitoring inventories, and in some cases, videotapes. Hopefully, patients can learn to repeat such feedback themselves as often as necessary to compensate for deficits in attention, memory, or comprehension. Repeated, structured self-observations also help patients to objectify the evaluation of their own performance, to figure out what it is they're doing "right" and "wrong." In such cases, Cicerone points out, overt self-observation may compensate for a loss of internalized self-monitoring.

Cicerone (1989) cites Pine's (1985) recommendations for working with the so-called "fragile" patient, and has attempted to apply these principles to the treatment of brain-injured patients (see also Miller, 1992a, 1992b; Robbins, 1989; Shapiro, 1989; Werman, 1984; see Chapter 12). In this therapeutic framework, first, the range of associations to an interpretation should be limited, since the classical, open-ended, interpretive approach may precipitate cognitive disorganization in the brain-injured patient. Instead of psychodynamically interpreting a patient's emotional response, the therapist should cognitively restructure the meaning of that response, so as to aid the patient in clarifying his or her own motives, feelings, and actions.

Second, interpretations should be postponed until an agitated or withdrawn emotional state has subsided, allowing the patient to gain composure and control, to be less defensive and more amenable to "hearing" the interpretation. During a relatively neutral or nonthreatening interlude in the session, the therapist can refer back to the emotionally charged event, employing the distance of time as a psychological buffer.

Third, the therapist should maximize the patient's preparedness and the supportive aspects of the environment, i.e., potentially challenging statements or suggestions by the therapist should carry with them the understanding that the patient has some leeway in accepting them — at least for the moment, or until he or she is better able to deal with the subject.

Neuropsychodynamics and the Limits of Interpretation

According to Bennett (1989), organically based cortical disinhibition may result in the reemergence of previously resolved psychological issues, perhaps dating back to childhood This may mislead the therapist into believing that "unresolved issues" underlie the patient's current complaints, spurring the therapist to embark upon an inappropriate program of psychotherapy. The error is in addressing old psychological issues that have reappeared in the patient's consciousness due to cortical disinhibition as if they are the patient's primary psychodynamic focus, all the time not realizing that it is the cognitive deficits that are the primary problem underlying the difficulties in coping. The therapist lacking knowledge and experience with brain injury may even go so far as to "expertly" assert that neither cognitive nor emotional changes could result from such a "minor" head injury; indeed, this diagnostic error is committed disconcertingly often by supposedly knowledgeable neurologists and psychiatrists (see Chapter 2).

The proper approach in such cases is to be appropriately supportive, but refrain from traditional insight-oriented therapeutic modalities until the patient's cognitive processes recover to the point where he can productively participate in such therapy. More generally, Bennett (1989) speculates that the process of resolution of psychological issues is facilitated by active cortical inhibition (interestingly, a similar theory was first proposed by Pavlov, 1927).

RESISTANCE AND DENIAL

Denial and Defense

The traditional concept of resistance in psychodynamic psychotherapy is that it represents an active, protective, psychical force that keeps repressed, disturbing, primitive instinctual material from coming into conscious awareness. Small (1980) points out that brain damage often results in behavioral regression due in large part to the dissolution of higher integrative cognitive skills necessary for complex adaptational tasks. Even as recovery and improvement in cognitive functioning occur, the patient may cling to the more regressed mode because it has become predictable and manageable. Careful encouragement, support, and step-by-step training may be necessary to enable such a patient to utilize his or her recovering capacities.

Forcing a too-early renunciation of "immature" defenses and coping patterns, argues Small (1980), may precipitate a catastrophic reaction and lead to massive resistance toward further progress. Denial, especially when severe and pervasive, is probably the most difficult of the defenses to deal with, and organic denial is typically refractory to any psychotherapeutic approach. In other cases, denial serves a more psychodynamically based, ego-protective function, which, however, may be maladaptive because it prevents the development of a realistic self-concept and impedes efforts to focus on areas where true progress might be made.

Cicerone (1989) points out that brain-injured patients who may freely acknowledge their physical symptoms may, at the same time, deny any cognitive, behavioral, or emotional disability. Patients may also acknowledge problems with memory much more readily than problems with thinking and personality. Perhaps problems with physical functions and memory are more objectifiable, more easily separated from the person's sense of self, and therefore less psychologically threatening. However, Cicerone suggests, it might also be that the comprehension of our own thought processes and personality attributes requires a greater capacity for self-reflection, and therefore represents knowledge that is less acceptable to the patient with greater conceptual impairment, or with organic lack of awareness. In still other cases, denial may represent an emotional reaction and protective response in the face of increasing recognition of disability and emotional distress.

Confronting denial in a brain-injured patient, says Small (1980), is often a delicate matter because the therapist risks pushing the patient over the edge into a catastrophic reaction, resulting in a further entrenchment of the denial. Small suggests avoiding confrontations and challenges in favor of a gradual focusing on reality that continually monitors the patient's ego tolerance as it proceeds. Partial insights and interpretations should take precedence over ultimate ones, so that sufficient time is allowed for a reaction to each interpretive piece to be elaborated and judged.

In this therapeutic vein, a particular technique recommended by Small (1980) is to encourage the substitution of a more "negotiable" defense, such as rationalization, for outright denial. One 55-year-old head injury patient insisted for some time that he could return to his old job, involving a highly skilled, blue-collar, technical machinist trade, even though his current level of impairment rendered such a prospect clearly out of the question. He adamantly refused to consider any other kind of less demanding work, strenuously insisting that he had been a loyal contributor to his company for many years, and if "they won't let me go back to my old job, I'm not doing a damn thing."

By capitalizing on his strong sense of entitlement, I was able to gradually swing him around to the idea that he had indeed "paid his dues" in that particular job and that he probably now deserved to lay off and take it easy for a while. This permitted him the psychological leeway to undertake tasks he could deal with more easily during this "semiretirement," and from there move to jobs he could perform competently in a real employment setting, albeit, in his appraisal, "on the side—just to keep my mind occupied." Here, it was a matter of reframing the denial in a more ego-supportive context. One very practical bonus of this accommodation, I learned later, was that he was able to stay with his company long enough to earn his pension and retirement benefits—something his family appreciated and thus led to a marked reduction of stress and worry at home.

This kind of modality should be used with caution, however, as certain patients may react to the therapist's well-intentioned reframing efforts as a form of clinical hucksterism designed to belittle the patient and "twist my mind around," as one patient put it. Here again, knowing your patient well and having gained his or her trust will effectively lubricate the complex machinery of these clinical intervention strategies.

Another therapeutic approach is to forget altogether about insight vs. denial, per se, and instead focus on goals. Here, says Small (1980), it is extremely important that the series of sub-goals leading to the main objective be broken down into small enough chunks so that the patient can accomplish them competently, but not so simple that the patient feels he is being patronized. I'm always impressed by the uncanny ability of many otherwise obtunded patients to discern when they're being treated like "babies."

The Premorbid Personality

Prigatano et al. (1986) point out that many of the failures in psychotherapy with brain-injured patients are seen in individuals who had major psychiatric problems before their injury. However, not all of these patients may have shown obvious signs of such problems beforehand. Their relatively stable job and family routines, as well as their general cognitive compensatory skills may have allowed them to keep those problems under control. But when the brain injury undercuts their cognitive abilities, the underlying psychiatric disorders or behavioral disturbances emerge in an unrestrained fashion, and these may irreparably sabotage the therapy process. In contrast, the patients who seem to benefit most from psychotherapy are those who are committed to becoming independent, who can take a realistic view of themselves, who can utilize their strengths and tolerate their weaknesses, and who can work diligently at cognitive remediation and other therapeutic tasks—an apt description of "good" psychotherapy patients in general (Blau, 1988; Kottler, 1991, 1992; Miller, in press d).

Similarly, Lewis and Rosenberg (1990) emphasize the effects of patients' premorbid personalities in determining whether therapy—and the therapist—are seen as a benefit, or as a threat and a burden. Patients whose preexisting level of ego organization was only in the borderline range to begin with probably have never fully developed the capacity to use ideation and self-reflection in the service of adaptation. In psychotherapy they are encouraged to reflect on their experiences and they consequently view therapy as a painful challenge to their vestigial faculties for thinking in the service of self-understanding, problem-solving, and planning a course of adaptive behavior. Some patients may become—indeed, perhaps always were—characterologically unable or reluctant to engage in such effort, and the therapist must then continually tread a fine line between stimulating the patient's latent and genuine capacities for adaptive thought and action, and pushing the patient beyond his or her limits, thereby creating the set-up for a catastrophic reaction (see also Miller, 1992a, 1992b; see Chapter 12).

Resistance to Change

Similar to Small's (1980) argument, Lewis and Rosenberg (1990) point out that many brain-injured patients experience psychotherapy as a threat to the relative safety of their dependency. The neuropsychological dysfunction and associated functional disabilities may exempt them from many of the demands life places on the average adult, thus providing an acceptable modus operandi for having their dependency needs met by others. The process of psychotherapy, with its implicit thrust toward growth and autonomy, may therefore be viewed by such patients with some degree of ambivalence, if not outright aversion. A related fear is that if they make even those changes and functional gains that are genuinely within their capacity, then others will perceive them as more intact and competent than they really are, and consequently abandon them.

Prigatano et al. (1986) point out that for the brain-injured patient plagued by guilt or remorse, the injury may be perceived as a sort of cosmic atonement. Psychotherapy, with the implicit promise it holds for a fuller, more productive, and happier life, may therefore be resisted. Accordingly, these authors say, the patient's guilt and feelings of "badness" should be addressed in psychotherapy, but this, I find, can be difficult for a number of reasons.

First, the ability to achieve the requisite reflective distance and self-evaluation that true remorse implies may be adversely affected by cognitive impairment (Miller, 1988a). Second, some of the patient's feelings of "badness" may be reality-based, as traumatic brain injury sometimes comes as the capping event of a career of impulsive hell-raising and callous abuse of other people (see Chapter 5). Third, where true remorse exists for, say, the death of an innocent passenger in a car accident, the patient's functional incapacitation may be the intrapunitive "compromise" he accepts to forestall a more virulent decompensation. Well-meaning therapeutic attempts to disencumber such patients of their self-imposed Sisiphyean stone may be met with ferocious resistance, as this penance may be all that is holding the patient's psyche together in the face of otherwise unbearable guilt. Here, the therapist must be extraordinarily sensitive and creative in broaching and dealing with this issue, which will vary in its particulars from case to individual case.

SPECIAL PSYCHOTHERAPEUTIC PROBLEMS

Concreteness and Rigidity

Carberry and Burd (1986) have described two problems that may complicate the psychotherapy process with brain-injured patients. The first is rigidity of thought processes, which refers to the impaired flexibility in thinking frequently seen in a patient who appears "unreasonably" unyielding in his opinions and actions. In such cases, these authors suggest, the therapist can ask the patient to list as many alternative views and choices as possible on significant issues to encourage flexibility. Brainstorming and listing alternatives in a spontaneous fashion, trying out opposite behavioral ideas as an experiment, and using therapeutic humor can be useful techniques to facilitate less egocentric and rigid thinking.

However, one problem with these exercises arises from a single observable fact: There is a big difference between rehearsing cognitive strategies in the therapeutic session and internalizing these strategies for future spontaneous use in the real world. This, of course, is part of the broader problem of lack of generalization faced by cognitive rehabilitation specialists (see Chapter 1).

Also, be careful about using humor. Organically impaired patients may not "get" the joke in more abstract and metaphorical kinds of humor, and their concreteness and egocentric personalization may cause them to perceive themselves as being made fun of. The result may be the unintended further alienation of an already hypersensitive patient. I had this experience in a group therapy setting where I sometimes use cartoons from magazines to highlight certain topics. One patient failed to see the humor in a particular cartoon and became indignant that I was mocking her disability — fortunately, the other group members bailed me out. Later, it became clear that the offended patient had misinterpreted the "funny" point of the cartoon, focusing instead on some aspect of the joke that painfully tapped into her own issues regarding relationships with men.

In general, however, I find humor a valuable therapeutic adjunct if used judiciously. Also, even such clumsy but well-intended blunders may be excused by patients if there exists a solid therapeutic relationship based on trust. More on the use of humor and related "paradoxical" kinds of techniques in psychotherapy as a whole can be found in the volume edited by Fry and Salameh (1987).

Deficits in Empathy

The second therapeutic obstacle identified by Carberry and Burd (1986) involves deficits in empathic response, which is especially likely to be seen following frontal lobe damage (Grattan & Eslinger, 1989; Mattson & Levin, 1990). The cognitive rigidity of the brain-injured patient often manifests itself socially as egocentricity and limited empathic reciprocation in interpersonal relationships. One strategy recommended by Carberry and Burd (1986) is for the therapist to consistently ask questions such as "How does your wife feel about this?" or "What feelings did your friend talk about when you said that?" In trying this approach, I've found that some patients respond favorably, that is, they actually pause and try to reflect on what the other person might have been experiencing. Other patients seem to miss the point entirely, while still others get frustrated and angry at the therapist's "changing the subject," i.e., focusing on someone other than the self-absorbed patient himself. These differences probably relate to a combination of factors such as injury severity and premorbid personality.

Carberry and Burd (1986) also favor specific training in empathy, carried out by asking the patient to anticipate how the therapist might react to a particular event that occurred in the session. At the same time, they suggest tying the deficits in empathy to problematic events in the patient's life, which may spur the patient to tune into other people's feelings and recognize that others have separate, often different, emotional reactions. Connecting difficulties in expressing empathy during the therapy session with similar empathic communication problems out in the real world also fosters generalization.

Immaturity and Childishness

Frontal lobe patients, especially those with minimal deficits in other areas, may show relatively normal performance on standard intellectual tests, even though their judgment and comportment in practical daily tasks and real-life social interactions is contrastingly abysmal (Ackerly, 1964; Eslinger & Damasio, 1985; Stuss & Benson, 1984). Yet these patients may use their intact test performance to argue—often in a narrowly technical, concrete, and "lawyerlike" manner—for their overall intactness of cognitive and psychosocial functioning and attendant rights to full adult privileges. The therapist may then have no choice but to be gently but firmly confrontive regarding how the patient's behavior is disruptive or maladaptive, and to work with the patient in relearning self-monitoring. Bennett (1987) suggests building complexity through the use of such tasks as meal planning and preparation, and gradually expanding the tasks to include more and more normal self-management activities.

The kinds of immature, childish behavior often seen in frontal lobe and other brain-injured patients can interfere with interpersonal relationships both within the therapy setting and outside of it (Prigatano & Klonoff, 1988). One factor is whether the patient can see the "big picture," or simply apprehends and understands small, restricted aspects of a given situation. For example, if the patient overreacts to very small details and does not understand the complexities of human interaction—misses the interpersonal forest for the trees—establishing an adult relationship is problematic. Establishing normal human intimacy is also difficult if one adult is childish and does not appreciate the normal, mature aspects of relationships (similar problems are reported by families of Alzheimer patients and patients with some types of personality disorders). In many such cases, the only alternative is to take a directive and reeducative approach, to train the patient to at least "go through the motions" of normal adult interpersonal behavior until, hopefully, some of this behavior becomes reinternalized.

Paranoia and Suspiciousness

The cognitive impairment sustained in brain injury—again, particularly injury involving the frontal lobes—frequently confronts the patient with an altered interpretive lens through which to evaluate not only his own feelings, motives, and abilities, but also the utterances, nuances, actions, and reactions of others. When this interpretive ability becomes sufficiently distorted, paranoid and other delusions may result. According to Lishman (1978), a number of brain damage-induced factors contribute to the development of paranoia. The patient loses cognitive flexibility and has difficulty shifting from one frame of reference to another, a prerequisite for empathy (see Grattan & Eslinger, 1989). Cognitive concreteness nails the patient to the immediate situation and causes his attention to be captured by incidental impressions and events. Inability to extract essentials and discard trivial or redundant aspects of a situation is further compounded by the deficiency in abstract conceptualization that ordinarily permits a person to transcend immediate impressions and implications of an utterance, action, or event. All this provides fertile cognitive ground for the development of overvalued ideas of reference or frank paranoid delusions.

Clinicians understand that paranoia is often fueled by feelings of inadequacy and inferiority, and the typical brain-injured patient has much to feel inadequate about as he is regularly confronted with situations he can no longer handle—or at least handle as well as before. Patients also may become extremely defensive about their new dependency on other people and the loss of control over their lives that this entails. In many cases, caretakers come to assume responsibility and decision-making for more and more areas of the patient's life. Worse, this increased dependence on the few is exacerbated by increasing isolation from the many, as friends and family drift away, workmates are no longer seen, and even doctor visits become less frequent.

All this leaves the patient removed from the larger social world and in daily, almost continuous, contact with weary caretakers who may themselves be experiencing a smoldering resentment, if not outright hostility, toward the patient, borne of dashed expectations for recovery and general burnout. Not surprising then, that paranoia may develop as the dominant personality characteristic in the patient, which further ticks off the caretakers and propels a vicious cycle of recrimination and despair (see Chapter 4).

Not that this is inevitable. Prigatano et al. (1988) believe that premorbid personality plays a role in posttraumatic paranoia and that neuropsychological deficits are a necessary but not sufficient condition for producing paranoid delusions after brain injury. Certainly, it appears that some patients adjust much better than others, even with seemingly equivalent levels and types of physical and cognitive impairment. One would expect that patients with premorbidly low self-esteem and coping resources would lash out more catastrophically to yet another stab at their ego integrity than patients who have a more solid and yet flexible psychical structure capable of absorbing such blows.

In dealing clinically with the paranoid brain-injured patient, Prigatano et al. (1988) recommend that first, a consistent, structured, working alliance be established between patient and therapist. This includes strict adherence to appointment times, specific review of daily work assignments, and avoidance of vague interpretations about feeling states. Once such a consistent, reality-based relationship is established, the therapist can gradually help the patient to verify his perceptions. For example, patient self-generated qualifying statements such as "I don't know if this really happened, but . . ." or "This may be a delusion, but . . . " are utilized by the therapist to help the patient increase his self-monitoring skills—especially to encourage the patient's ability to preemptively modify inaccurate perceptions before they develop into fixed delusional beliefs.

My only qualification to this approach has to do with the "reality" aspect. Sometimes, there are several realities that confront the patient, the three most common of which are the patient's own reality, the therapist's reality, and the patient's family's reality. Even in traditional psychotherapy, all too often these worlds collide, and the therapist must carefully evaluate and piece together a coherent, composite reality that accommodates all three to some degree. Trying to compel a brain-injured patient to conform to a reality that has been falsely presented to the therapist by a manipulative or even a well-meaning, but confused, family risks blowing the whole "reality trip" and propelling the patient into the relative safety of his delusion.

Prigatano et al. (1988) regard some of the techniques of behavior modification valuable in handling paranoia, while others may be worse than useless. Positive aspects consist of focusing on practical goals, mutually agreed upon by patient and therapist. This helps the patient measure his success and get direct feedback about how he is progressing toward his goal. In contrast, placing a cognitively impaired paranoid patient on a rigid behavioral contingency program can easily reinforce the notion that he is in fact being controlled or manipulated by others. These authors find that putting fewer rather than more demands on these patients is very important in establishing a therapeutic alliance. In fact, this kind of informed therapeutic flexibility is useful in dealing with psychotherapeutic control issues in general (Kottler, 1991; Miller, in press d).

Emotional Outbursts and Instability

Another problem area involves anger and temper outbursts. According to Bennett (1987), these can be dealt with using much the same kinds of techniques that help nonbrain-damaged patients deal with anger control.

One approach is stress management and relaxation training, which may result in a lower level of arousal to frustrating events and thus a higher threshold to reacting explosively to potentially anger-evoking situations. By self-monitoring, the patient can learn to recognize when his threshold is being approached and then utilize the relaxation training. Learning to identify anger-inciting events, and then either avoiding them or relaxing before they occur can be helpful. Cognitively rehearsing strategies to be used in stressful situations also decreases the likelihood of anger outbursts occurring. Teaching the patient to recognize and deal adaptively with potentially anger-evoking situations is the key to avoiding many maladaptive responses. For more intact patients, more sophisticated cognitive-behavioral approaches, like the one described by Potter-Efron and Potter-Efron (1991) may be useful. Anger and its management are discussed in more detail in Chapter 5.

Helplessness and Hopelessness

Doubt about performance and indecision in situations requiring any risk or responsibility may develop in brain-injured patients who are fearful of further loss and/or have experienced failure in situations in which they were consistently successful before the injury (O'Hara, 1988). In essence, a "learned helplessness" is produced, which may inadvertently be reinforced by family members who themselves have been psychologically traumatized by the patient's injury. For families who fear additional risk-taking and who assume responsibility for the patient, further reinforcement of the patient's dependency in decision-making is likely to occur. With such patients, particularly in preinjury dependent personalities, the psychotherapeutic liaison must be carefully monitored and structured to allow the patient to gradually experience successful risk-taking and goal-setting, with the therapist's support and assistance.

Self-Image and Identity

The impairment in coping produced by decreased efficiency of information processing, impaired memory, and diminished reasoning ability may constitute a savage blow to the self-image of a previously intelligent, well-educated, and high-functioning patient (Bennett, 1987). A type of patient I'm seeing more and more often is a premorbidly high-achieving, almost compulsively successful, "Type A" executive or professional whose injury has resulted in perhaps a 10 or 15% loss of cognitive efficiency, as near as can be determined by the tools of assessment. Indeed, IQ and other test performance, even after the brain injury, is likely to be in the superior range on many indices. But this is a person that is used to "giving 110 percent." Ninety-five percent, or even 105 percent, is just not enough to keep this individual at the top of his highly competitive game. Several such patients have described to me, in almost identical words, how the effects of the brain injury have dulled their "edge." To the extent that maintaining this edge is vital to the patient's peak performance and self-image, even a minor brain injury can produce a gaping narcissistic wound.

For this and other types of patients, as Bennett (1987) points out, the realization that the self is different leads to fear and uncertainty about the future and a feeling that "I can no longer accept or understand myself, so how can my family or friends possibly do so." In a desperate attempt to cope, the patient may try to ward off painful feelings by erecting psychological barriers between himself and his family or friends. Another strategy is to "program" himself to make others think he is normal, all the time knowing that this is a charade. The patient may go to great lengths to put on the appearance of normalcy as a way of countering what he mistakenly believes to be a loss of sanity, not realizing that the emotional and cognitive turmoil is an expectable component of the postconcussion syndrome and not a sign of going crazy. Here again, accurate information provided by a skilled and sensitive psychotherapist is crucial.

Existential Issues

Many of the problems involving life after brain injury concern fundamental issues of life and meaning (Baumeister, 1991). Yalom (1980) has identified four central concerns of the psychoexistential orientation to psychotherapy: death, isolation, meaninglessness, and freedom. I was going to attempt to develop Yalom's theme as it applies to brain-injured patients, when I discovered that Nadell (1991) has done precisely this in a thorough and insightful way. Much of the material in this section, therefore, is adapted from that source, along with my own comments and observations (see also Chapter 11).

Death   As much as any threat to physical survival, traumatic brain injury underscores our finite nature. Unlike orthopedic injuries which affect isolated functions, brain injury can impact numerous functional systems in devastating ways, forcing the individual to come to grips with mortality in a most radical and sudden fashion. One of the most common comments made by brain-injured or other seriously injured or ill patients is that they can never look at life the same way again. They envy other, healthy people with their mere petty everyday concerns, who are perceived as living in a now-unreachable fantasy land, an almost Edenic garden of ignorant bliss that they, the patients, have been cast out of.

Freedom   Freedom is the conscious striving for actualization of possibility within the confines of necessity, of life's conditions, and here the brain-injured patient is presented with a dual challenge. Above and beyond the boundaries with which we must all struggle, brain injury can impose severe limitations in almost every important sphere of existence, including basic functions, such as feeding, ambulation, sexuality, toileting, and hygiene, as well as more complex activities like work, recreation, and communication. The limitations imposed by brain injury can be so dramatic that they may, for a time at least, crush the psychological capacity of the individual to self-create, even in conjunction with a skilled helping professional. In such cases, the best course is often not to "push it"; the therapist must sometimes bide his or her time and wait for the right existential opening to begin the process of dealing with limitations.

Meaninglessness   For the brain-injured patient, changes in cognitive capacities such as memory and symbolic thought can ravage what were previously sources of life's meaning (see Baumeister, 1991). The alterations in the interpersonal, vocational, and recreational spheres of existence that often follow brain injury can strike insurmountable blows to the terrestrial meaning experienced by the brain-injured patient prior to the injuring event.

Although we sometimes glibly advise brain-injured patients to "relax" and "enjoy life," what we might regard as safe and pleasurable situations are, as Forrest (1987) points out, often risky and frightening for the patient haunted by a global sense of impairment that intrudes into every enjoyable aspect of life. Even seemingly simple pastimes, when analyzed neuropsychologically, are "brain tests" of one sort or another. For example, think of the faculties required for reading novels, appreciating ballet or theater, playing cards or board games, crocheting, taking a drive, building model ships, or playing tennis, golf, chess, or billiards. Even network television — which some would argue represents the epitome of mindlessness — may be confusing to the cognitively impaired patient who can't follow the plots of cop shows or comprehend complex conversational sitcom humor. One of my patients lamented that she could no longer enjoy her two favorite TV shows, "Cheers" and "Designing Women," while her comprehension of "Roseanne" and "Oprah" were relatively intact. Perhaps someone should do a study ranking the cognitive sophistication of television programs based on reports of brain-damaged subjects.

Isolation   According to Nadell (1991), alienation or isolation from self encompasses the separation of the individual from that which is an extension of himself, including skills, talents, abilities, and the familiar material reality that one has created. Given that brain injury is often accompanied by changes in social skills, cognitive capacities, and physical appearance and abilities, alienation becomes almost inevitable, as well-established connections to others may erode. This interpersonal alienation can in turn intensify feelings of self-alienation, as the self-structure is in part an internalization of the appraisals held of us by others. Self-alienation may further distance the brain-injured patient from others, as the individual may be unwilling to reach out and socially engage, defending against the pain of anticipated rejection—yet another vicious cycle.

Existential Psychotherapy of the Brain-Injured Patient   Ordinarily, says Nadell (1991), we are able to gradually confront and integrate the existential realities of mortality and vulnerability in a more timely manner, through the deaths of elderly loved ones, less dramatic life changes and illnesses encountered in the normal aging process, and with the comfort of spiritual, philosophical, and religious belief systems. Therapy can address the matter by helping the patient to get in touch with the precarious grasp we all have on life and the precious nature of the gift of life.

According to Prigatano et al. (1986), no matter what their particular religious persuasion, the concept of God has extraordinary psychological significance for many brain-injured patients. God can represent a coming to grips with reality, a connecting of one's self to something beyond a limited biological existence. When this takes place, the patient has a sense of integration and individuation (in the Jungian sense) that is necessary for acceptance of the tragedy of his life. The patient can then move ahead psychologically. (My caveat: Be sensitive to the possibility of heightened religiosity after brain injury, secondary to temporal lobe seizure activity—I haven't seen this commonly in traumatic brain injury, but it has occurred in at least one case I know of.)

As a result of this elevated awareness, the patient's sense of the urgency of the moment may help him seize satisfaction in what may have previously gone unnoticed. The taste of food, the sights and sounds of nature, the companionship of friends and family, a favorite song, the reading of a good book, and so on may all be experienced with a greater intensity, enhancing the quality of life. This enhanced quality of life may in turn allow the patient to cope more effectively, softening the blows of his ever-present limitations and deficits, easing his depression, and enabling him to channel more of his energies into rehabilitation.

While recognition of losses is a painful process for the patient, one can emphasize the qualities that are still, in part or in whole, defining features of who he was and still is. Among these essential characteristics may be various aspects of his personality, interests, knowledge, skill areas, and so on. Through this exploration process, the gap between the patient's premorbid and postinjury self can be partially closed, reducing the sense of self-alienation, isolation from objectification of self, and the accompanying ego-dystonic states. At some point in the therapy process, I find it useful for the patient to begin to develop a few short- and long-term projects that can serve as concrete sources of accomplishment and satisfaction. Here, the therapist treads another thin line, this time between empowering the patient by potential success and the risk of psychic disembowelment by potential failure. Needless to say, good clinical judgment and empathic skill is required to reduce the chances of such pernicious set-ups.

The centrality of meaning to life makes it incumbent on the psychotherapist working with the brain-injured patient to act as a vehicle for helping the patient reconstruct a viable sense of terrestrial meaning. While important, the issue of cosmic meaning, says Nadell (1991), should not be encouraged or discouraged, but only validated by the therapist to the degree that it is important to the patient as a source of strength, motivation, and support, and serves to reconstitute a sense of meaning for the patient. In helping the patient formulate a sense of meaning in life, it is important for the therapist to avoid forcing his or her own values and goals on the patient, serving instead as a sounding board for, and facilitator of, the patient's creative self.

I'm usually skeptical about attempts to romanticize catastrophic adversity, especially by healthy clinicians working with injured patients. However, I can appreciate the sentiment expressed by Nadell (1991) that through such existential explorations, psychotherapy is able to approximate its most noble aspirations, maximizing the patient's quality of life. Similarly, Bennett (1987) notes that brain injury, at least minor brain injury, may be an opportunity for personal growth. After several years have elapsed and the recovery period and residual deficits have been put in perspective, most minor head injury patients will assert that the injury was not the worst thing that ever happened to them—similar beliefs are apparently expressed by spinal cord patients, according to Trieschmann (1984). The brain-injured patients believe that some good things have resulted; some have told Bennett that the injury "knocked some sense into them," which may represent the adaptive coping strategy of making lemonade out of lemons; alternatively, it may reflect an internalization of the sentiments of others. In any case, while significant personal growth is possible during the recovery period, this should not be "expected" and additional undue existential pressure should not be placed on the patient. (Recently, a brain tumor patient complained to me that everybody keeps expecting her to be "noble.")

According to Bennett (1987), having had a minor brain injury may leave one with a greater appreciation of life and a greater respect for its fragile nature. This is a sobering experience, which may render the patient more serious, overall. Indeed, the new seriousness is one reason why some adolescent and young adult brain injury patients lose friends; they seem too mature. (My caveat: Don't mistake organic emotional flattening and loss of abstract humor appreciation for existential seriousness.) The greater appreciation of life and the experience of abandonment, says Bennett, can leave the brain-injured person exquisitely sensitive to the needs and feelings of others. (My caveat: Sometimes the opposite occurs, i.e., egocentricity and cynicism.) Finally, Bennett notes, for the patient who has a good recovery, the brain injury may signal a time to settle down and to be more goal directed, in a sense forcing the question, "What do I want to do with my life?"

My main qualification regarding this whole approach is that the extraction of existential meaning from adversity is something that should ultimately come from the patient, not be foisted upon him by the therapist. Such "conversions by the sword" are usually unconsciously motivated by a need to reinforce the therapist's own meaning system, not the patient's, or they may be part of a therapeutic rescue fantasy in which the patient is "saved" by being given the magical gift of a new George Bailyean outlook on life. We can't expect all or most of our patients to become philosophers after their injuries—how many therapists would respond this way? But human beings do crave meaning, and if a philosophical or religious orientation can nourish the patient in his or her journey back to the land of the living, then our therapeutic role must stretch to include some measure of guidance in affairs of the spirit.

CHAPTER 4

Significant Others: Family Problems and Family Therapy

As we've seen, brain injury never occurs in an interpersonal vacuum. From the first critical stages of the injury to whatever ultimate, long-term resolutions are reached, the patient's significant others—spouse and children, parents and in-laws, friends and lovers—play a crucial role in determining the kind of life that person will have postinjury. By the same token, the patient's response to his injury will have a profound impact on the family dynamics that ensue after he has returned home and things are supposed to have "settled down." Rehabilitation clinicians, mostly operating in postacute, inpatient settings, understandably tend to focus their evaluative and remediative efforts on the patient; if anything, "significant others" are usually taken to mean anticipated jobsite personnel, rather than family. However, as this chapter will make clear, any effective, comprehensive program of psychotherapy and rehabilitation must involve the patient's family and his wider social sphere.

MAJOR PATIENT PROBLEMS
REPORTED BY FAMILIES

The brain-injured patient presents the family he returns to with a set of problems that the family members may be ill-equipped to handle by reason of temperament, maturity, lack of experience, or, usually, some combination of the above. The following are the problem areas most often

70

cited by families themselves as interfering with the patient's adjustment at home.

Awareness and Responsiveness

The types of cognitive problems that families report most often in their brain-injured relatives are disturbances of awareness and impairment in learning and memory. One kind of awareness problem may be seen where the patient's organic disorientation for time and place makes him unmindful or oblivious to his actual surroundings (restaurant, movie theater), and he behaves in ways appropriate to where he *thinks* he is (usually home), or simply without regard to the feelings, sensibilities, or reactions of others.

A more complex manifestation of impaired awareness is the development of an immature, childlike egocentricity, what Lezak (1988) calls a "Copernican perspective," with the patient at the center of his emotional and interpersonal universe. The behavior may resemble that seen in a young child, who as yet fails to perceive other people as distinct personalities and individuals, with needs, desires, and rights of their own.

A previously healthy, mature, and self-sufficient adult man or woman who now habitually acts like a complaining, demanding child understandably has a draining effect on the caretakers. Often, the family, with good intentions, will at first indulge the patient's wishes and demands ("After all, he's been hurt"), but soon come to realize that the patient, like an egocentric child, is not capable of reciprocating, of being grateful, of giving them "credit" for their efforts to help (Pasnau et al., 1981). The result is that caretakers spend long hours ministering to the needs of the patient with scant acknowledgment or appreciation on the part of their ward — and indeed, in some cases, actually abused for their efforts (see below).

Learning and Memory

But even a child eventually learns which types of behaviors are consistently reinforced and which tend repeatedly to lead to punishing consequences and should therefore be avoided. Brain-injured patients, however, typically fail to learn from experience. They don't remember the consequences of their actions — if, indeed, the actions themselves — and thus seem to get into the same kinds of trouble again and again, requiring the family to mobilize continual alertness on the patient's behalf (Lezak, 1988; Livingston & Brooks, 1988; McKinlay & Hickox, 1988).

Lezak (1988) cites a common blunder made by families in these kinds of situations, namely, treating the adult patient like an irresponsible adolescent who should be "allowed to make his own mistakes," and thereby "learn what the real world is like." Unfortunately, repeated failure on the patient's part or the well-meaning, "character-building" withholding of bailouts by the caretaker has little effect on these patients' behavior. Instead, rooms go uncleaned, laundry undone, food unprepared, bodies unbathed, work or school or doctors' appointments unkept, bills unpaid, and so on. At some point the family comes to realize that in order to forestall total deterioration, they must intervene repeatedly and remain always on the lookout for potential trouble. It just doesn't seem to get any easier, and the constant vigilance of the caretakers takes its toll (Brooks et al., 1987; Lezak, 1988).

Emotional Changes

A variety of emotional changes occur after brain injury that families may find difficult to comprehend or tolerate (Lezak, 1988). These include apathy, silliness, irritability, anger, and depression. Making matters worse is the frequent impression by family members that these emotional displays are in some sense deliberate, even spiteful, and *could* be controlled by the patient if only he "would put his mind to it," "knock it off," or "cut the crap." A further complication is that in some cases, there may actually *be* a certain willfulness behind the obnoxious emotionality—the patient, is, in effect, taking advantage of, or "using" the symptom to express his anger or resentment. Some typical emotional problems are as follows.

Anxiety   When the mental functioning of a previously introspective, self-aware, and autonomously behaving person has been impaired by brain injury, his experience of himself and the world necessarily changes, and this kind of internal disorientation can produce tremendous anxiety. As Lezak (1988) points out, anxiety arising from awareness of one's altered mental status tends to erode the patient's self-confidence, to make him overly cautious and vigilant, and to foster feelings of inadequacy, confusion, and even fears of "going crazy." Anxiety may also stem from fear of losing control, especially in patients who retain some insight into their deficits and are thus only too aware of how their behavior and their control over their lives has crumbled away. Families may then be faced with an overanxious, overcautious patient who resists their best attempts to sooth, reassure, or cajole him into a more "realistic" attitude.

Depression   Probably the commonest early response by patients to brain injury—indeed, to most serious injuries or medical illnesses—is depression. Organic depressions can result from damage to different parts of the brain involved in the experience and expression of mood states and emotional behavior. For example, agitated, anxious, and angry depressions, often accompanied by language disturbances, may occur with left frontal lobe lesions (Robinson, 1986; Robinson et al., 1984, 1985), while more apathetic, amotivational, and emotionally "flat" depressions may be seen with damage to the right hemisphere (Ross, 1981; Ross & Rush, 1981; Ross & Stewart, 1987; Ross et al., 1981).

Organic, as well as reactive depressions—the patient's response to the realization of his altered functional state—may present the family with emotional behavior that is unsettling and difficult to deal with (Lezak, 1988). Depression also tends to feed on and exacerbate the patient's other emotional and social maladjustments, setting up yet another of many vicious cycles. Perhaps more than any other emotional response, says Lezak, the patient's depression tends to erode family members' self-esteem and fuel their feelings of guilt and inadequacy, since the depressed mood and behavior seem so refractory to their best efforts to relieve it. "We've done everything humanly possible, and more, so why doesn't he snap out of it already?" is a common family refrain.

Changes in Personality

"He's not the same person," is another plaint often voiced by families, this time referring to changes in the patient's personality that may be highly disturbing to the family members. In fact, patient personality changes typically constitute more of a burden on the family than physical disability or impairment in intellect, memory, or speech (Brooks, 1984; Fahy et al., 1967; Livingston & Brooks, 1988). Moreover, personality changes appear to be relatively longstanding, being reported by up to three-fourths of families as long as five years after the injury (Brooks et al., 1986, 1987).

While, in a few exceptional cases, brain injury may render the patient quieter and more tractable than before, most postinjury personality changes are perceived by families as disruptive and destabilizing, particularly problems with irritability, temper, aspontaneity, restlessness, and overall "childishness" (Brooks, 1984; Thomsen, 1974). Irritability, in particular, seems to climb to the top of the family complaint list as time goes on (McKinlay et al., 1981). Some typical personality change problems are as follows.

Anger and Aggressiveness   Aggressive behavior syndromes after brain injury can occur for a number of reasons, such as paroxysmal episodic dyscontrol, frontal lobe disinhibition, or exacerbation of premorbid personality traits (Miller, 1990e; also see Chapter 5). With regard to families, Lezak (1978) points out that many patients are frustrated and frightened by their condition, feel like an unworthy and unwanted burden to their families, and are demeaned and humiliated by the care they need, yet fearful of losing it. As ever-present reminders of their dependency and incompetency, caretakers may become the focus of the patient's bitterness. As a result, family members, particularly the spouse and dependent children, may be abused by the patient.

Attacks on the caretaker commonly take the form of belittling, rejection, hostility, endless complaints and demands, and accusations of unfaithfulness and neglect (Lezak, 1978, 1988). The patient may frequently threaten physical violence, but actual violence is relatively rare. Most patients act out their anger by shouting, gestures, and diatribes, although an occasional kick or jab may punctuate the outburst. But even nonphysical expressions of anger, Lezak points out, can be extremely distressing and demoralizing to a conscientious caretaker, sensitive family member, or bewildered child.

Newer evidence suggests that family violence and brain injury may be more closely associated than previously thought. Rosenbaum and Hoge (1989) found that 61% of their sample of male patients referred for evaluation of spousal violence had histories of what they termed "severe" head injury, a rate far exceeding that in the general population. In this sample, alcohol abuse was significantly associated with head injury, consistent with other research supporting a strong relationship among impulsive behavior, alcohol and drug abuse, and head injury (Bond, 1984; Galasko & Edwards, 1974; Galbraith et al., 1976; Jamieson, 1971; Miller, 1989b, 1990b, 1992e; Potter, 1967 — see Chapters 5 and 6).

Paranoia   After brain injury, many families report that the patient has become overly suspicious of caretakers and others around him. This can range from mild circumspection to outright paranoid delusional psychosis. Patients with left hemisphere damage, often accompanied by aphasia, may develop organic paranoid syndromes (Benson, 1977; Leftoff, 1983). However, for most patients, more subtle perceptual and language deficits, combined with impairment in insight, feelings of worthlessness, and fears of rejection create a combined cognitive-emotional set-up for the development of paranoia (Lezak, 1988). Paranoia may become a special problem for married men who have become sexually impotent after brain injury. Here, the suspiciousness may express itself as an obsessive concern about the fidelity of his wife, although female patients whose sexuality has been affected by brain injury may become similarly hypervigilant.

In a number of these latter cases, however, I've noted that these concerns have some basis in fact. That is, sexually deprived husbands of brain-injured wives are more likely to seek satisfaction elsewhere than are similarly deprived wives of brain-injured husbands. There also seems to be an age effect, younger wives of brain-injured men seeming to have affairs more frequently than older wives—then again, this may simply reflect the overall demographics of infidelity in the general population. To date, I know of no systematic research that has attempted to examine the basis for these anecdotal observations.

Paranoia and suspiciousness may also develop over money matters, and in my experience this is a more common problem than sexual suspiciousness. In some cases, legal wrangles may ensue, with the patient making all sorts of "protective" provisions for his assets which, by reason of organically impaired judgment, are ill-advised, if not downright disastrous. The family, appalled at this financial mismanagement, acts to intervene—sometimes in their own interest, sometimes with the best of intentions for their loved one—which only serves to stoke the patient's paranoia still further, setting up a vicious cycle of animosity and recrimination. Accusations fly, more lawyers and doctors are called in, incompetency hearings may be scheduled, in-laws and distant cousins may enter the fracas, and before long the patient's behavior has hopelessly deteriorated and the family's good will totally drained.

Dependency   Brain injury often imposes an uncomfortable and unwanted state of dependency on once-assertive, self-assured, independent people, and this may take a variety of forms (Lezak, 1988). Organic deficits involving both cognitive and emotional components of behavior reduce the patient's capacity for spontaneous recall and forethought, and thus restrict his mental existence to the immediate here-and-now. Other patients may retain relatively intact orientation for time, but have difficulty organizing, ordering, and integrating their thoughts and experiences. Till others have a greatly diminished ability to spontaneously generate ideas or initiate activities. Many of these patients also have difficulty with any activity involving planning, and are therefore further unable to take adequate charge of their lives.

Most moderately-to-severely impaired patients, Lezak (1988) points out, are in fact dependent on their families or caretakers for at least some important aspects of their physical care or financial support, and still others have come to begrudge the patient the help or support they nevertheless feel duty-bound to provide. But when the patient's needs finally exceed the family's capacity to fulfill them, and the patient's care must be obtained from agencies outside the family, many caretakers then feel guilty and ashamed for what they regard as their failure to "do right by" their loved one.

In other cases, families may actually reinforce the patient's lack of independence and autonomy. Childlike dependency that is intolerable to the spouse may be perfectly acceptable to parents (Brooks, 1984), and may thus be encouraged, directly or tacitly. For many parents of adolescent or young adult brain injury survivors, caring for the now-dependent offspring is their only way to "rescue" or "get back" their son or daughter whose behavior had perhaps previously been seen by the parents as out of control (see Chapters 5 and 6). Although Lezak (1988) warns of the battles that may rage between parents and spouse around their sharply differing attitudes towards the patient's dependency, I have found that in many cases the spouse, too, may be gratified by the husband's or wife's dependency because of the new sense of control it gives the caretaker. Indeed, in my experience, it's not unusual for spouse and parents to collude in keeping the patient as helpless and dependent as possible, ostensibly for his or her "own protection."

Impulsivity and Impaired Control   As will be discussed in Chapter 5, impulsivity is a common sequel of brain injury. In some cases this relates to focal frontal lobe damage, but some degree of disinhibition may be seen with almost any kind of injury to the brain. Typically, the relationship of premorbid impulsive personality traits to posttraumatic impulsivity is a complex one (Miller, 1987, 1988b, 1989b, 1990e, 1992a, 1992e).

According to Lezak (1988), almost any activity may be affected by impulsivity or lack of control. Some patients become impulsive eaters, gorging on everything in sight. The family's attempts to impose healthy or reasonable-sounding dietary restrictions may be met by angry demands for more food or specific kinds of food, overwhelming the caretaker's resolve. In this regard, I have noted that in some cases the brain injury is viewed by the patient as an excuse to engage in all kinds of unhealthy habits like smoking, drinking, and junk food bingeing: "What the hell do I have to lose?" is the typical rationalization.

Sexually impulsive patients are at best a nuisance, at worst a danger to the community and a source of constant vigilance and anxiety for the caretaker. One male patient I knew, a physically enormous, yet premorbidly gentle, "teddy-bear"-like young adult, ran up repeated posttraumatic arrests for attempted rape and eventually had to be institutionalized entirely on the basis of his sexual behavior. He was not physically aggressive, did not actually harm the women involved, retreated at the least resistance to his advances, had never been known to strike or otherwise physically injure anyone, and was, in fact, quite tractable, cooperative, and pleasant in almost every way, even after his head injury. But he had the disconcerting postinjury habit of rather blatantly and crudely soliciting sexual favors from neighborhood women, which, combined with his size, made him appear sufficiently dangerous to be put away.

Parents of adolescent or adult female patients, says Lezak (1988), may be tormented by worries about these girls' or women's heightened susceptibility to the unscrupulous charms or outright sexual depredations of others, although it is more common in my experience to see female patients become sexually "turned off" following brain injury. Still, I know of at least one case involving brain damage due to herpes simplex encephalitis, where the family members spent a good part of their time tracking down their young adult daughter, a former honors student, to biker bars and similarly grim hangouts, where she characteristically retreated for days at a time. Although I did not formally evaluate or treat this patient or her family, my impression from speaking with them was that this was due only partly to organically impaired judgment, and was more a matter of depression and devastated self-esteem being acted out in a rageful, self-destructive, "see-how-bad-I-can-get" way.

Patients who spend money impulsively may need to have credit cards confiscated or destroyed, bank accounts closed, and power-of-attorney assumed by relatives, who then may become the objects of scorn and abuse (Lezak, 1988; also see Chapter 11). Other patients may run up huge phone bills (the sexually solicitous patient described above was a constant patron of dial-a-porn services), go for long cab rides, or shoplift items from stores. Substance abuse may complicate the picture (see Chapter 6).

REACTIONS OF FAMILIES TO CARING FOR AND LIVING WITH A BRAIN-INJURED PATIENT

While the reactions of families to the brain-injured loved one are in some respects unique to each individual family situation, some characteristic clusters of family reaction patterns can be identified.

Denial

Usually, families want to believe that their impaired spouse or child will get better, will "return" to them in some reasonable semblance of his or her former self. *Denial* generally has a pejorative connotation to most psychotherapists, but denial can be adaptive when it preserves family stability, keeps the family members from being overwhelmed, and maintains appropriate role functioning of the family members. But denial becomes pernicious when it hinders progress toward functional independence or stands in the way of realistic planning for the future. Such pathological denial should be considered when the family's response to the injury clouds an accurate perception of the patient's abilities and deficits (Rosenthal & Young, 1988).

Denial, at least in the initial stages, may be a way of maintaining the fragile stability of a family system that might well become unglued by forcing an abrupt, all-out acceptance of the patient's incapacity from the outset (Rosenthal & Young, 1988). Force-feeding reality to the patient's family may only serve to overwhelm them and probably stiffen their resistance to becoming optimally involved in any productive treatment program. Such a shaken family, for example, is unlikely to make the necessary adjustments and compromises to accommodate a daily regimen of home cognitive remediation because "it's hopeless anyway."

Family denial may be prolonged by fantasies that the patient will return to his former self, if only given enough time, care, and encouragement, or if only the right treatment, or a new breakthrough, can be discovered (Romano, 1974). Such denial hinders treatment insofar as it prevents family members from setting realistic goals. The families may then collude with the patient's own denial system in which he is unable to accept anything less than complete recovery. This then leads to interminable shopping around for doctors, treatment facilities, medicines, quack remedies, and so on, as a way of avoiding the need to set less-than-perfect, but realistic goals (McKinlay & Hickox, 1988).

Feeling Trapped

At one time or another, feeling trapped is an almost universal reaction of family members to living with and caring for a brain-injured person (Lezak, 1978). At best, even when pursuing a full-time career or active social schedule, the caretaker may feel tied down to a particular job situation or tethered to the homesite by the patient. A frequent lament I hear is "I know I'll never take another vacation." At worst, the caregiver's whole individuality, interests, and personal needs may be swallowed up by the demands of the patient. In such cases, disintegration of the family's stability may be rapid, although sometimes there evolves a kind of quasiadaptive symbiotic relationship seen in other kinds of mutual dependency syndromes, where the caretaker achieves the fulfillment of some psychological need by catering to another's demands, often in a martyrlike fashion.

Isolation

Family members may feel themselves to be—indeed, may become—socially isolated as a result of caring for the brain-injured patient (Lezak, 1978). Some housebound patients require full-time attention. Other patients, who are less of a bother at home, may embarrass the family in public, get lost or panicked in unfamiliar places, or become belligerent with strangers. In such cases, the family soon decides that it's just easier to stay home. Worse, guests and visitors drift away in the face of repeated obnoxious or embarrassing behavior by the patient, or when aphasic disorders or orientation problems make him a less-than-enjoyable companion.

Even relatively unbothersome patients may nevertheless not be able to fulfill the role of normal companion when couples go out together for dinner, to the movies, or especially for activities that require some degree of mental and/or physical ability, such as playing cards or bowling. One friend of a patient's spouse told her that going out with her and her husband was "like going out with a spoiled kid."

Not just friends, but even extended family members—aunts, uncles, cousins, in-laws—may stop coming around after a while. One family got a stark glimpse down the social road ahead when they spent their first post-injury Christmas dinner alone. Worse, outside relatives who take a hands-off attitude with respect to day-to-day caretaking responsibilities may, on their occasional visits, overflow with critical advice on how the immediate family should be doing its job. This then produces secondary fallout in terms of family bitterness and resentment.

Jealousy and Guilt

Immediate family members who live in the same household may come to envy and resent the attention that the patient receives (Livingston & Brooks, 1988). This may alternate with periods of remorse over being too hard on the patient: "After all, I'd rather be intact, independent me than brain-damaged, care-dependent him." Other family members may feel that they are in some way to blame for the patient's injury (McKinlay & Hickox, 1988), and in some cases this may have a basis in fact (see below). Also, hostile fantasies, acknowledged or suppressed, may produce in family members oscillating cycles of anger and remorse, especially among siblings.

These conflicts may be further fueled by parents who keep reminding the uninjured, but neglected, sibling just how "lucky" he or she is.

Family Depression

Just as brain injury may be a source of depression for the patient, so it may be for the family. Most family members who live with a personality-disordered, brain-injured patient suffer some degree of depression (Lezak, 1978). The family's mood may become yoked to that of the patient, with rollercoaster ups and downs occurring several times a day. It is the symptoms of depression—the anxiety and agitation, obsessive rumination, lethargy and fatigue, disturbed sleep and appetite—that otherwise stable family members often interpret as signs of "going crazy."

Family Role Changes

Brain injury may involve a loss of important qualities that were part of the patient's premorbid intellectual, cognitive, and personality pattern, and this may force other family members into unaccustomed and unwanted roles (McKinlay & Hickox, 1988). For example, a previously dependent and submissive family member—usually the wife—must now assume responsibility and make decisions. In other cases, the new role and family power relationships may be relished and jealously guarded, with the result that the goal of optimal rehabilitation is pursued only halfheartedly by the caretaker, if not actually sabotaged.

Within extended family situations, spouses of brain-injured patients may come into clashes with in-laws due to the overprotectiveness of the patient's parents, who may actually find the new dependency of their son or daughter gratifying, while the spouse struggles valiantly to make the patient more independent (Rosenbaum & Najeson, 1976)—although, as noted above, I have not personally found this type of conflict to be as common or serious a problem as interfamilial collusion over maintaining dependency.

However, occasionally such clashes do occur with a vengeance. One wife of a patient in his late 30's who had a stroke and underwent brain surgery for an aneurysm reported numerous pitched battles between herself and her husband's parents who repeatedly accused her of "pushing" their son "beyond his limits." Thinking to provide a kind of shock-treatment cure for this continual back-seat carping, the wife encouraged the parents to take care of their son at the parents' house while she took her children on a two-week trip to visit out-of-state relatives. Expecting to find, on her return, a pair of exhausted, distraught, and contrite in-laws begging her to take back her husband on any terms she cared to name, she was instead stunned to discover her husband aslouch in his wheelchair in front of the TV, all rehabilitation home-practice tasks laying undone for the last two weeks, and being hovered over indulgently by both parents who had apparently devoted their every waking moment to making their son "comfortable," and thereby setting the example of how they expected the wife to treat their offspring from here on in. Expectably, the situation quickly deteriorated when the wife took her husband home and tried to get him to resume acting "responsibly."

Family Expectations

Caretakers and family members may harbor certain expectations regarding the patient's outcome that are at odds with either those of the patient or with reasonably expectable reality. Immediately following the acute stage of the trauma, the atmosphere may be one of relief and even joy at the patient's survival, and family members are then typically solicitous and indulgent while the patient struggles to regain his health (Lezak, 1978). This mood soon sours, however, when the patient becomes irritable and demanding, and no longer seems to make an effort to resume his normal responsibilities. Caretakers who fail to understand the difference between illness and invalidism may reinforce a lower level of functional competence than the patient is actually capable of, or abet the development and maintenance of chronic pain and somatization syndromes, as well as medication dependence (Miller, 1990c, in press a, in press b, in press c; see Chapter 7).

Problems Experienced by Specific Family Members

Although the family may go through the process of coping with their brain-injured loved one together, the actual experience of each family member is likely to be somewhat different, as each member stands in a different relationship to both the patient and the other family members.

Parents   Having a child suffer any serious illness or injury can be a devastating experience for a parent. With brain injury, there are several unique aspects as well (Lezak, 1988). If the injury has caused permanent deficits, there is the distressing realization that caring for the child may never end, that the parents will never have freedom in their later years to enjoy their retirement, to move about as they wish, or to have uninterrupted privacy and independence. When the brain-injured child is living at home, the caretaker, usually the mother, is likely to become the focus of competition between the injured child and the other parent and/or other children for her attention. Marital conflicts often result as parents disagree over who is to care for the injured child and how, and one parent, usually the father, feels neglected by the exhausted mother who copes with the child all day long. Thus, Lezak finds that it is not unusual for marriages to dissolve within a year or two following the onset of a significant brain impairment in a child.

Apparently, the child's physical and cognitive impairments tend to stress the family far less than the disturbing emotional and behavioral sequelae of the brain injury. Perrott et al. (1991) found that childhood brain injury affected behavior, school performance, and adaptive living skills far more profoundly than intellectual and cognitive functioning in their study sample. Furthermore, these brain-injured children placed much greater demands on their parents and were more active and distractible than their siblings. Several years postinjury, about half of the parents were still experiencing stressed family relationships, which they attributed directly to their child's head injury. Indeed, two of the mothers rated their level of caretaking stress as "almost intolerable," and both of these mothers were observed by the investigators to be "visibly distressed" during the interview and clearly in need of support.

Children   The relatively high incidence of brain injury in the young adult population assures that a good number of parents of young children will be affected (Urbach & Culbert, 1991). The brain-injured parent may be detached and disinterested, preoccupied and self-absorbed, moody and irritable, volatile and explosive, confused and forgetful, or strange and delusional. Depending on age and other factors, the child may be overwhelmed by a disruption of primary bonding, a loss of stable object relations, an impairment of affectional ties, the bizarre characterological and behavioral alteration of a major identification figure, or a disturbing confrontation to reality testing. The greatest potential disruption for a child may be the increased likelihood of marital conflict, separation, and divorce.

All these ingredients make for a toxic psychological brew of object loss, unresolvable grief, heightened performance expectations, and a sense of competitive inadequacy. Consequently, the child may display a syndrome of argumentativeness, decreased frustration tolerance, heightened sensitivity, passive-aggressive household chore refusal, declining school performance, withdrawal, and ruminative fears about safety.

Sadly, young children often bear the brunt of the family's problems with the brain-injured parent-patient (Lezak, 1978). They may be ignored by the patient and inadvertently neglected by the healthy parent who is trying to keep the family going singlehandedly. Added to neglect may be abuse. Some patients bully and belittle their offspring in childish competition for the spouse's attention and affection, trying to grasp a few shreds of self-respect as they observe their growing children's competencies begin to surpass their own.

Older children may suffer less because they can get out of the house and otherwise avoid the disabled parent more easily, or because they have already had a number of years of good parenting as a foundation, or because they can understand the realities of the situation better than their younger siblings. However, where problems arise, older children and teenagers tend to act out the family's distress in the form of school truancy, failing grades, delinquency, and prematurely leaving home. One 17-year-old girl deliberately got herself pregnant and married her boyfriend just to "get the hell out of that nuthouse."

For most children, brain impairment in a parent brings a sharp reduction in attention from other family members, an increase in responsibilities, and an uncomprehended shame and guilt. This is further compounded by frustration and anger at having a "different" family, at being unable to bring friends home, at not participating in school or community activities requiring a parent because one parent is occupied by the other parent's care, and at the absence of parties or picnics and other kinds of good times the family had previously enjoyed (Lezak, 1978).

Siblings   When the brain-injured patient is a child (see also Chapter 8), the reactions of the patient's siblings may vary, and, as with other family members, much depends on the existing family dynamics (Pasnau et al., 1981). Many siblings at first experience a sense of relief that the injury happened to their brother or sister and not to themselves; this may soon turn to guilt over having been spared and daring to feel "happy" about it. Other siblings, especially younger ones, may fear that the same thing or worse could happen to them; again, guilt feelings may further fan these flames of fear. In other cases, resentment and anger against the patient may ensue because of the added caretaking responsibilities imposed on the sibling, who is now expected to be more "grown up" than his or her friends. Once again, guilt may feed into this, creating still another vicious cycle.

Unfortunately, sometimes guilt may have a basis in reality. Three siblings and one friend, all adolescents, were involved in an auto accident in which the oldest sibling was driving while stoned on beer and marijuana. The boy's younger brother was killed and his sister and the friend both suffered serious brain injury, while the driver himself escaped with some broken bones, but no head trauma. Not only did the driver blame himself, but the full fury of the family's existential outrage was for a time directed against their son, who came close to killing himself. In such cases, the therapist must address the family's loss, their rage against the "guilty" member, and that member's own crippling remorse. In this case, the driver and the family were able to deal effectively with issues of responsibility, guilt, atonement, and forgiveness. This young man eventually became active in caring for his injured sister and in anti-drug, designated-driver, and other such causes.

The Spouse   In the majority of cases, the overwhelming brunt of caring for and coping with the adult brain-injured patient falls on the spouse. As we've seen, unlike parents, who will probably love and care for their injured child come hell or high water, such impairment may be more than the husband or wife had "bargained for" in terms of the marital relationship. Indeed, studies (Panting & Merry, 1972; Thomsen, 1974) show that husband-wife relationships tend to be less stable in the face of brain injury than parent-child relationships, and this makes for some special problems (Lezak, 1978, 1988; Pasnau et al., 1981).

If the spouse—especially the wife—has been accustomed to depending on the patient, there is often an initial postinjury period of numbness and disbelief, followed by anger over the reversal in the relationship. Isolation is a major problem inasmuch as the brain injury may have cheated the spouse out of the active companion that she is used to living with, but leaves her roped by social convention to the still-living marital partner and therefore not free to pursue other intimate relationships. As noted above, married friends may drift away, as "couple activities" become more and more difficult.

Other people may not endorse the legitimacy of the spouse's grief, since the patient has obviously survived: "You ought to feel lucky he wasn't killed." The kind of support that usually surrounds bereavement by death is thus not forthcoming. Even divorce may not be an easy option, the spouse often feeling fettered by responsibility, guilt, family pressure, fear of social condemnation ("Can you imagine—she deserted him in his time of need!"), or financial and child custody considerations.

Special problems revolve around sex. In brain injury, interpersonal difficulties tend to account for far more sexual problems than physical incapacity, the latter being more of a concern with spinal injuries (Rosenbaum & Najeson, 1976). It is usually the wives that report dissatisfaction with marital relations after their husbands' brain injuries, and this may occur for a variety of reasons (Lezak, 1978, 1988; Rosenbaum & Najeson, 1976; Rosenthal & Young, 1988). The loss of empathic sensitivity and the childlike emotionality and behavior of many brain-injured patients may strain any feelings of intimacy. The patient's organic egocentricity may prevent him from genuinely expressing affection and giving pleasure; instead he may behave self-gratifyingly, "like a horny monkey," as one spouse put it. Sexual demands may be tinged with anger at the perceived rejection by the spouse, leading in some cases to a catastrophic reaction and possible violence. Patients who cannot perform adequately may blame the spouse, yet pursue them all the more vigorously to "prove themselves"—indeed, wives typically find it easier to live with sexual indifference than with the patient's compulsive sexual harassment.

The "Posttraumatic Sexual Indifference Syndrome"   I have observed a particular change in a number of men and women after "mild" head injuries, consisting of an overall marked lowering of sex drive with, for men, an accompanying inability to sustain an erection during lovemaking. This seems to occur in patients of all ages, in both reportedly happy marriages and not-so-happy ones, and may persist for at least one year postinjury. Affected men can achieve erection and orgasm, but require greater stimulation and feel less pleasure than before. Affected women can physically engage in sexual activity and get some enjoyment out of the intimacy involved, but, again, sexual pleasure per se appears to be diminished. Both sexes report that they rarely think about sex spontaneously and may only become aware of the "problem" when it becomes an issue for the spouse. Most attempt to participate in sex for the spouse's sake, but the noticeable lack of ardor strains the lovemaking situation. Spouses may feel rejected, which fuels further disappointment, guilt, and recrimination.

It is tempting to dismiss this *posttraumatic sexual indifference syndrome*, or PTSIS (if I may coin both the term and its acronym), as a standard manifestation of depression, and indeed, many of these patients show depressed mood. But whether sexual dysfunction is produced by depression or vice versa is another of those ubiquitous chicken-and-egg questions in the field of brain injury rehabilitation and therapy. In most cases I've seen, the other, classic "vegetative signs" of major affective disorder are typically not much in evidence, and most of these patients report good appetite and relatively normal sleep patterns, although the latter may show some disturbance in a few cases, which is probably an independent sequel of head injury (see Chapters 1 and 2).

I wonder to what degree this syndrome relates to subtle organic disruption of normal hypothalamic-endocrine and other limbic system functioning due to centripetal physical effects of traumatic brain injury (Parker, 1990; see Chapter 1) or possibly superimposed neurophysiological consequences of severe psychological trauma (Kolb, 1987; Miller, 1993b; Parker, 1990; see Chapter 2). In fact, recovery from this syndrome does seem to occur in many cases, often in parallel with recovery of other posttraumatic cognitive and emotional deficits within the classic six- to 18-month window of recovery from head injury. In still other cases, a standard major depressive disorder may account for, or contribute to the problem.

In a few refractory cases, focused sex therapy and/or dealing with general sexual and emotional intimacy issues has proved helpful. Also, different patients will react to his problem in different ways, and so will their spouses, based on a combination of premorbid personalities and the overall dynamics of the marriage. Some patients, usually men, "freak out" at this further assault on their masculinity and sense of control, while other patients, usually women, may actually welcome the "excuse" to withdraw from what may have been unsatisfying sexual or emotional intimacy in the marriage all along. But I've seen the reverse reaction in either gender: A few men are happy to blame their sexual indifference or dysfunction on "brain damage," and a few women are crushed by their inability to fulfill the sensual aspect of their female persona and/or perceived wifely role.

Probably the most important intervention, I find, is to attack the inevitable vicious cycle of bad sex = bad mood = worse sex = worse mood, etc., that occurs in these situations. In some cases, where the sexual problem has become the core around which a large chunk of interpersonal psychopathology has crystallized, more intensive marital and family therapy may be called for. This will be considered further below.

PRINCIPLES OF FAMILY THERAPY
IN BRAIN INJURY

As Rosenthal and Young (1988) point out, the appropriate family intervention is one that assists the family in realistically appraising the impact of the injury on family functioning and the patient, and in maximizing the family's capability in managing the multiple disabilities that have emerged out of the brain injury.

Educative and Supportive Measures

An important, if frequently neglected, component in the therapeutic and rehabilitative process is the education and training of the family in the care and "handling" of the brain-injured relative. Over half the relatives interviewed by Panting and Merry (1972) felt that supportive services had not been adequate. The most common complaint was that doctors did not supply sufficient information, particularly with regard to the patient's prognosis and about the kinds of difficulties that should be anticipated. Indeed, by far the most frequent complaint I hear is: "Why didn't my doctor tell me that?" and much of the neuropsychologist's task with brain-injured patients and families often consists of explaining the nature of the injury, its expected effects, and the implications for future rehabilitation and adjustment.

Supportive family counseling recognizes the debilitating impact brain injury can have on an otherwise reasonably healthy family structure, and should assist the family in dealing with feelings of loss and helplessness, and in facilitating the family's ability to adapt itself to the disability and its potential consequences (Rosenthal & Young, 1988). Family members should be given the opportunity to express and work through their feelings of sadness, loss, guilt, and anger, while being helped to accept a realistic picture of the brain injury. Ongoing counseling of this type can be especially important in the early stages of the patient's discharge from the in-patient treatment facility when he or she will be returning full-time to the family system.

In this regard, Lezak (1978) points out that while the patient is still in the hospital, and during the first few "honeymoon" weeks or months after returning home, the family may ignore, deny, and even resent well-intended professional advice about the nature of the task ahead at home, since they may be unwilling to let go of the optimistic anticipation of substantial progress by their loved one. This attitude may impede eventual adjustment to the family setting, and Lezak recommends that the therapist take a firm hand in seeing to it that the family knows what it's in for. As noted previously, I have found that such an approach, though well-meaning, may too often be perceived by the family as professional strongarming and thus possibly jeopardize their ability and willingness to profit from professional input in the future. Sometimes the therapist or counselor simply has to back off and wait till the family is ready to listen. However, I agree with Lezak that, at some point, there are certain things the family needs to hear.

First, anger, frustration, and sorrow are natural emotions that relatives of brain-injured patients should expect to experience. Second, caretakers must take good care of themselves if they are going to be of continued optimal benefit to the patient. Third, in the inevitable conflicts with the patient and disagreements with other family members, the caretaker must ultimately rely on his or her own conscience and judgment—I would add that the caretaker should remain open to constructive input from others, but without necessarily feeling bound by any given piece of advice if it doesn't seem right. Someone's got to be in charge and make the command decisions.

Fourth, everyone must try to understand that the family role changes necessitated by the patient's brain injury can be emotionally distressing for all the family members—I often emphasize to families that seeking help in dealing with these stresses is not the same as "knuckling under" to adversity, but rather represents an adaptive, courageous response. Fifth, there are realistic limits to what the family members can do to change the patient's personality or behavior, and so they need not feel guilty or ineffective when their care does not result in dramatic improvement. Finally, when it appears that the welfare of dependent children is at stake, the family may have to tackle some tough choices about where the best place for the patient may be for all concerned, at home or in a long-term care facility—I find that many families need professional permission even to begin thinking about the implications of "putting away" their loved one.

A large part of educative and supportive counseling involves dealing with the unrealistic expectations the family may have about the patient's future and theirs (McLaughlin & Schaffer, 1985). Families—and some rehabilitation staff, too—may harbor expectations of complete personality overhaul, a veritable remolding or rebirth of the brain-injured patient. There are several possible reasons for this. Premorbid behavior may have been antisocial or disruptive, and the family now seizes on the patient's enforced invalidism as an opportunity to make him over in their own, more socially correct, image—some families I've talked to literally expect their loved one to have been "scared straight" by the injury and they therefore look forward to the postinjury period with actual, if ill-founded, relief: "Thank God it's over now."

Also, many patients go through a recovery period that seems to replicate normal development, i.e. learning to walk, talk, take care of themselves, and so on. Recovery may be seen by the family as a chance to nurture the patient toward becoming the "right" kind of person, a sort of second chance at parenting, especially when there is guilt or regret over having misused the first chance. In such cases, families need to be dissuaded from trying to effect a total personality makeover of the brain-injured patient; instead, they should be encouraged to proceed at the patient's own pace in developing his or her existing potential. I find that this can best be accomplished by focusing the family's attention on what can realistically be attained right now, leaving open the question of whether further, ultimate changes can be made. Taking it "one step at a time"—if the "steps" are truly doable—can divert some of the energy from wishful thinking to productive rehabilitation.

Family Psychotherapy

Of course, many families go through emotional and interpersonal crises having nothing to do with injury or illness, and these ordinarily constitute the bulk of the typical family therapist's caseload. Brain injury can stretch the adaptive capacity of the family system to its limit, compounding whatever problems already exist and quite often serving as the key issue around which family pathology crystallizes. Where educative and supportive measures are not in themselves sufficient — and they rarely are in most real families in the real world — more extensive and intensive family therapy approaches may be indicated (Miller, 1991b).

Where the brain injury impacts on a preexisting history of family problems, and/or where the family's reaction to the brain injury results in maladaptive patterns of interaction, family therapy can help resolve dysfunctional communication that may be causing or exacerbating difficulties among the family members and between the family and the patient. Rosenthal and Young (1988) emphasize several approaches to, and goals of, family therapy in brain injury.

First, family members must be encouraged to assume mutual responsibility for the family's problems and must learn how to shift the burden of causality from the identified patient to the dysfunctional areas of the family system. Second, the positive, adaptive, and healthy aspects of the family system should be strengthened and capitalized on. Third, dysfunctional interaction patterns can be explored by the reenactment of family conflicts and by assisting the family members to substitute conflict-resolution strategies that are appropriate to their particular family system. Finally, practice exercises or homework assignments outside the sessions can be assigned to foster generalization of behavior change — although my own experience with all such out-of-session therapeutic "homework" has not been encouraging, as many families feel they have enough to do already. Too much reliance on homework — especially written homework — may be counterproductive in these cases, giving them one more thing to fail at and leading to compromised motivation and cancelled sessions. This is something that should be evaluated for each individual family.

One key task of family therapy is to ease the transition of the patient into his new role within the family, and facilitate adjustment to changed roles on the part of the other family members (Lezak, 1988). This usually requires a certain reworking of each family member's old feelings, expectations, and reaction patterns so that new, more realistic perceptions and understanding can take their place. Such dissolution and reintegration can be a difficult task, and is rarely accomplished right away (Pasnau et al., 1981). Interventions introduced at too early a stage of the adjustment process must run interference among a horde of unrealistic expectations and fantasies, denial and raw shame, guilt and catastrophic reactions on the part of the family. The family healing process takes both time and skill.

Sometimes erupting spontaneously, sometimes emerging only with careful probing on the therapist's part, guilt, reactive blaming, and demandingness are typically found in family members, along with marked anxiety around discussing these difficulties directly (Pasnau et al., 1981). These feelings may contribute to splitting among the family members, as well as to the bombardment of the therapist and other clinicians with demands and complaints of inadequate care. This in turn may lead to the pitting of doctors against one another, clinicians fighting to avoid or dump the patient, the family becoming angrier and more desperate, and the therapist feeling that the case is hopeless because of "reality issues."

The first place to intervene is in the initial workup, but here the therapist must be careful that the family not perceive this as a humiliating, accusing, or demanding interrogation: "So, what's *your* particular role in this family mess. . . ?" Pasnau et al. (1981) recommend empathic contact with each individual family member, including the brain-injured patient, as a way to nonjudgmentally draw out and explore the fears and fantasies that may be getting in the way of progress toward adjustment.

For example, patients should be gently queried about their fears of the family trying to get rid of them or wishing that they could, or that the family is conspiring to steal the patient's money (reality issues *are* important here). Families should be encouraged to express their guilt over resenting the "poor, injured patient," often related to the also inadequately faced fear that caring for the patient will exhaust the family's energy, finances, and good will, and "steal my life from me," as one stoke patient's husband put it. Obviously, hostility and resentment may need to be faced as well. Also, family members may need help to get in touch with anxieties about no longer being able to depend on the injured person, financially or emotionally.

The therapist, recommend Pasnau et al. (1981), should, at the outset, empathize with such disowned fearful fantasies without attempting to discredit or dismiss them, and thus enable the family to work toward the time when these fantasies can be acknowledged as conscious anxieties to be openly dealt with. At some point in the process, the family should be ready to face more productively the reality-based management issues involved in caring for and living with the patient. In this regard, requirements of the family members should be made explicit and should be challenged if they unduly constrict family members' activities, or if they occur in response to uncontrolled outbursts by the patient. Naturally, the patient's capacity and motivation to take responsibility for his or her actions must be taken into account as well.

Special Treatment Problems: Sex and Anger

Sex   As noted in a previous section, sex after brain injury is a delicate issue for patients, spouses, and clinicians alike, and it is therefore not surprising that experts differ as to their recommendations for how and when to deal with sexual issues and who should bring it up. Rosenthal & Young (1988) feel that it is important to address marital and sexual issues from the earliest stages of recovery. Though some spouses and significant others may be unable to confront these problems during this stage, it at least lets the family know that the subject is not taboo and that the therapist is available to discuss these issues at a later date when the family is ready. Often, however, family members are more receptive and willing to work on these issues after the patient has been home for a while and they have accommodated to the reality and permanence of the changes.

Where the spouse is cooperative, I find that formal sex therapy by a competent, qualified, and specially trained professional can sometimes make the difference between a life of marital misery and at least some satisfaction. Often, however, patients and spouses are reluctant to take the referral, or drop out at the first signs of frustration. In many such cases, as noted above, the marital relationship may have already been shaky before the injury, and the patient's new invalidism is now used as an excuse, by either party, to avoid all further intimacy. Here, the problem is less one of sexual performance than a personality/relationship issue, and should be treated accordingly.

Anger   Management of anger depends on its source. As will be described in Chapter 5, at least three main syndromes of angry, aggressive behavior may be seen after brain injury: (1) an intermittent explosive disorder due to electrophysiologic disturbances in limbic brain areas; (2) undercontrolled, disinhibitory affect and behavior seen with damage to the frontal lobes; and (3) accentuation of premorbid impulsivity and antisociality. In addition, an initial stage of frustration and learning to cope with deficits may manifest itself as angry behavior during the early stages of recovery. Although different aggressive syndromes have different treatment indications (Miller, 1990e; see Chapter 5 for more detail), some general recommendations with regard to family issues can be made.

Behavioral management is the trusty standby of functional rehabilitation, and when used appropriately, can be a powerful therapeutic tool, especially when the family can be trained to maintain the program at home. However, resistance to using these methods can be quite strong among many family members, who may resent or feel pity at having to treat their loved one "like a trained dog," as one family member told me. A better plan — where he or she is capable — is for the patient to be taught his or her own anger-management strategies. In this regard, McKinlay and Hickox (1988) employ a behavioral program they call **A-N-G-E-R**:

A = Anticipate the situations that can trigger an angry outburst.

N = Notice the signs of mounting anger in yourself; this can be accomplished by gradual training in self-monitoring.

G = Go through your "temper routine," which includes relaxation exercises, breathing techniques, and finding alternative ways of handling the situation.

E = Extract yourself from the situation if all else fails.

R = Record how you coped and reflect on what lessons might be learned for next time.

Another approach recommended by McKinlay and Hickox (1988) relies on assertiveness training. The premise here is that in many cases temper outbursts are a socially unskilled form of assertion; therefore, acceptable assertive behaviors and other social skills are taught to broaden the patient's social interaction repertoire for adaptively getting his or her needs met. Of course, the program is tailored to the level of the individual brain-injured patient. It should be noted that these kinds of self-management and skills-training approaches are in principle little different from the techniques now being applied in many treatment settings, such as substance abuse and chronic pain (Clarke & Saunders, 1988; Hanson & Gerber, 1990; Miller, 1990c, 1991e, in press a, in press b, in press c; Monti et al., 1989; Philips, 1988; see Chapters 6 and 7).

BRIGHT SPOTS AND FUTURE DIRECTIONS

One gets the impression from reading the literature that the outlook for family adjustment to brain injury is almost always poor, and my own clinical experience suggests that family therapists who require regular large doses of success and gratitude should steer clear of the brain injury field. However, even if the exception rather than the rule, the positive outcomes we do sometimes see as the result of our assiduous efforts at helping can sustain the promise of optimism in each new case.

Nor are the reports from the field uniformly grim. Research shows that even some very severely injured patients make excellent recoveries, and their families are not unduly burdened (London, 1967). In another study, family relationships that had shown disruption at one year had settled down again at a two-year follow-up (Oddy & Humphrey, 1980). Weddell et al. (1980) found that a group of head injury families selected for rehabilitation actually enjoyed closer involvement after the injury, and in two cases studied by Fahy et al. (1967), previously paranoid, aggressive, and assaultive behavior underwent a change for the better, the patients becoming good-tempered and compliant after the brain injury—although I suspect that in these latter two cases focal damage to limbic system structures may have produced an acquired organic placidity (Kluver-Bucy syndrome).

So the good news is that it's not all bad news. The challenge is to discern the factors that contribute to good recovery: premorbid personality, family environment, social support, professional intervention, and so on. Perhaps those clinicians who work solely or mainly in acute and postacute rehab settings see the tough cases before time and proper treatment have allowed things to mellow out. Too often, any systematic therapeutic work ends when the family carts the patient home from the treatment facility. Contributing to this is the growing reluctance of third-party providers to underwrite such outpatient services as psychotherapy, family therapy, sex therapy, aggression management training, and so on, thinking that physical and vocational rehab is all that's needed to return the patient to "maximum functional capacity."

But a patient whose cognitive difficulties are further impacted upon by depression over impaired sexual performance, whose will to go on is sapped by constant family bickering, who feels beaten and demoralized and unsure of what miseries each new day might bring—this person will not be one of your more reliable wage earners, no matter how much jobsite retraining is provided, and cannot be a caring, loving parent or spouse because every adaptive resource is being continually pounded down. If the therapist can help change the patient's and the family's life from a disastrous defeat into at least a fighting struggle, then a crucial corner has been turned.

PART III

Special Problems

CHAPTER 5

Out of Control:
Impulsivity and Aggression

THE ABILITY TO CONTROL IMPULSES is one of the things we ordinarily regard as making a person human. When this capacity is lost — or voluntarily surrendered, for example, through excessive intoxication — those we thought we knew may seem to become virtually different persons, even to the extent of what we might describe as a "Jekyll-and-Hyde" transformation. Indeed, that very story illustrates the archetypal distinction we make between "civilized" control and "bestial" disinhibition. Thus, it can be particularly scary to see someone we know and love lose those vestiges of civilization to a brain injury.

Aside from the transient state of confusional combativeness that occurs in the postacute interval following a traumatic brain injury, usually after an acute period of unconsciousness (Bond, 1984, 1986; Lishman, 1978; Strub & Black, 1981), persisting aggressive, violent, or impulsive behavior is a frequent problem complicating long-term recovery — that is, after the patient is supposed to have "gotten better."

In some cases, sudden, storm-like explosive outbursts confound psychosocial adjustment that may be proceeding adequately in other respects. Alternatively, impaired judgment and self-control produce a pattern of childlike, impulsive behavior that may include violent tantrums and other forms of "trouble-making." In still other cases, the posttraumatic aggressive behavior seems to be a continuation and exacerbation of a previous lifestyle pattern of antisocial acting-out. This chapter will review the main types of post-brain injury aggressive syndromes — their causes, clinical manifestations, and recommendations for treatment.

97

EXPLOSIVE AGGRESSIVE DISORDER OR
EPISODIC DYSCONTROL

Clinical Features of Episodic Dyscontrol

The type of syndrome known in *DSM-III-R* (APA, 1987) as *intermittent explosive disorder* can occur without a prior history of traumatic or other damage to the brain. However, when episodic rage does follow a head injury, it is most commonly reported in association with damage to the medial portion of the temporal lobes, which contain limbic system structures important for regulating emotion and motivation (Mark & Ervin, 1970; Wood, 1987).

In some cases, the underlying pathology can be documented by radiological or EEG abnormalities, but there are many instances of brain injury in which objective neurologic signs may not be present to account for the episodic aggression. In such cases, the connection with head injury must be inferred by comparison to the patient's premorbid personality and behavioral functioning. However, there is now ample evidence that brain injury may be one of the predisposing factors in the development of the *episodic dyscontrol syndrome*: a pattern of intermittent attacks of violence due to an electrophysiological disturbance in the brain (Elliott, 1982, 1984; Mark & Ervin, 1970; Monroe, 1982; Pincus & Tucker, 1978; Williams, 1969; Wood, 1987).

The clinical presentation in episodic dyscontrol varies in severity and form. More severe aggressive behaviors can appear as sudden, often unprovoked outbursts, primitive and poorly organized in nature — flailing, spitting, scratching, etc. — and usually directed at the nearest available object or person. The act itself can be quite destructive to furniture, pets, or people who happen to get in the way, but human injury is usually the result of the misguided efforts of observers to subdue the patient during an episode. In such cases, the wild thrashing of limbs that inflicts the injurious blows probably represents a desperate attempt to escape restraint, rather than a directed assault against a particular individual, although sudden, directed, but usually unsustained attacks may occur. The outbursts are typically short-lived and may be followed by feelings of regret and remorse when the individual becomes aware of what he has done.

Another kind of dyscontrol episode may resemble the type of aggressive response familiar in persons known for having a "short fuse," that is, individuals for whom it takes less than the usual degree of irritation, frustration, or provocation to elicit a violent response. In such cases, the behavior may appear less out of control, more organized, and more clearly directed against the source of the antagonism.

Awareness of the actual period of violent behavior varies from patient to patient, usually in association with the severity of the dyscontrol episode itself. Some patients claim total amnesia for the episode, while others report a vague, dreamlike recollection of what they were doing while the episode was in progress. Still other patients maintain clear awareness of the outburst but report being powerless to stop it—these are often the patients who express the greatest remorse after the attack. In many cases, the individual may retain sufficient control to momentarily suspend or redirect the violence, e.g., "take the fight outside" or switch the target of the attack from a spouse or child to a chair or wall.

One patient would regularly destroy items in his basement during episodes of dyscontrol. Many of his attacks were preceded by an aura, or warning sensation, whereupon he would race to that subterranean refuge and "take it out" on the various pieces of old furniture he collected around the neighborhood and stored there for just such occasions. Rather less foresight was shown by another patient, hospitalized for drug abuse in addition to episodic violence, who also happened to be a Vietnam vet and an avid gun collector. During one dyscontrol attack precipitated by a combination of cocaine use and spousal conflict, he brandished a loaded M-16 at his wife and children and felt, as he put it, that "I was just going to blow them away—there was no way I could stop it." Yet he was able to restrain himself long enough to run outside where he proceeded to perforate his station wagon, because, he reflected, "I really love my family—I guess part of me wouldn't let me hurt them." Unfortunately, not all such episodes have such relatively benign outcomes.

Episodic Dyscontrol, Seizures, and Brain Dysfunction

The presence of auras preceding many cases of episodic dyscontrol raises another issue. The relationship between episodic dyscontrol and "true" epileptic seizure disorders is as yet not completely clear, but probably represents a continuum between normal behavior with normal EEG findings on the one side, and frank seizures with clearly epileptiform EEG patterns on the other. In fact, EEG recordings of patients with episodic dyscontrol often show this "in-between" pattern of electrophysiological irregularities—that is, not exactly normal, but not clearly epileptiform (Mark & Ervin, 1970; Pincus & Tucker, 1978).

Lishman (1978) differentiates between aggressive attacks that are a component of seizures or seizure-like brain activity vs. more "normal" manifestations of aggression. The former typically begin abruptly and have an explosive character, whereas more normal aggressive responses often occur after a gradual build-up of anger, and the mayhem may involve some premeditation (cf. the proposed legislation in some states for a mandatory "cooling-off period" for gun purchases). Unlike normal aggression, epileptic aggression usually ends as abruptly as it begins, with quick resumption of the patient's normal personality. However, as mentioned above, any strict dichotomy between epileptic and normal aggression is negated by the many intermediate cases where both behavior and EEG patterns may contain elements and blends of either or both extremes (Elliott, 1982; Pincus & Tucker, 1978).

Wood (1987) emphasizes the distinction between "organic" episodic violent attacks and the habitually aggressive behavior of aggressive psychopaths (antisocial personality disorder in *DSM-III-R*). In the latter case, the aggression is rarely spontaneous and explosive, but rather occurs as part of a more general pattern of personality disorder and social maladjustment, usually to obtain some goal. In the case of episodic aggression due to traumatic temporal lobe damage, however, the aggression is unpatterned, is not confined to particular situations or times or individuals, and occurs with minimal provocation, certainly without premeditation.

Again, research and clinical observation reveal numerous violations of this diagnostic "rule," as many aggressive psychopaths without acquired brain injury show EEG abnormalities (including temporal lobe signs) and neuropsychological deficits, and also may display an impulsive, short-fuse character in many of their aggressive and other antisocial acts (Elliott, 1982; Mark & Ervin, 1970; Miller, 1987, 1988b; Pincus & Tucker, 1978; Williams, 1969). All this suggests caution in making any firm distinctions between acquired vs. constitutional behavior disorders (Miller, 1990e, 1990f). This will be discussed further below.

Possibly more common, but less easily recognizable, is the temporal lobe abnormality that does not produce an immediate outburst of physical aggression, but causes an abrupt change of mood (Wood, 1987). Some patients describe mood swings, occurring for no apparent reason, that produce a marked change in behavior, attitude, and frustration tolerance. This change in mood may make the patient more vulnerable to stress, which in turn may lead to an outburst of uncontrollable fury that later leaves the individual feeling remorseful and depressed.

Such a pattern may be related to the slow, progressive, smoldering build-up of angry or other dysphoric feelings that occurs via electrophysiological *kindling* (Adamec & Stark-Adamec, 1983; Post, 1980; Racine, 1978). In this process, repeated stimulation of temporal lobe limbic structures, particularly the amygdala, produces a cumulative increase in excitability and a lowering of the seizure threshold, so that a subsequent minor event, insufficient in itself to cause a seizure-like response, serves as the final straw that breaks the camel's back, inciting the brain into paroxysmal activity with correspondingly uncontrollable behavior. (See Miller, 1991f for a more comprehensive discussion of the psychopathological and psychodynamic implications of kindling.)

AGGRESSION DUE TO
FRONTAL LOBE IMPAIRMENT

The Frontal Lobes and Behavioral Inhibition

As noted, the frontal lobes have traditionally been characterized as the seat of higher abstraction, judgment, planning, sustained motivation, and self-regulation—the so-called "executive functions" of the brain (Luria, 1980; Mattson & Levin, 1990; Nauta, 1971; Stuss & Benson, 1984). Rosenthal (1987) points out that the return of basic intellectual functioning to the normal range by six to 12 months postinjury is often taken to indicate that long-term cognitive sequelae are absent. However, the relative resilience of standard IQ scores may be due to the predominance of frontal lobe injury in many of these patients that spares more posterior brain regions. Formal, psychometrically assessed intelligence is often relatively unaffected by brain damage that is confined to the frontal lobes, as many routine skills and items of previously acquired knowledge are largely retained (Lezak, 1983; McFie, 1975). Instead, what is more commonly seen in such frontal cases are less-easily documentable problems in attention, planning, judgment, self-monitoring, and in initiating and carrying through activities in the real world, especially in complex, nonroutine situations where a greater degree of cognitive flexibility and novel problem-solving is called for.

Bond (1984) has identified aggressiveness as one feature of frontal lobe damage due to brain injury. It is inferred that generalized brain damage occurring in head trauma impairs the mechanisms that inhibit or regulate emotional response, and that the frontal lobes may be especially vulnerable (Mattson & Levin, 1990; Pollens et al., 1988; Posthuma & Wild, 1988). One consequence of this, argues Bond (1984), is that the patient has little, if any, control over sudden shifts of mood or the rapid changes in basic drives that direct behavior. This includes a lower threshold for aggressive behavior.

This release or disinhibition aspect of frontal lobe aggression is, according to Wood (1987), essentially what distinguishes it from the episodic dyscontrol syndrome discussed above. The latter seems to be actively generated or elicited as a result of some paroxysmal electrophysiological event. Frontal aggression, on the other hand, seems to represent an "escape" of aggression, along with other impulsive emotional behavior, because of the brain's impaired ability to maintain an emotional equilibrium or to control the behavioral expression of changes in mood. It is because of this that frontal patients typically overreact to minor provocation or frustration.

Clinical Features

In its most usual presentation, an external irritant — a frustrated goal, an obnoxious person — provoke an emotional response from the frontal patient, which quickly escalates beyond the magnitude that most people would regard as "appropriate" or proportional to the seriousness of the provoking circumstance. Once started, the patient seems to have little or no control over the behavior. In contrast to episodic dyscontrol, the external source of provocation is usually apparent, and the attacks are usually directed toward that source.

The quality of the behavior differs, too, in that serious violence and destructiveness are seldom seen in frontal lobe outbursts. Rather, shouting, crying, cursing, fist-pounding, and throwing of reachable objects are the most common manifestations — the overall impression is more of a tantrum than a directed, violent attack. Insight into, and remorse over, the outburst is rare, and the patient's labile affective state can easily switch from rage to mirth with the right kind of prodding and cajoling. In fact, the distractibility and truncation of the outburst by appropriate social stimulation is one of the features that distinguishes frontally disinhibited angry outbursts from episodic dyscontrol. The latter attacks, once started, typically manifest a "life of their own" and seem to have to run their course. But intact frontal lobe functioning is necessary for both sustaining and restraining emotional states — hence the lability of affect and behavior seen in frontal damage, and the relative ease with which these emotional states can be externally manipulated in either direction.

PREMORBID AGGRESSION AND ANTISOCIALITY

Causes and Effects

Perhaps the single most vexing conundrum in clinical theory and practice with brain-injured patients is the relationship between behavior disorder and brain damage, particularly frontal lobe damage. Indeed, the argument for the frequency of frontal lobe impairment in traumatic brain injury stems largely from the commonly observed concreteness, cognitive inflexibility, impulsiveness, poor organization and planning, impaired problem solving, and lack of adequate behavioral self-control shown by many of these patients (Mattson & Levin, 1990; Pollens et al., 1988; Posthuma & Wild, 1988). These "executive control" deficits are commonly presumed to be a more or less direct result of the brain injury itself, and many cognitive rehab programs for retraining behavioral control functions are based on this assumption (e.g., Goldstein & Levin, 1987).

As discussed in Chapter 2, personality traits commonly associated with traumatic brain injury include irritability, impulsivity, socially inappropriate behavior, unawareness of personal impact on others, deficits in sustaining motivation, and emotional lability. Typically, these "postconcussion personality" characteristics are attributed to the effects of the brain injury itself and are thought to have a basis in the executive frontal lobe functions.

However, clinicians and researchers are beginning to recognize that these impulsive and sometimes aggressive behavioral tendencies and personality characteristics may in fact have predated the injury (Bond, 1984; Miller, 1989b, 1990e, 1992e; Prigatano et al., 1986, 1987; Wood, 1984, 1987). In such cases, frontal disinhibition or paroxysmal electrophysiological disturbances may merely be further disinhibiting or exacerbating a behavioral pattern that has already existed for some time. Demographic data suggest a high incidence of sociopathic behavior in this patient group prior to injury, and many of these same supposedly postconcussional traits are found in groups of individuals identified clinically as psychopaths or antisocial personalities (Begun, 1976; Cleckley, 1976; Miller, 1987, 1988b; Millon, 1981) — in whom there is, in turn, an associated high rate of substance abuse (Cloninger, 1987; Craig, 1982; Miller, 1985, 1989b, 1990a, 1991e — see Chapter 6).

Correspondingly, many of the neuropsychological and personality patterns may reflect this premorbidly impulsive, thrill-seeking, emotionally and behaviorally labile, and often antisocial cognitive style, as opposed to being solely attributable to the effects of the brain injury itself (Miller, 1987, 1988b). Deficits in "executive control," therefore, may characterize the thought and behavior of those individuals most likely to incur a traumatic brain injury in the first place (Miller, 1989b, 1990e, 1992a, 1992b, 1992e; see also Chapters 6 and 12).

Neuropsychological Studies of Antisocial Populations

Adjudicated male delinquents have been found by Berman and Siegal (1976) to be impaired in their ability to comprehend, manipulate, and utilize conceptual material. Violent male penitentiary prisoners are more impaired than nonviolent prisoners on measures of cognitive, language, perceptual, and psychomotor abilities (Spellacy, 1978), and assaultive delinquents have a greater number of EEG abnormalities, poorer verbal memory, and increased perseveration, as compared with nonassaultive subjects (Krynicki, 1978). The significant finding of frontal-like impairment in another series of delinquents led Yeudall et al. (1982) to speculate that delinquents and other antisocial individuals may have particular problems in planning their actions, perceiving the consequences of those actions, and altering those actions in the face of changing circumstances. Gorenstein (1982) further established the presence of frontal-like deficits in a group of adult psychopaths, using a variety of neuropsychological measures.

Bryant et al. (1984) has found that more impulsive, assaultive subjects in an adult male prison population show significant impairment, compared to less violent prisoners, on tasks requiring complex integration of information from the visual, auditory, and somesthetic processing systems, as well as in the ability to create, plan, organize, and execute goal-directed behaviors and to sustain attention and concentration. These investigators point out that the types of behavior disorder described for the more violent offenders resemble those reported in acquired organic frontal lobe damage. Sutker and Allain (1987) replicated this work in a nonprison population, showing that psychopathic inpatients at a Veterans Administration alcohol and drug treatment program perform more poorly than nonpsychopathic inpatients on a variety of measures sensitive to frontal lobe impairment, even when IQ is controlled for. In these studies, the deficits are generally found in the absence of identifiable head trauma or neurologic injury—indeed, overt organic pathology by examination or history is ordinarily used as an exclusion criterion in studies of this type.

I (Miller, 1986a, 1986c, 1988c, 1990f, 1991c, 1992b) have argued that studies in psychiatric neuropsychology that use neurocognitive measures to identify impairment, especially localized impairment, in nonbrain-injured populations must be interpreted with caution. Rather than inferring "lesions" in this or that hemisphere or lobe, the findings of such studies should be taken to suggest that the underlying brain organization that contributes to the personality and cognitive style of each person is a unique one, shaped by heredity, developmental factors, and whatever acquired organic damage may occur in the person's life.

Certain regularities of neuropsychological functioning and cognitive style may indeed be found in members of particular clinical groups. However, characterologically impulsive, antisocial individuals do not have injured frontal lobes in the same pathophysiological sense as a stroke or gunshot victim. Rather, they possess a particular constitutional neuropsychodynamic organization underlying the impulsive cognitive style, one main component of which is an underdevelopment of, or deficiency in, frontal lobe control over behavior. To the extent that this neuropsychodynamic pattern affects test performance as well as general behavior, we may see "frontal"-like deficits on some neuropsychological measures.

Premorbid and Acquired Behavior Disorders: Interaction Effects

Often, preexisting impulsive traits or behavioral difficulties go unnoticed or are glossed over until after the brain injury. It's quite possible for someone to get away with marginally antisocial behavior as long as he is able to use what barely functional neurocognitive abilities and coping skills he possesses to keep from crossing the line into really deep trouble. Then comes the brain injury, which diminishes even these rudimentary adaptive skills. What remain are the impulsivity, aggressiveness, egocentric childishness, and frustration intolerance without any real measure of compensatory judgment or restraint.

Now the behavior gets *really* bad. Antisocial acts are committed wantonly, previously concealed or controlled drug abuse becomes blatant and excessive, and before long the person winds up in serious trouble at work, at home, or with the law. At this point, friends and family cannot help but notice the "new" turn for the worse. All the problems may then be dumped on the brain injury itself, often accompanied by a defensive idealization of preinjury behavior on the part of patient and family alike: "He was such a good kid until the damn accident, then everything changed. Well, sure, he got in a little trouble now and then, but what kid doesn't? Boys will be boys . . . his bad friends influenced him . . . the drugs made him crazy," and so on. Of course, a careful review of the patient's history will often reveal that the present bad behavior hardly originated with the brain injury, but rather represents an extension and amplification of a previous pattern.

Thus, to the extent that head injuries tend to happen preferentially to people with premorbidly impulsive and often aggressive lifestyles, it is hardly surprising that superimposed injury to the brain would serve to intensify and exacerbate this pattern, whether through frontal disinhibition or lowered threshold to paroxysmal brain activity, or both. A vicious cycle if ever there was one—those most prone to sustain a brain injury are those most likely to have the worst reaction to it (Miller, 1989b, 1990b, 1990e, 1992a, 1992b, 1992e, see Chapter 12).

One way in which this interaction may manifest itself is shown in a study by Allen et al. (1988) who compared organically impaired and nonimpaired long-term psychiatric hospital patients on several dimensions of problematic behavior associated with treatment difficulty. These included psychotic withdrawal, severe character pathology, violence and agitation, and suicidal depression. Four of the five patients in the violent subgroup were young men, and this subgroup showed great diversity in psychiatric diagnosis and pattern of behavioral dyscontrol. The organic impairment was of diverse etiologies, predominantly longstanding, and often subtle and difficult to diagnose precisely. Only one patient had a true epileptic dyscontrol syndrome, i.e., violence associated with paroxysmal, seizure-like disturbance.

Despite the diagnostic and symptomatic heterogeneity in this violent subgroup, the patients showed strikingly similar psychological profiles. They were each described as emotionally immature or "childlike"; each clung to a wish to remain sheltered and nurtured, feeling inadequate to face the challenges of young adulthood. All were afraid and ashamed of their poor emotional control and tried to hide or deny it. Many were also hampered by intellectual limitations that prevented them from meeting cognitive challenges successfully or living up to their own and others' expectations for achievement. These patients had not developed adequate controls over affect, but rather relied on primitive and ineffective defenses, including constriction, denial, avoidance, and dissociation. They responded to blows to their self-esteem by developing grandiose fantasies, e.g., of intellectual superiority, or by externalization, blaming others for their failings, which often involved lashing out violently in words and actions. In general, the pattern was similar to that of the psychodynamic "primitive personality" described by Robbins (1989) (see Chapter 12).

In some rare cases, clinicians have seen previously hell-raising individuals who seem to have been "scared straight" by the brain injury, but how long these postinjury reformations last is unknown and, at any rate, they are the exception. If anything, the preponderance of the evidence suggests that, in most cases, brain injury makes a person "more like himself"—i.e., accentuates preexisting personality traits—rather than producing any dramatic alterations in personality (Bond, 1984; Oddy, 1984; Wood, 1987). Previously compulsive persons may become fanatical control freaks after the injury, somatizing individuals may develop a panoply of hysterical and "psychosomatic" symptoms to complicate their organic difficulties, and previously impulsive patients may become wildly out of control.

TREATMENT OF BEHAVIOR DISORDERS

While some treatment principles are specific to behavior disorders related to brain injury, others are applicable to dealing with impulsive and aggressive behavior disorders in general.

Treatment of Episodic Dyscontrol

In the treatment of episodic, explosive aggression, Eames (1988) and Wood (1987) argue that pharmacotherapy or behavioral management methods are inadequate if either is used alone. Instead, they recommend a combination of anticonvulsant medication, particularly carbamazepine (Tegretol) plus behavior therapy. When patients who have unquestionable seizure-related aggressive behavior disorders are treated with anticonvulsants alone and not subject to continued, consistent behavioral control — for example, when the patient's outpatient behavioral follow-up is insufficient or erratic — then the behavior problems frequently respond poorly. Anticonvulsants can control seizure activity, but they can't teach new, adaptive modes of behavior.

I have seen this phenomenon most clearly when a patient with a paroxysmal disorder does well on medication within a structured inpatient milieu, only to fall apart behaviorally when discharged to the family who may be unable or unwilling to maintain the continuity and consistency of behavioral management because they believe that "the medication will make him better." For this reason, I strongly recommend working closely with the family well in advance of the anticipated discharge date so as to coordinate as smooth a transition as possible from inpatient to outpatient management.

Treatment of Frontal Lobe Behavior Disorders

Managing the type of disinhibited aggression seen in frontal lobe-injured patients really represents a subset of the management of frontal lobe behavior in general. As Wood (1987) points out, given the problems one sees in frontal patients maintaining an adaptive behavior pattern even when relying on external guides and constraints, one can only imagine the difficulties these individuals must experience in *self*-control.

In such cases, explicit and consistent external guidance is the key, especially in the early stages following the injury. In my experience, improvement often depends on sufficient neurological recovery from the postacute effects of the brain injury; training the frontal patient in more adaptive behavior often fails to meet expectations because the issue is not really one of a deficit in skill-learning, per se. Rather, the very ability to use skills and knowledge in a self-regulated and goal-directed way is what has been affected. With regard to aggression and other impulsive behaviors, the patient frequently "knows" that the reaction is inappropriate, especially after it has occurred. What is impaired is the ability to self-modulate emotions and behaviors in accord with internal need states and the exigencies of the outside world (Luria, 1980; Nauta, 1971).

According to Wood (1988), the thinking of frontal-injured patients is too concrete and egocentric to allow subtle forms of social perception to change behavior. Such cognitive impairments as diminished insight or loss of social awareness prevent the patient from perceiving the subtle antecedents that control human behavior or the consequences of their own behavior for others. Therefore, many of these individuals revert to a more automatic and stereotyped style of behavior, characterized by poor judgment and a superficial way of thinking. They fail to see beyond the immediate and the actual, and therefore do not anticipate the wider and long-term implications of their actions.

Thus, continued external guidance may be necessary for adaptive behavior to be maintained. Of course, the outcome will vary from patient to patient, depending on the extent of the impairment, the premorbid level of functioning, and the resources of the present environment. Family members often have to be trained as a kind of surrogate frontal lobe system for the patient in order to enable him to use his retained cognitive abilities in a productive fashion. In some cases, the establishment of a predictable routine at home or at work is helpful in reducing the number of frustrating situations that might set off an impulsive, aggressive episode.

Another problem to watch for is the squeaky-wheel-gets-the-grease phenomenon. According to Eames (1988), it's not too difficult to identify a patient who is screaming obscenities and assaulting staff and other patients as exhibiting a "behavior disorder." On the other hand, the patient who sits quietly, withdrawn from the environment, yet giving polite responses to questions, is not often so identified and may be ignored, as staff or family attention is directed to the "trouble-makers."

This is unfortunate, because the patient whose refusal to cooperate results from frontal lobe *abulia* (lack of spontaneous activity or initiative) may be neurologically quite able to respond to encouragement, exhortation, or a formal positive reinforcement program. In addition, to the extent that this disorder reflects disruption of the diencephalic dopaminergic pathways activating the anterior cingulate cortex (Fisher, 1982), medication with the dopamine agonist bromocriptine may produce increased levels of activity and interaction. Finally, the patient whose difficulties with the organization of everyday domestic tasks stem from a severe attention disorder may make little progress from simple repeated practice. However, if formal retraining of attention is undertaken, remediation in activities of daily living may be more fruitful.

Treatment of Premorbid Impulsivity
Exacerbated by Brain Injury

Individuals with premorbid patterns of impulsivity and violence pose a special treatment problem because it is here that the whole tangle of neuropsychological impairment, electrophysiological abnormalities, and personality pathology becomes one of the thorniest of clinical issues. In many such cases, rehabilitation is really *habilitation*, since what is being trained for the first time is the ability to behave adaptively according to the rules and constraints of the real world—for many patients a startlingly novel experience forced upon them only by reason of their injury.

Such cases require attention to cognitive rehab variables, substance abuse factors, medication effects, behavioral management, psychotherapy, and forensic issues. One particular problem I've observed with many of these patients is a tendency to endorse their impairment and use it as an excuse for continuing and even escalating previous patterns of antisocial behavior. As one patient genteelly put it: "Hey, I was a mean motherfucker before my accident, and now I'm one fucked-up, brain-damaged, biogenetically dangerous dude." Often compounding the problem are patterns of malingering, somatization, chronic pain, and drug abuse that further frustrate attempts at psychosocial habilitation. Not surprisingly, long-term prognosis in such cases is typically not encouraging.

Even so, for some patients in this class, albeit a minority, the brain injury may turn out to be the key life event that fosters a reevaluation of priorities and goals. If the therapist and rehab team can seize this existential initiative (see Chapter 3) and if the patient retains sufficient psychological resources to sustain motivation and effort toward recovery, such lives may be turned around for the better.

General Principles of Behavioral
Management

Behavior therapists tend to favor an orderly, organized, step-by-step, and empirically validated approach to clinical problems. While this treatment modality is not appropriate for all types of problems seen after brain injury, management of impulsive and aggressive behavior of diverse etiologies can often be facilitated by behavioral techniques. Burke and Wesolowski (1988) have identified the main steps in the behavioral analysis process: (1) identify the target behavior; (2) measure the frequency of the behavior; (3) analyze the behavior; (4) develop an intervention; (5) program generalization of the behavior; (6) empirically evaluate the results.

Focusing more specifically on anger management, Carberry (1983) lays out the following strategy:

1. Avoid getting into a power struggle or battle of wills with the patient.
2. Ignore negative, attention-seeking comments and complaints, while reinforcing the patient's positive comments and behavior.
3. Involve the patient in a number of small steps aimed at helping him feel less helpless.
4. In conversation with the patient, avoid the areas of resistance and negativism and try to tie in with the patient's own positive interests and concerns.
5. Develop a plan with the patient that allows him to have as much input as possible.
6. Try to know and understand the patient's major belief systems.
7. Where appropriate, employ paradoxical techniques that consist of going with the resistance rather than using counterretaliatory techniques.
8. Use reframing—rephrasing or restating the problem in another way—to defuse anger, resistance, and negativism.

Extinction and Reinforcement

In behavioral terminology, *extinction* refers to the reduction in the frequency of behavior due to withholding of reward, or reinforcement. The utility of combining extinction of unwanted behavior with encouragement and reinforcement of wanted behavior is illustrated in a controlled case study by Lewis et al. (1988) that compared three different behavioral strategies directed at reducing the socially inappropriate talk of a brain-injured patient. Socially inappropriate talk was defined as any unintelligible, foolish, or absurd statement not fitting the context of the situation.

In the *attention and interest* condition, the therapist responded to socially inappropriate remarks by smiling, maintaining eye contact, and saying things like, "That's interesting," "You're too much," "You're too funny," and so on. In the *systematic ignoring* condition, the therapist broke eye contact for three seconds and then initiated a conversation on an appropriate topic. The therapist administering the *correction* contingency responded to maladaptive talk by saying in a neutral tone of voice: "You're talking nonsense when you say. . . . People can't understand you. Now start again and tell me about something that makes sense." During the final week of the study, each therapist administered the correction condition.

The results of this study showed that, irrespective of the therapist, the correction contingency consistently produced the greatest diminution of socially inappropriate talk. Systematic ignoring, a successful procedure for reducing attention-seeking behaviors, was somewhat less effective than correction. As expected, attention and interest greatly exacerbated the problems and demonstrated that the high rate of inappropriate talk observed in the neutral environment was likely maintained by social reinforcement.

In practice, this kind of approach requires great skill and patience to implement productively. Behavioral managers must be alert to avoid inadvertently reinforcing unwanted behaviors. Also, notwithstanding the cut-and-dry descriptions of such processes given in published reports, the real-life implementation of behavioral control regimens are often met, especially at the outset, with messy emotional displays that must be dealt with in their own right. My experience is that these systematic behavioral interventions work best — certainly in the start-up stages — in institutional settings where the staff has the requisite knowledge, skill, patience, and resources to implement the program effectively. Once in place, transfer to the family setting may be facilitated, and hopefully the family will be willing and able to follow through. But where such programs are carried out lackadaisically, haphazardly, and with insufficient knowledge of behavioral principles, they may end up doing more harm than good.

Modeling and Shaping

According to Wood (1988), modeling is frequently used by rehabilitation therapists when instructing a patient how to approach a task or social situation. In a behavior modification protocol, modeling is used to accelerate the process of learning because the desired response is demonstrated by the therapist in a manner and at a level of complexity that the patient is most likely to understand. Modeling combines processes of operant reinforcement and observational learning. It is applicable not only to patients but to family and staff.

Modeling techniques usually incorporate *shaping*, a technique for reinforcing successive approximations to the target behavior. This has proven a useful strategy in the progressive development of complex behaviors in the brain-injured. Most functional behaviors involve a complex response pattern, and brain-injured patients find it particularly difficult to initiate and display complex behaviors. Therefore, reinforcement is aimed at the subelements of a complex behavior or at attempts to initiate the behavior.

I would add the recommendation that the therapist be careful to insure that what takes place is true modeling, not just imitation. The latter involves a concrete, situation-specific aping of behavior or parrotting of speech that shows no internalization or generalization outside the specific therapeutic setting. Of course, imitation is the first step to modeling, but should not be mistaken for the whole of it. The therapist should have the patient gradually practice the modelled behaviors in situations that are similar in type, but not concretely specific to the learning session, then attempt generalization to other settings.

Proactive Approaches

Hogan (1988) maintains that taking a proactive approach to the problems of frustration tolerance and aggression can yield more positive results than trying to deal with situations after they occur. In behavior training sessions, with the patient's prior knowledge, the patient may be placed in situations that would typically result in loss of control of aggression. The goal is to increase the patient's tolerance level by small increments and reward any improvement in performance. Similar kinds of proactive approaches have had wide applications in the behavioral medicine and addictions treatment fields, where they are respectively known as *stress inoculation* and *relapse prevention* (see Chapters 6 and 7).

One technique to build such practice into the program consists of *behavioral games*. These games, guided by clear rules and clear consequences, combine repetition and recreation with peer pressure to maintain behavioral control. For example, in "floor hockey," verbal aggression results in a visit to the penalty box, and the aggressor's team is at an obvious disadvantage. In particularly sensitive areas, desensitization techniques and stress management training may be employed as well.

Self-Talk

According to Hogan (1988), the notion that people's feelings are created internally as the result of their ideas and internal verbalizations, and that the individual can learn to control his thoughts, can translate into an effective behavioral technique (see also Chapter 12). Emphasizing the nonproductive and possibly destructive nature of negative or irrational thinking patterns in contrast to the benefits of positive, goal-directed thinking begins the process of turning over control of one's "feelings" to the individual, according to this view. Role playing and psychodrama, done in groups, appear to be particularly effective approaches, given attentional deficits and the benefits of active involvement in therapy. Both methods allow for repetition, practice, and immediate reinforcement of appropriate, adaptive behaviors.

Changing the Environment

Eames (1988) notes that there are often two interacting factors that lead to the exhibition of disordered behavior. On the one hand, there is the brain state that drives or allows the behavior, on the other hand, the environmental stimuli that precipitate it. Often, therefore, the disordered behavior can be prevented or reduced by dealing with either factor. In planning management, it is essential to consider what might be gained or lost by the patient from each of the options available. This in turn is determined largely by the stage of recovery that has been reached.

Early after injury, disturbed behavior is best managed by attempting to eliminate environmental precipitants (e.g., pain, full bladder or bowel, alien surroundings, insensitive or authoritarian handling) and letting the passage of time take care of the confusion itself. Later on, however, it must be remembered that the goal of rehabilitation is to return the patient to the highest possible level of independence, not only physically, but socially. Ordinary society will simply not tolerate disturbed or aggressive behavior, nor is society prepared to avoid provocation, since this is inherent in many social settings where irritating and obnoxious people may abound. It is therefore necessary to deal with this kind of behavior disorder in a more direct way, to eliminate the *tendency* to respond maladaptively, not just try to play behavioral catch-up after the behavior occurs. Here again, the family's cooperation and participation must be enlisted for this approach to be effective.

Family Involvement

It is obvious from Chapter 4 just how important the family is in facilitating or inhibiting the patient's postinjury recovery and readjustment. In dealing behaviorally with family-related issues, Wood (1988) points out, the therapist must combine appropriate treatment methods with a degree of common sense. In any inpatient or day hospital program, therapists ultimately have to rely on family members to cooperate with treatment staff and to extend therapeutic progress into the home setting. *Behavioral contracting* can provide guidelines that a family can follow and that link the activities of the treatment staff with the role that relatives can play at home, thus helping to maintain the necessary degree of continuity in the patient's social environment.

Behavioral contracting establishes an agreement between therapist, patient, and family as to the appropriate goals of treatment and the best way to achieve them. Such an agreement allows families to adopt the clinical procedures used in the institutional setting and implement them in a clear and unambiguous way in the home—provided sufficient thought is given by the treatment team as to how the methods used in the facility translate to the home environment. Another advantage of behavioral contracting is that it gives families a degree of confidence that they are working *with* the treatment team and not at cross purposes.

Generalization

With regard to families and to wider community generalization, Hogan (1988) points out that many brain-injured patients experience a "revolving door" syndrome—in and out of several programs during the course of their rehabilitation. The problem appears to be less a general ineffectiveness of the programs themselves (although programs do vary in quality) than a broader failure of treatment to generalize to the community environment. The chances of this happening without at least some kind of support are slim. To ensure successful reintegration, rehabilitation programs need to provide more of these kinds of community and home-based services.

Behavior Management and Psychotherapy

But, after all, you can't just treat people like machines, and patients and families alike will sooner or later balk at approaches that rely exclusively on managing contingencies of reinforcement. Hogan (1988) notes that psychotherapy and behavior modification are often thought of as being mutually exclusive modalities. However, both approaches may complement each other as long as careful attention is paid to the timing and type of counseling or therapy needed. The ability to generate a consistent, positive, and caring atmosphere can certainly make the difference between an effective behavioral program and an exercise in futility.

Problems, Hogan (1988) says, are best viewed as opportunities to treat and teach. Within such an atmosphere it is possible to build close, trusting relationships between staff and patients. Often, that trusting relationship is the one ingredient that fosters behavior change. When a patient, as a result of cognitive impairment, is truly unable to comprehend the problem that the inappropriate behavior presents, that patient may take the leap and make an effort to change based only on his trust of the therapist, rather than on reasoning or coercion.

Counseling and psychotherapy can provide that needed trust. But, Hogan (1988) warns, it can also reinforce inappropriate behaviors if the two approaches are provided at the wrong time. Rather than counseling the patient immediately following the targeted behavior, it is desirable to wait until the patient is in control and has been "caught" performing positively. Reinforcing this desired behavior avoids the risk of attending to unwanted behavior. In this way, the clinician may reinforce the appropriate behavior and then add, "Let's talk about what happened earlier today." My only qualification here is that after too long a wait, many brain-injured patients may no longer remember or care about the original incident.

In both group and individual therapy, Hogan (1988) says, the clinician may deal with the patient's reaction to the injury so as to reduce confusion and provide strategies for dealing internally with the problems. It is extremely important early on in the process to explore with patients what has happened to them and how their injuries have affected their ability to function. Prigatano et al. (1986) similarly emphasize providing an explanatory model for what has happened to the patient.

It is also important, Hogan (1988) notes, to focus on the future and on the patient's ability to change things for the better. Just as patients may be unaware of the problems resulting from a brain injury, so may they also be unaware of subsequent gains and improvements experienced in treatment. To focus on improvements and successes as they occur and contrast them with performance levels upon entry into treatment can add perspective and increase motivation. It may seem obvious, but patients need to be supported for what they're doing right, as well as being corrected for what they're doing wrong. Indeed, I find that having some valued goal to strive for often makes the difference between a patient's fighting tooth and nail against all behavioral interventions vs. enduring temporary failure, disappointment, and indignity for the sake of a better future.

CHAPTER 6

Bad Medicine:
Alcohol and Drug Abuse

ACCORDING TO A 1988 survey by the National Head Injury Foundation's Substance Abuse Task Force (NHIF, 1988), there was not one facility in the United States that specifically addressed the substance abuse treatment needs of the brain injury population. This is not for lack of need. The NHIF Task Force found that approximately half the total number of brain injury patients had at least some preinjury trouble with substance abuse and many had been heavy users. This pattern typically continues after brain injury. Traditional head injury rehab facilities report difficulty in managing their substance abusing patients, while at the same time, traditional drug and alcohol treatment programs have poor success rates with cognitively impaired patients. Despite this growing awareness, close to half of U.S. trauma centers fail to routinely screen for alcohol use (Soderstrom & Cowley, 1987). Alcohol problems figure prominently in the high unemployment rates reported for postinjury patients (Ben-Yishay et al., 1987; Brooks et al., 1987; Kreutzer et al., 1991).

This chapter will examine the role of substance abuse in contributing to, and complicating recovery from, traumatic brain injury, and will explore some of the treatment options for patients with combined brain injury and substance abuse syndromes. Happily, in the last few years, this problem has begun to be addressed in the brain injury treatment field, but there is still far to go.

ALCOHOL, DRUGS, AND BRAIN INJURY: CAUSES AND EFFECTS

A number of factors conspire to make brain injury and substance abuse a volatile mix. As most reported research has been with alcohol, this chapter will reflect that emphasis.

Effects of Drinking on the Brain and Brain Injury

Research suggests several ways that alcohol can impact with head injury. First, alcohol use is the best established predisposing factor that places an individual at risk for traumatic brain injury. Roughly half (findings in different series range from 29 to 68%) of all such injuries occur during a state of intoxication. In addition, about half of the victims of such injuries have previous histories of alcohol abuse (Brismar et al., 1983; Field, 1976; Hillbom & Holm, 1986; Kerr et al., 1971; Rimel et al., 1981; Tobis et al., 1982). Because the symptoms of brain injury and alcohol intoxication often overlap, it is possible that a significant proportion of alcohol involvement in acute brain injury goes undiagnosed (Jernigan, 1991).

Alcohol and drug abuse also appear to be relatively frequent among the ranks of nonbrain-injured but physically handicapped persons, but in many of these cases the abuse is related more to overuse or misuse of prescription medication, to depression over loss of function, or to the tacit or explicit encouragement of friends, family, and even some clinicians who may well-meaningly recommend a few drinks for relaxation or "cheering up" (Greer, 1986; Greer et al., 1988; Motet-Grigoras & Schuckit, 1986). Ironically, increased independence arising through recovery and rehabilitation in brain-injured and other handicapped persons may increase substance abuse by virtue of increased mobility and accessibility of drugs and alcohol (Kreutzer et al., 1991).

Second, alcohol can complicate the brain injury itself, as well as physical recovery. Patients with a significant blood alcohol level (BAL) at the time of the injury have a lower grade of consciousness when admitted to the hospital, remain in coma longer, and have longer hospital stays (Brismar et al., 1983; Edna, 1982). Alcohol can lead to fluid and electrolyte abnormalities, which can exacerbate cerebral edema (Steinbok & Thompson, 1978). Chronic, long-term alcoholism has been shown to be associated with cerebral atrophy and other structural brain changes (Ron et al., 1982; Wilkinson, 1987), which can lead to increased risk of brain injury-induced hematoma due to increased capillary fragility, decreased brain counterpressure, and possible alterations of blood clotting mechanisms (Elmer et al., 1983;

Markwalder, 1981). Alcohol dilates peripheral blood vessels, which reduces blood pressure and blood loss tolerance, increasing the risk of brain hypoxia (Elmer & Lim, 1985); this may be further exacerbated by alcohol-induced respiratory depression (McQueen & Posey, 1975). Finally, alcohol inhibits neutrophilic migration and other bactericidal activities of blood, thereby increasing the risk of infection (Brayton et al., 1970; Johnson et al., 1969).

Sparadeo and Gill (1989) report that over half of a large sample of patients admitted to a hospital trauma center had a documentable BAL, and if the BAL was at the intoxicated level (.10 or more), complications of the medical course occurred that contributed to increased cost of treatment. These included longer length of stay, longer duration of agitation, and lower cognitive status at discharge. Longer duration of agitation is likely to lead to additional consultations and specific management procedures, which increase the cost of hospitalization, for example, continual staff-intensive observation, psychiatric consultations, and use of medication for behavioral management. Medication, in turn, may slow down cognitive recovery and increase the length of stay. In addition to focusing on costs, it would be instructive to know what aspects of clinical outcome were affected by BAL during brain trauma.

Third, aside from structural brain changes, chronic abuse of alcohol can produce cognitive deficits (Franceschi et al., 1984; Miller, 1985, 1989b, 1990a, 1991e; Parsons, 1987a; Tarter & Edwards, 1985), which interact with the neuropsychological impairment produced by the injury itself, and which may interfere with behavioral and psychosocial recovery from brain injury. Typical impairment patterns found on neuropsychological testing include deficits in attention and concentration, visuospatial and perceptuo-motor functioning, learning and memory, verbal reasoning and abstraction, conceptualization, and behavioral control. A patient already cognitively compromised by a history of alcohol abuse may have even less capacity to compensate for the effects of a brain injury and fewer intact abilities to utilize in rehabilitation.

Indeed, Parsons (1987b) has pointed out that many long-term alcoholics, even without complicating brain trauma, may have inordinate difficulty in dealing with the demands of standard alcohol treatment programs, which, to accommodate dwindling insurance coverage, are increasingly tending toward 28-day, short-term programs. The result is that the patient may be close to discharge just at the point where he is beginning to cognitively clear sufficiently to obtain some benefit from milieu treatment. How much poorer must be the outcome of someone in such a program who has additionally sustained a traumatic brain injury and, conversely, how much more discouraging the prognosis for someone in a traditional brain injury rehab program who has been abusing alcohol since before the injury and continues to do so afterward.

In fact, the NHIF Substance Abuse Task Force (NHIF, 1988) reports that sending a brain-injured patient out to a standard 28-day substance abuse treatment program hardly makes a dent in overall adjustment difficulties. These programs are typically too fast-paced and require writing, memory, organization, and abstract conceptualization skills that are beyond the capabilities of many brain-injured patients—virtually the same criticism Parsons (1987b) has leveled against many traditional alcohol and drug treatment programs. Parsons recommends more long-term treatment approaches, tailored to the slowly-improving neurocognitive skills of the recovering alcohol abuser, and in fact, this kind of approach has been put into practice with nonbrain-injured alcoholics by Gordon et al. (1988).

Similarly, the NHIF Task Force recommends that a more effective treatment strategy for substance-abusing, brain-injured patients might be to build the alcohol and drug program right into the brain injury rehab program. Length of treatment and type of treatment modalities used would be determined by the individual patient's needs, taking into account such a patient's decreased ability to absorb, process, and generalize. Unfortunately, in the present economic climate, bottom-line considerations too often outweigh clinical ones; however, as will be discussed in the final section of this chapter, a few innovative programs are beginning to integrate substance abuse treatment into brain injury rehab.

Effects of Brain Injury on Drinking

Interestingly, some investigations have revealed that the frequency and quantity of drinking actually decreases after brain injury, in some groups at least. For example, Kreutzer et al. (1990) found that nearly three times as many patients in their sample were abstinent postinjury as preinjury. In addition, the number of patients considered problem drinkers declined by a third postinjury, while the total proportion of light or infrequent drinkers stayed about the same as before the injury, and many patients who were moderate drinkers preinjury drank less or gave up the stuff entirely after injury. Nevertheless, considering the potentially adverse effects on long-term outcome, the number of postinjury problem drinkers or heavy drinkers was still relatively large, including up to a fifth of the sample. In a follow-up study, Kreutzer et al. (1991) replicated the finding of a general decline in alcohol use after brain injury. However, an intriguing pattern emerged: While a greater number of preinjury light drinkers became postinjury teetotalers, the number of moderate and heavy drinkers remained about the same. Preinjury marijuana use showed an overall decline post-injury.

In accounting for these findings, the authors point to several factors. First, postinjury evaluation took place an average of six years following injury and the frequency of marijuana use tends to decrease with age as a general finding from national samples. Second, patients may have limited access to drugs and alcohol because of physical disability, financial hardship, or tighter family supervision. The usually deleterious social isolation that so often follows brain injury may have one bright side if it keeps the patient's former drug contacts away, and some drug dealers may actually feel pangs of conscience about "selling shit to a gimp," as one of my patients put it (the dealer in question had a brother whom he described as a "retard," which apparently served to instill a peculiar sort of empathy). Some patients — far too few, though — may discontinue drug and alcohol use in compliance with recommendations from medical professionals as well as increased interest in maintaining personal health. These are typically the same patients who come to view their brain injury as a form of existential transition event (see below and Chapter 3; see also Miller, 1991e).

Premorbid Impulsivity and Antisociality

Excessive, dysfunctional drinking seems to be largely a young man's game. Young adult males as a whole have the highest drinking rates in this country, with 19% meeting the criteria for classification as heavy drinkers (Johnson et al., 1977). According to the U.S. Bureau of Census (1986), of all persons arrested in 1985 for driving under the influence, 85% were between the ages of 18 and 44. This age group also accounted for more than 75% of all arrests for public drunkenness, disorderly conduct, and drug-related violations.

Brooks (1984) has reviewed some of the evidence linking premorbid antisociality and substance abuse with an increased risk for traumatic brain injury. Heavy drinking appears to be particularly common at the time of such injuries, and head injury victims are often habitual heavy drinkers (Galasko & Edwards, 1974; Galbraith et al., 1976; Potter, 1967). Fahy et al. (1967) found that 12 out of their series of 32 head injury cases had been "socially maladjusted" prior to the injury. Five had shown "chronic neurotic" symptoms, four had histories of heavy drinking and petty crime, one showed "low intelligence," one had been epileptic, and one had received psychiatric treatment for chronic schizophrenia. Jamieson (1971), in an account of 1,000 consecutive head injury admissions to a rehab unit, discovered that many of the patients were known to the police before admission. A number of them had records of violence and other antisocial behavior. They also tended to come from broken homes, to have poor school records, poor martial stability, and a higher rate of domestic and industrial accidents than a control group.

Bond (1984) cites Field's (1976) report that in Britain (whose statistics on brain injury and behavior disorder are roughly comparable to that of the U.S.), about half the total number of traumatic brain injuries are the result of motor vehicle accidents, and males outnumber females by a ratio of five to one, with more than half under age 20. Significantly, antisociality as a general characteristic shows a similar male predominance and young age of peak prevalence (Begun, 1976; Miller, 1987, 1988b; Millon, 1981). Cartlidge and Shaw (1981) note that being male and under 25 carries with it the greatest risk of brain injury.

Two studies have specifically examined the relationship among traumatic brain injury, aggression, and alcohol abuse. Alterman and Tarter (1985) used a specialized diagnostic interview to ascertain the presence of familial alcoholism in a group of alcoholic inpatients at a VA treatment facility. Goodwin (1979) had originally hypothesized that familial and nonfamilial alcoholics comprise different subtypes of alcoholism. Since then, evidence has accumulated that familial alcoholics manifest more dependence, more immaturity, and lower social competence than nonfamilial alcoholics. They show more severe alcoholism, including earlier onset, and are more likely to have childhood histories of hyperactivity and attention deficit disorder, as well as greater degrees of cognitive impairment on neuropsychological testing (see also Cloninger, 1987; Tarter et al., 1985). Tarter et al. (1984) had previously found that adolescent sons of alcoholics, who were not themselves alcoholics, were more likely than sons of nonalcoholics to have experienced physical abuse from their fathers and to have suffered from loss of consciousness due to traumatic brain injury.

In the present study, Alterman and Tarter (1985) found that familial alcoholics were more likely than nonfamilial alcoholics to have sustained a closed head injury, although the reasons for this association were unclear. The authors speculate that antecedent conditions such as hyperactivity or conduct disorder, or perhaps adult antisocial personality, augment the risk for coincidental trauma. Not surprisingly, a history of traumatic brain injury has been found to be associated with impaired cognitive performance in alcoholics relative to nonbrain-injured alcoholics (Grant et al., 1984).

One important area where the interaction between premorbid personality, substance abuse, and head injury becomes relevant is that of family violence. Rosenbaum and Hoge (1989) studied a group of male patients referred for evaluation of spouse abuse, and found that 61% had histories of severe traumatic head injury, far exceeding the head injury rate in the general population. Although the relationship between child abuse and head injury did not reach statistical significance, it did indicate a trend toward a positive relationship. In this sample, alcohol abuse was significantly associated with head injury—consistent with the body of literature documenting a strong relationship between alcohol, aggressive behavior, and traumatic brain injury (Bond, 1984; Field, 1976; Galasko & Edwards, 1974; Galbraith et al., 1976; Jamieson, 1971; Miller, 1989b; Potter, 1967).

The present study's investigators suggest that one way of explaining the relationship among alcohol abuse, head injury, and marital violence is that alcohol predisposes both to head injury and aggressiveness. Alternatively, oversensitivity to alcohol is associated with a variant of the episodic dyscontrol syndrome (see Chapter 5), the *pathological intoxication syndrome*, in which uncontrolled, violent behavior can be triggered by even small amounts of alcohol (Monroe, 1982; Pincus & Tucker, 1978). A third possibility is that alcohol and head injury each independently promote aggressive behavior, and the two together have a synergistic effect. Finally—yet another vicious cycle—violence-prone individuals may be more likely to engage in dangerous activities that increase the risk of traumatic brain injury. For example, in the present sample of spouse-abusers, several subjects reported victimizing individuals other than their wives or other family members, suggesting that spouse abuse may be underreported by virtue of being masked by more generalized violence.

Sociocultural Factors

Neurobiology is not necessarily destiny, however, and predisposition is not predestination (Miller, 1990f). Sociocultural factors almost always interact with constitutional predisposition to produce behavioral outcomes.

According to Bond (1984), certain cultural factors related to drinking, risk-taking, and thrill-seeking may increase the risk of traumatic brain injury among young men. For example, excessive heavy drinking is widespread among young men in the west of Scotland and is closely related to injury caused by motor vehicle accidents and assaults, especially among lower socioeconomic groups. In Australia, high-speed auto driving during drinking bouts is a frequent cause of accidents that result in serious injury or death among adolescents and young men. In both groups, prior records of criminal and civil prosecution are often copious, indicating that young men who sustain traumatic brain injuries have had more encounters with the law than others (Jamieson & Kelly, 1973).

One need hardly comment on the glorification of "life in the fast lane" that deluges the American public through advertising and the media. Jernigan (1991) points out that the alcohol beverage industry spends approximately two billion dollars per year to promote its products. In ads, alcohol use appears in conjunction with high-risk activities such as skiing and auto racing. Depictions of an unhelmeted motorcyclist holding a beer, or of skiers doing flips down a mountainside are virtual how-to guides for traumatic brain injury. Targeted marketing enables the alcohol industry to identify key groups of consumers, most prominently ads and promotions linking alcohol with blue-collar men, a group already at relative risk for alcohol-related auto and industrial accidents, and to target them with culturally appropriate messages—for example, commercials linking beer with the prominent American car culture. No surprise, then, that impulsivity, drinking, driving, and traumatic brain injury all tend to go together in the U.S. and elsewhere (Donovan et al., 1983; Finkle, 1982; Landrum & Windham, 1981; Richman, 1985; Selzer & Barton, 1977; Zelhart, 1972; Zelhart & Schurr, 1977).

TREATMENT OF ALCOHOL AND DRUG PROBLEMS IN THE BRAIN-INJURED PATIENT

Education

As I've noted throughout this book, despite intensive—sometimes oppressive—contact with the health care system, brain-injured patients and their families typically receive woefully inadequate information about the nature of their condition and the implications for recovery. This is even more true for lifestyle issues such as sexual relations and drug use. Only quite recently have rehab professionals begun to wake up to this informational-educative aspect of treatment.

Substance abuse prevention is considered to be an essential part of Langley et al.'s (1990) comprehensive traumatic brain injury rehabilitation program. They recommend presenting alcohol information in a small group setting with consideration of the cognitive abilities of the group members. Inasmuch as the desire of brain injury patients to return to life as usual is typically quite strong, it is important for the clinician to have a clear picture of the patterns that patients consider part of their "normal" preinjury lifestyle.

For example, one brain-injured patient told me with pride that he had not been drinking for the last four months. Yet his breath clearly reeked. When I gently confronted him on this point, he looked at me quizzically and proceeded to school me that having a few beers wasn't really "drinking"; the latter designation was reserved for hard liquor. Subsequent inquiry revealed that, in the culture this patient came from, smoking pot wasn't considered drug use, either, since "everybody does it, like smoking cigarettes or [no irony intended] drinking beer." In such cases, the clinician must decide on the relative costs and benefits of trying to compel such a patient to buck his culture, as against accepting at least a lower level or less dysfunctional pattern of drug and alcohol use than before, and working therapeutically within those limits.

Altering Beliefs and Fostering Motivation

According to Langley et al. (1990), only when the education phase is completed is the brain-injured patient encouraged to make a commitment to modify his alcohol use pattern. For many, such a commitment will be rejected out of hand. Research and clinical observation generally show that using scare tactics or strongarm methods on patients in educational groups is not effective in changing alcohol use behaviors. Rather, interventions applied in a nonthreatening, nondemanding, informational format are more likely to help thaw resistance to alcohol-related behavior change. If a low-risk patient—i.e., one who does not have a history of serious alcohol abuse—rejects the notion of total alcohol abstinence, Langley and colleagues suggest avoiding a tug-of-war over the issue. Rather, they recommend that the clinician provisionally respect the patient's decision in the hope that the education that has been provided will at some future time help the patient see major alcohol-related trouble coming before it's too late.

High-risk brain injury patients—i.e., those with current or preinjury histories of dysfunctional alcohol abuse—who resist modifying their alcohol consumption, are strongly encouraged through counseling and education to reconsider their decision. Some helpful counseling and educational techniques offered by Langley et al. (1990) include a review of the consequences of preinjury alcohol abuse, discussion of pros and cons of continued drinking, and exploration of the impact of alcohol use upon functional deficits. In this regard, W. Miller's (1983, 1988, 1989) similar technique of *motivational interviewing* may prove useful with some brain-injured patients.

For those patients who do decide to modify their alcohol abuse pattern, assistance will probably be needed to bolster resolve and facilitate change. One method recommended by Langley et al. (1990) is to help patients restructure their beliefs about the effects of alcohol use following brain injury. This is actually not as robotic as it sounds, but is related to the educative aspect of treatment discussed above. Quite frequently, patients mistakenly believe that alcohol can enhance functioning, improve problem-solving and socialization abilities, or release tension, rather than recognize the actual decrease in cognitive, physical, and behavioral functioning that occurs after drinking. It is important for the clinician to counter inaccurate and often harmful expectations in a systematic and concrete way, by providing contrasting information and teaching new coping skills. Instructions, modeling, role-playing, feedback, and homework tasks can all be used to teach patients new behavioral skills when confronted with typical alcohol consumption scenarios (see also Monti et al., 1989).

According to Langley et al. (1990), the brain-injured patient can be expected to experience some degree of ambivalence about alcohol use, with potential adverse consequences being counterbalanced by perceived benefits of use. Rather than using direct confrontation to break down expectations or denial, the clinician should collaborate with the patient to weigh costs against perceived benefits of alcohol use and then make a decision about what needs to be done. In order to ensure retention in memory, the patient can be videotaped making the commitment, and the tape then used as a prompt. For some patients, however, I find that videotaping is perceived as a threat, kind of like a taped confession at a police station—not beyond the actual experience of a number of such patients. Once again, modifying the approach to the particular patient is likely to yield the best results.

Craving

Clinicians who work in substance abuse treatment settings know that for many users of alcohol or other drugs, craving during abstinence can be the chief obstacle in the path of successful recovery (Clarke & Saunders, 1988; Monti et al., 1989). Brain-injured users are no exception. One technique used successfully by Langley et al. (1990) is cue exposure and response prevention, that is, presenting alcohol but preventing its consumption, which will supposedly extinguish craving. Cue exposure and response prevention utilize a simple extinction paradigm, making it useful with brain-injured patients unable to maintain vigilance, carry out problem solving, or employ self-control interventions during unexpected craving situations.

Coping Skills, Maintenance, and Relapse Prevention

Langley et al. (1990) point out that brain-injured alcohol abusers are likely to experience a variety of high-risk situations that increase the potential for relapse upon discharge; these are situations in which the person has characteristically used drinking as a coping response. Although the circumstances themselves may not be inherently stressful, the absence of an effective coping repertoire typically leads to a decrease in self-efficacy. In general, coping skills training is most effective when behaviors are trained in relation to specific situations, as opposed to providing general information or global strategies—the same applies, as we've noted, to cognitive rehabilitation and behavioral management of conduct disorders. Strategies to help patients learn to cope with high-risk situations include modeling, role-playing, and strategy rehearsal. The idea is to play out potential risk situations for relapse and have the patient actively rehearse strategies for dealing with them, using as many variations on the real-life themes as possible (Monti et al., 1989).

Family Systems and Social Support

Langley et al. (1990) point out that with abstinence, family disturbances, conflicts, or difficulties previously concealed by the alcoholism may now be exposed. In such cases, the family has to learn a range of interactional and conflict management skills before it can reconstitute itself as a newly functioning family system. Family members require much of the same education that the brain-injured survivor receives, particularly with regard to the increased risks for alcohol use. Often, families need to be helped in identifying potential high-risk situations and be trained to use relapse prevention techniques to prepare patients for coping with these situations following discharge (see also Potter-Efron & Potter-Efron, 1991).

According to Langley et al. (1990), specific training for family members should also include how to deal with potential setbacks, e.g., compromised behavior or other decreased functioning, following relapse. Families should be familiarized with the warning signs of chemical dependency and know where to go for help in their community. In some traditional approaches to substance abuse problems, family members are encouraged not to interfere, but to allow the abuser to stumble over the consequences of his behavior. I have already criticized this approach with regard to behavior disorders in the brain-injured (see Chapter 5). Similarly, Langley and colleagues recommend that family members not ignore dysfunctional drinking, but rather increase their involvement in intervention if substance abuse is posing a health or safety risk to the brain-injured family member. It is also helpful to discuss the specifics of alcohol-serving practices within the family; holidays and family celebrations may be particularly difficult.

Twelve-Step Programs and Support Groups

Langley et al. (1990) question the appropriateness of the standard Alcoholics Anonymous (AA) format for most brain-injured patients. In cases where AA participation is recommended, some modifications and additional supports are usually required in order to make it effective. It is recommended that attending the meetings of a single group, rather than multiple groups, might reduce confusion associated with different formats and agendas. Training a sponsor or other AA members to work with brain-injured patients could also help maximize the value of AA. Interestingly, in working with sponsors of brain-injured, recovering drug and alcohol abusers in AA and NA (Narcotics Anonymous), I've noted that the sponsors and other group members often don't seem all that surprised by the symptoms and behavior of these patients, as many such manifestations of "brain damage" are apparently quite familiar in newly clean-and-sober recoverers.

I also thoroughly concur with Langley et al. (1990) that, even though the brain-injured patient himself may require options other than AA, family members may still benefit from involvement in groups such as Alanon, Alateen, and brain injury support groups. A practice that these authors have found to demonstrate some success and that warrants further exploration is that of incorporating substance abuse issues in an ongoing brain injury support group setting. Families can also be referred to a number of other organizations such as Mothers Against Drunk Driving (MADD) and Remove Intoxicated Drivers (RID). Patients and their families can also play a key role in coalitions advocating alcohol policy change and should be provided with information about local and national organizations through which their experiences and concerns may find a voice in the policy-making process. My own experience here leads me to caution that making substance recovery issues a formal part of brain injury support groups may alienate certain other members, as drug and alcohol abuse are still associated with a certain degree of stigma in our society. However, specialized subgroups are a workable alternative.

Professional Advocacy

According to Langley et al. (1990), prevention advocacy often places the health professional in strange territory. Medical, nursing, and other professional school curricula seldom include courses on citizen advocacy, press relations, or coalition building. But having availed oneself of training in these skills—combined with the credibility that comes with a degree in the health professions and experience on the front lines of head trauma care and rehabilitation — health professionals may play a key role in changing the alcohol and drug environment.

Neuropsychological and Personality Predictors of Alcoholism Treatment Outcome

It seems almost axiomatic that brain injury will have an effect on the success of substance abuse recovery efforts. Although I'm aware of no systematic studies that specifically address the impact of traumatic brain injury and its associated psychosocial variables on substance abuse treatment outcome, some insight on this matter has already been provided by alcohol researchers themselves. In these cases, the cognitive and psychosocial deficits in question are presumed to either result from the deleterious effects of long-term alcohol use on the brain, or to be associated with developmental cognitive disorders that may predispose to alcohol and other drug abuse (Abbot & Gregson, 1981; Chastian et al., 1986; Donovan et al., 1984; Gregson & Taylor, 1977; Kupke & O'Brien, 1985; Leber et al., 1985; Macciocchi et al., 1989; Parsons, 1987b — see Miller, 1991e for a review).

The worst treatment outcome, increased likelihood of relapse, lower educational and employment status, and poorer quality of life in general are associated with lower intelligence and lower levels of cognitive efficiency, particularly in the functions of abstraction, problem-solving, perceptuomotor integration, complex memory, behavioral self-monitoring and self-regulation, language skills, and verbal reasoning. In the case of alcoholics without acquired brain injury, this probably represents premorbid, constitutional features of cognitive style that predispose to a lifestyle of dysfunctional substance abuse. However, as discussed in Chapter 5, these same features also predispose to traumatic brain injury.

Thus, individuals with deficient ability to perceive problems and conceive solutions to them, who lack the capacity to verbally self-monitor, reflect on, and self-regulate their impulses and behaviors, who have difficulty maintaining a goal-oriented mind-set due to impaired ability to anticipate future consequences, who are likely to perceive important events in their lives as beyond their control, and who as a result have a fragmented self-identity, impaired ego-autonomy, and a nonreflective, impulsive cognitive style may be especially likely to employ psychoactive substances to help modulate their thought processes and feeling states.

In particular, skills involving planning and language appear to play a key role in the cognitive profile of good-outcome alcoholics, perhaps related to their ability to use self-articulatory inner speech as a tool of reflective self-evaluation and self-control (Joseph, 1982; Miller, 1988c, 1990a, 1991c; Vygotsky, 1962). Indeed, what many neuropsychological tests may be measuring is a kind of generalized "cognitive competency" factor that seems to be predictive of outcome for a wide variety of syndromes and problems (Miller, 1990f, 1992a).

For example, a study by Harder et al. (1990) compared the prognostic potential of ten demographic and clinical factors previously associated with psychiatric outcome in a mixed group of psychiatric patients at a community mental health facility. Intellectual level, social class, and the capacity for close interpersonal relationships were the only predictors to show significant correlations with outcome measures of symptom severity and overall adjustment at follow-up, beating out such measures as sex, age, diagnostic severity, race, and stressful life events. It is intriguing that alcohol treatment outcome studies show that cognitive competence, as inferred from high neuropsychological performance, tends to be associated with successful self-recovery, while intense group affiliation seems to provide the external support necessary to maintain abstinence for those whose internal coping resources are less well developed (Miller, 1991e). Perhaps we're already seeing two clusters of substance abuse populations that may require markedly different forms of intervention.

These neuropsychological indices of recovery are also related to premorbid personality factors which, as we've discussed, are in turn related to outcome of brain injury (Chapter 5). Many studies indicate that psychological characteristics associated with poor alcohol and drug abuse treatment outcome include antisocial or borderline personality, depression, and concomitant substance abuse, i.e., polysubstance abuse (Berglund, 1988; Berglund & Leijonquist, 1978; Burling et al., 1989; Cloninger et al., 1978; Craig et al., 1990; Edwards, 1986; Edwards et al., 1981; Grande et al., 1984; Hesselbrock et al., 1985; Hodgeson et al., 1978; Kosten et al., 1989; McClellan, 1986; Powell et al., 1982; Robins et al., 1984; Rounsaville & Kleber, 1986; Rounsaville et al., 1987; Schuckit, 1972, 1985, 1986; Schuckit & Morrissey, 1976; Schuckit et al., 1969; Weisman et al., 1980; Winokur et al., 1971 — see Miller, 1990a, 1991e for more comprehensive reviews). In addition, almost any kind of psychiatric disturbance, if severe enough, bodes ill for substance abuse recovery. Conversely, subjects with higher levels of self-efficacy (Bandura, 1982) or ego autonomy (Miller, 1988c) do well in treatment and maintain abstinence goals in the period following treatment. In fact, given an adequate kernel of self-efficacy to start with, substantial increases in this trait may be observed as the result of proper therapy (Miller, in press d).

Substance Abuse Treatment Programs Relevant to
Brain-Injured Patients

One treatment approach that seems to be effective with many brain-injured patients is the cognitive-behavioral relapse prevention (CRP) program, originally developed by Marlatt and Gordon (1980, 1985) and adapted and elaborated by George (1989). CRP derives from social-cognitive theory (Bandura, 1986), which, in turn, combines ideas from cognitive psychology, social psychology, and behavior modification. With regard to substance abuse, the key theoretical assumptions of CRP are the following: Addictions are jointly caused by past learning, situational antecedents, reinforcement contingencies (rewards and punishments), cognitive expectations (beliefs), and biological influences. The behavior exists on a continuum between nonproblematic expression (e.g., social drinking) and addictive or otherwise dysfunctional expression (e.g., frank alcoholism). Therefore, the same principles can be used to explain acquisition and maintenance of both nonaddictive and addictive behavior. Addiction, in this view, is a maladaptive coping response to life stressors and problems. Presumably, more adaptive coping responses are not utilized and the addictive behavior has evolved as a habitual replacement response for this deficiency (see also Miller, 1990a).

An underlying and pervasive feature of all CRP treatment is *self-efficacy enhancement*—which is also an important ingredient in working with brain-injured patients whose self-conceptions have been shattered by their disabilities. To promote the individual's self-efficacy, employment of the various training techniques of CRP are accompanied by instructions to imagine that the rehearsed experience is associated with mounting feelings of competence and confidence. As a result, the patient experiences heightened expectations of successful coping in future, real-life situations, thereby reducing the probability of relapse.

Another alcohol relapse prevention program that is based explicitly on self-efficacy theory is that of Annis and Davis (1989). Their model proposes that when a patient enters a high-risk situation for drinking, a process of cognitive appraisal of past experiences is set in motion that culminates in a judgment, or "efficacy expectation," on the patient's part of his ability to cope with the situation. This judgment of personal efficacy determines whether or not drinking will take place.

The program makes a point of recognizing that it may be more effective with certain types of patients than with others. Accordingly, a crucial part of the evaluation process consists of careful screening for patient suitability. The model of behavior change that underlies the program assumes the existence of adequate motivation, that the patients see some benefit in working with the therapist toward greater control of their drinking behavior. It is therefore unlikely that such an approach would be effective with, say, a homeless alcoholic who has few incentives to stop drinking, or an impulsive, antisocial, alcoholic offender who is remanded to treatment as an evasion of the criminal justice system. Thus, to the extent that sufficient internalized incentives exist for changing drinking behavior—in other words, that the patient believes he has something important to gain or to lose by his future behavior—this kind of relapse prevention program can serve as a means of narrowing the gap between contemplation and action, of demonstrating to the patient that change can be gradual and relatively nonthreatening, and thereby of motivating the patient to attempt to control his drinking.

This program also takes into account the belief system of the patient. Some patients feel strongly that their drinking problems are a reflection of deep-rooted psychological conflicts, and may insist on a psychodynamic approach to therapy, in which case relapse prevention procedures would be of little utility. Not that psychodynamic influences aren't important; rather, the drawbacks inhere in the potential temptation of patients to dwell on the past as a way of avoiding having to deal with the present. More commonly, patients will come to treatment expecting the therapist or the treatment program to take full control and solve their drinking problems for them—this, in fact, is the more likely attitude of many brain-injured patients. These individuals must learn that it is necessary for them to take an active role in designing and carrying out behavioral assignments in their everyday settings so that they, in effect, become their own therapists or maintenance agents, a concept not dissimilar to cognitive rehab and adaptive living skills training with brain-injured patients.

Relapse prevention training may be directed toward either an abstinence or a moderation goal, a clinical and philosophical flexibility that might alienate patients and therapists wedded to a disease model and/or to the AA orthodoxy of total abstinence. In fact, the evidence suggests that patient adherence to the rigid AA credo of "one drink, one drunk" is associated with higher, not lower, probability of posttreatment relapse (Heather et al., 1983)—why stop at one or two drinks when you've already "blown it"?

However, such twelve-step affiliations certainly don't preclude benefitting from relapse prevention training, as long as participants accept the basic premise of learning to prevent relapse by dealing more effectively with high-risk drinking situations. Finally, research on the relapse prevention model suggests that patients who have clearly defined areas of drinking risk tend to benefit more from brief relapse prevention training than patients whose drinking is more generalized across situations.

Another important component of the relapse prevention program is identifying the strengths, resources, supports, and coping skills already available to the patient, which then form the groundwork for the development of successful homework assignments. Again, such assessment-derived treatment planning is also the accepted methodology in brain injury rehabilitation. Coping responses that the patient may have been using successfully in other areas may be quite effective, with only minor alterations, in addressing problematic drinking situations. Significant others, such as a spouse or employer, may be willing to provide support, encouragement, and even active involvement in helping the patient deal with high-risk situations.

One important patient resource identified by Annis and Davis (1989) as being important to the success of relapse prevention is called *cognitive coping*. This describes the ability to reason things out, to see connections between actions and consequences, and to plan alternative ways of dealing with situations. The patient should be able to appreciate the positive benefits of not drinking and believe that he would personally benefit from abstinence or control. When confronted with urges or temptations to drink, the patient should be able to distract himself by thinking of other things, or by imagining a positive outcome — the kinds of strategies employed by those individuals who self-recover from alcoholism without therapy or support groups (Ludwig, 1985; Tuchfield, 1981 — see Miller, 1991e for a review). It is here that all the cautions and recommendations about generalization of treatment gains from cognitive rehab and adaptive living skills training dovetail with those related to control of drinking and other substance abuse.

With regard to effectiveness of relapse prevention training, a study by Annis et al. (1987) randomly assigned a group of alcoholics who had recently completed a three-week inpatient program to receive either relapse prevention training or more traditional counseling on an outpatient basis. Each patient was classified as having either a "generalized profile" (similar drinking across all types of high-risk situations) or a "differentiated profile" (greater drinking risk in some types of situations than in others). Results at six-month follow-up showed no differences for subjects with generalized profiles across the two treatment conditions in the daily amount of alcohol consumed. However, subjects with differentiated profiles showed a substantially lower alcohol intake with relapse prevention training than with traditional counseling.

In sum, we must acknowledge that, as substance abusers — brain-injured or not — differ, so must our handling of them (Miller, 1990a, 1991e). Those with sufficiently developed ego autonomy, and with cognitive styles conducive to reflection, future-orientation, frustration-tolerance, communication skills, internal locus of control, and goal-maintenance might benefit optimally from flexibly structured, self-directed forms of day-treatment type programs. Conversely, the impulsive, cognitively deficient, internal resource-poor alcoholic or drug abuser would be more suited to a tightly structured, externally supportive inpatient program. Our brain-injured patients are most likely to be representative of the latter group, but again, flexibility and adaptability of the treatment program to the individual needs of the patient and his circumstances are the keys to optimum effectiveness.

CHAPTER 7

Too Sick to Be Well: Chronic Pain and Somatization

CHRONIC PAIN IS A PROBLEM that affects tens of millions of Americans, disrupts job, family, and social functioning, and is responsible for four billion lost work days every year (Osterweis et al., 1987). Although it is not known exactly how many brain injury patients suffer additionally from chronic pain, the experience of clinicians in treatment settings suggests that these conditions quite frequently overlap—not surprising, considering that the main causes of both pain and postconcussion syndromes are typically automobile or industrial accidents.

This chapter will describe the nature of the chronic pain syndrome, outline the main kinds of psychological treatment modalities currently employed, and suggest ways of accommodating this type of treatment within a psychotherapeutic and rehabilitative model for brain injury patients (for more comprehensive reviews of the psychological evaluation and treatment of chronic pain in general, see Benjamin, 1989; Hanson & Gerber, 1990; Keefe & Williams, 1989; Miller, in press a, in press b, in press c; Philips, 1988). Although there are many kinds of regional pain syndromes that may occur after traumatic brain injury—headache and back pain are two prominent examples—the fundamental psychological issues surrounding persistent chronic pain are often equivalent across subjects and syndromes. Indeed, many of the problems complicating recovery and long-term psychosocial adjustment that are experienced by both chronic pain and brain-injured patients are strikingly similar.

THE CHRONIC PAIN SYNDROME

While traditional concepts of chronic pain have often been framed in terms of "organic vs. psychogenic," in the last two decades chronic pain has come to be viewed as a complex, multidimensional phenomenon involving not only sensory elements, but motivational, cognitive, and emotional components as well (Keefe & Williams, 1989).

Demographics

There appears to be a rather high prevalence of pain in the general population, especially headache, back pain, and dental pain (Hanson & Gerber, 1990). Younger people are more likely than older to experience almost every kind of pain, except joint pain (Taylor & Curran, 1985). Individuals suffering from daily stress are more likely to report a variety of types of pain and to suffer from more frequent pain episodes. Those with a more external locus of control—i.e., who characteristically see events as being determined by outside forces—report a higher incidence and severity of pain than those with a more internal locus of control, that is, those who view their experiences and actions as largely self-determined (Sternbach, 1986). Individuals who report lower levels of general psychological well-being have significantly higher scores on indices of back pain (Mechanic & Angel, 1987).

Physical and Psychological Causes

T. W. Miller and Kraus (1990) have provided a description of the typical evolution of the chronic pain syndrome that largely corresponds to what I've commonly observed in the histories of chronic pain patients, with or without brain injury. In fact, rehab clinicians will probably recognize many of the features of this pattern from their work with brain injury patients reporting persistent and refractory symptoms such as headaches, dizziness, fatigue, and cognitive deficits.

The problem typically begins with some accident or injury that produces acute pain requiring medical treatment. In a certain proportion of these patients, the pain and disability never seem to get better and, in fact, are reported by the patient to worsen with time. Various medical strategies are tried by the inpatient treatment team or by outpatient clinicians, but nothing seems to help. Excessive physical disability related to sleep and appetite disturbance complicate the picture and, in turn, are often exacerbated by the side effects of numerous medications.

The patient's ongoing struggle with continual pain frequently results in depression, obsessive somatic preoccupation, hypochondriacal concerns, death anxiety, and a tendency to formulate most life events and problems in the context of greater or lesser degrees of pain. This leads to a vicious cycle of helplessness, hopelessness, and despair. Each new treatment or physician briefly ignites hope, followed by disappointment when the procedure fails to cure the pain. Resentment and bitterness grow toward the medical profession and this antipathy is often reflected back, as doctors come to loathe and dread visits from the "crock." In fact, many of my own referrals for pain management are from physicians who can no longer handle these difficult patients.

Pain now becomes a central focus of the patient's life. External attachments and interests are abandoned, resulting in the patient's withdrawal from family and social activities. Interactions are fraught with tension and anger. Problems with medication and other drug and alcohol abuse may compound the problem by producing toxicity and addiction. Pain becomes a major coping mechanism, progressively allowing the patient to avoid any kind of stressful task or issue. This leads to even greater incapacitation, which aggravates the problem, alienates friends and family, and leads to the further decline toward total invalidism.

THE CHRONIC PAIN PATIENT: PERSONALITY, PSYCHOPATHOLOGY, AND COGNITIVE STYLE

The same kinds of nosological and phenomenological problems surround the identification of a "pain-prone personality" as with the "alcoholic personality," "postconcussion personality," or any other broad classification. However, certain clinical features of patients most likely to exhibit chronic pain problems can be identified.

General Features

Chronic pain patients cannot easily be dichotomized into those with either physical or psychological disorders: many patients have both, and a few appear to have neither (Benjamin, 1989). Pain is the commonest symptom in most medical settings (Merskey, 1980) and the second most common complaint of psychiatric patients. It is present in up to 40% of new psychiatric admissions (Delapaine et al., 1978), and less than half of these patients have an identifiable physical cause for their pain. In patients referred to pain clinics, about 60% have a diagnosable physical disorder, and at least half have some kind of mental disorder—a considerable overlap between these groups (Benjamin et al., 1988).

Using the MMPI, some researchers have found that chronic pain patients' profiles reflect a tendency toward marked somatic concern, the use of denial and repression as major psychological defenses, and the interpretation of problems of living in ostensibly rational and socially acceptable terms. This is associated with poor prognosis for remotivation and a contrasting appearance of being externally extroverted and sociable, while internally self-centered, demanding, and dependent (Naliboff et al., 1983). Although a somewhat greater number of histrionic and dependent personality disorder diagnoses may be found, the presence of virtually any type of personality disorder may be the salient characteristic of the chronic pain syndrome, rather than an exclusive association with a specific diagnosis (Reich et al., 1983)—a finding also true of "difficult" patients within traumatic brain injury and substance abuse populations (Miller, 1989b, 1990a, 1990d, 1991e, 1992a).

Pain and Depression

The most common diagnostic association of chronic pain is with depression (Benjamin et al., 1988; Fishbain et al., 1986; Kramlinger et al., 1983; Krishman et al., 1985). Depending on the subject series, between 10 and 100% of chronic pain patients report depression (Blumer & Heilbronn, 1981; Pilowsky et al., 1977). Rather than being of the strictly "endogenous" type, pain-related depression seems for the most part to improve with adequate rehabilitation, although antidepressant medication is also sometimes effective (Ward et al., 1979).

I have found it particularly important to distinguish between depression, in the clinical, syndromic sense, and the *demoralization* that frequently accompanies chronic pain. This need not be associated with personality disorder or significant psychopathology, but more commonly relates to living with a distressing and debilitating condition. It may often quickly respond to supportive psychotherapy. In cases of true endogenous depression, antidepressant medication often proves useful in taking enough of the edge off of the mood disorder so that behavioral medicine and psychotherapeutic approaches can be effectively applied. Also, many of the personality-disordered patients with chronic pain syndromes may have been coping with bouts of depression long before the pain syndrome began. In such cases, the depression is just another stable part of the preexisting clinical picture and should be treated accordingly.

Pain and Somatization

The second major diagnostic association of chronic pain is with somatization, or "somatoform disorder" in *DSM-III* (Miller, 1984a); this diagnosis is applied to between 10 and 15% of pain patients (Benjamin et al., 1988; Reich et al., 1983). These patients typically present with severe pain at single or multiple sites. Because these patients are presumably using physical complaints as a defense against psychological conflicts, they reportedly are quite reluctant to pursue a psychological course of evaluation and treatment.

Benjamin (1989) has adopted Sternbach's (1974) concept of "pain transactions" to explain some of the features of this syndrome. According to this conceptualization, some patients complain of pain in order to establish and maintain their invalid status with its ensuing benefits, or "secondary gain." They consult repeatedly with physicians, not to seek effective treatment, but to reaffirm medical endorsement of their invalidism. Their transactions involve a covert communication that usually invites the doctor to accept responsibility for treating and curing them—typically a preordained impossible task—while they, though appearing to be highly compliant, have in fact taken control of the treatment process. The doctor who fails to recognize this is likely to accept the responsibility and to end up trying many different treatments with only temporary benefit, thereby fulfilling the patient's needs.

Pain as a true *conversion* phenomenon—i.e., the psychodynamically symbolic transformation of an unconscious fear, wish, or conflict into a physical symptom—is thought to be rare in the present era (Coen & Sarno, 1989). However, I have seen a number of cases of accident-related conversion symptomatology accompanying chronic pain syndromes that could have sprung from the pages of Freud or Charcot. One involved a classic glove-and-stocking anesthesia in a female bookkeeper and computer operator with posttraumatic temporomandibular joint pain who had a history of sexual abuse and severe separation/individuation issues related to feeling trapped in her family business.

Another consisted of conversion paralysis of a single leg in a male truck driver with back pain who was experiencing conflicts about going back to work, anger at his job, and unrecognized dependency needs. Apparently, such syndromes are not necessarily time-limited phenomena, since about three years later I ran into this patient in a shopping mall. He had managed to graduate from a wheelchair to an elaborate brace-and-bandage arrangement that I had never seen before in any rehab setting. This contraption allowed him to at least limp along. He was still on disability, and still, he informed me, no doctor had come up with a definitive diagnosis to explain the impairment.

A third case involved a skilled male mechanic who, unable to find work in his specialized field, was compelled to take a lower-status and lower-paying construction job. Shortly after taking this job, he fell off a ladder, sustaining a back injury with pain, which was accompanied by conversion numbness and weakness of the right leg, as well as medically diagnosed hysterical pseudoseizures. In treatment, the connection between his disability, uncomfortable family separation issues, and legal maneuvering became apparent.

In other cases, an otherwise mild pain syndrome may summate with an otherwise mild postconcussion syndrome to produce overall severe psychosocial disability, as in the case of premorbidly hard-driving, successful individuals—typically upscale, "Type A" men—who sustain a number of cumulative nicks and dents in their competitive edge as a result of their injury. While a certain reduction in overall functional capacity may still permit a reasonably good adjustment potential for many people, a decline of even a few such cognitive and psychosocial "points" can be catastrophic for those whose preinjury go-getting lifestyles have involved always "giving 110 percent." In such cases, the combination of even a little cognitive slowness or confusion and a little pain and reduced activity can result in a devastating emotional and psychosocial crash.

One such case involved just such a supersuccessful, self-made, rags-to-riches entrepreneur who, in addition to amassing a business empire, was equally proud of his "man's man," Hemingwayesque lifestyle, in which he had traversed the jungles and civilizations of the world, escaped harrowing danger on numerous occasions, battled mercenary militias and tropical fevers—and who, ironically, met his undoing sitting quietly in his car with his wife at a stoplight and getting rear-ended by another vehicle. He suffered a whiplash injury, which produced upper back and neck pain, as well as what was neuropsychologically assessed to be "mild" cognitive impairment. However, the overall effect on his life was catastrophic. Heavily invested in his image of himself as a "110 percenter," his new reduced level of functioning knocked the psychological stuffing out of him, producing a deep depression and an accompanying refractory chronic pain syndrome.

I don't want to give the impression that every patient complaint that fails to achieve full-fledged medically sanctioned legitimacy should be automatically regarded as hysterical, psychosomatic, or the like. Far from it. Doctors make mistakes, miss organic diagnoses, and tend to dismiss what they can't understand. Every symptom should be adequately followed up, and even those for which no standard organic cause can be found should be treated on a psychological basis with the same provisionality that occurs in standard medical practice when response to treatment is used to evaluate the accuracy of a diagnosis. The history of medicine—neurology in particular—is full of "hysterical" syndromes that later turned out to have a pathophysiological basis (see Miller, 1991f). Thus, even when treating a conversion symptom or chronic pain syndrome psychologically, I urge clinicians to be sensitive to any signs or clues that might indicate the need for further followup. One must always tread that thin line between dismissing a patient's vague complaints without adequate evaluation vs. testing and testing and testing the patient unrelentingly in search of an elusive "cause." In each individual case, this is where the clinician's knowledge, skill, judgment, and empathy all come into play (see also Chapter 10). Finally, even "real" organic injuries and diseases are almost always affected by psychological factors (Weiner, 1992).

Role of Family and Social Systems

Like brain injury, chronic pain affects others beyond the patient and the clinician, particularly the family and other social systems (Miller & Kraus, 1990), and an energetic, productive individual may become a social and economic liability (Gallagher, 1976; Hendler, 1982). Family and work mates may have to make up for the loss of working capacity, which tends to weaken support for the pain patient and lead to anger and resentment.

Many relatives of chronic pain patients appear to derive what Benjamin (1989) refers to as *tertiary gain*, in which the patient's pain and disability help other family members deny or suppress their own conflicts. In fact, in some families the presence of an invalid serves to maintain intrafamilial homeostasis as the family becomes galvanized around the patient's pathology (Hughes et al., 1987; Roy, 1985). Interestingly, Benjamin (1989) points out, marital disharmony may actually have positive implications, since it frequently means that the spouse is refusing to endorse the patient's invalidism. By contrast, the presence of an overly solicitous spouse has been found to be the single most important predictor of a patient's failure to comply with a behavioral pain rehabilitation program (Funch & Gale, 1986). As noted in Chapters 4 and 6, similar patterns of family reaction to the patient's invalidism and maladaptive behavior are seen in the case of brain injury and substance abuse.

Litigation Issues

According to Miller and Kraus (1990), issues of litigation and compensation related to chronic pain may lead to increased suffering for the patient, which adversely affects prognosis. Pursuing claims, no matter how legitimate, may serve to rivet the patient's attention on having been wronged and thereby to seeking retribution and restoring his pride, rather than trying to adjust to a difficult situation while leading as normal a life as possible.

Contrary to the popular wisdom about the efficacy of "green treatment" in curing chronic pain, the majority of pain sufferers, according to most modern authorities, do not experience an automatic resolution of symptoms after settlement of their claims (Benjamin, 1989; Gotten, 1956; Hohl, 1974; McNab, 1964; Tunks, 1990; Woodward, 1982). Patients who are actively engaged in litigation tend to have about the same prevalence of symptoms as those who have had their cases settled, or who were never involved in lawsuits (Benjamin, 1989; Hohl, 1974; Schutt & Dohan, 1968). A number of studies have found that, after case settlement, many patients do not return to work, and many of those who do go back end up with lighter and/or lower paying jobs (Balla & Moraitis, 1970; Encel & Johnson, 1978; Mendelson, 1982; Tarsh & Royston, 1985). Here again, there is a parallel with traumatic brain injury: Despite the widespread belief in litigation-related malingering of cognitive symptoms, the evidence is mixed as to whether this occurs on a wide scale (Miller, 1990b; Oddy, 1984 – see Chapters 2 and 10).

My own experience has been that where the chronic pain syndrome derives most of its motivating force from the desire to evade work and other responsibilities, litigation issues by themselves can serve to entrench the invalidism. On the other hand, where the problem is more a part of overall poor adjustment or personality disorder, litigation issues are often less important from a monetary standpoint, but rather related to efforts at legitimizing the patient's outrage by suing and punishing the guilty party. In addition, in the litigious, game-show mentality that characterizes our society's popular notion of justice, sustaining a compensable injury is regarded by many patients – and their families and attorneys – as the equivalent of winning a lottery, with corresponding efforts to maximize the payoff (see also Chapter 10).

THE PSYCHOLOGICAL TREATMENT OF CHRONIC PAIN

Chronic pain need not be a permanently debilitating syndrome. In fact, for many patients it may be the "weak link" in the cycle of postconcussion invalidism that is most amenable to treatment. Sometimes, getting control of pain allows the patient to acknowledge the possibility of successfully coping with the postconcussion syndrome. Consequently, motivation for other aspects of treatment may be increased. This section can hardly review the entire literature on the psychological treatment of chronic pain—instead, I will focus on those applications that I've found to be most useful with brain-injured patients.

Operant and Cognitive-Behavioral Pain Management

Intervention approaches in this category generally follow one of two main courses. First, there are treatments based on the concept of operant pain behaviors (Fordyce et al., 1973, 1985). Following the operant model, behaviors related to pain may be reinforced by their desirable consequences, such as increased care, sympathy, nurturance, and avoidance of unpleasant job, family, or social responsibilities. Treatment therefore consists of changing environmental contingencies to stop the reinforcement of learned pain behaviors, while systematically rewarding well behaviors (Benjamin, 1989). As we have seen in Chapter 5, a similar approach has been applied to the treatment of behavior disorders in brain-injured patients by Wood (1987).

Cognitive or cognitive-behavioral approaches generally involve training the patient to identify inappropriate negative beliefs and expectations about pain, and to use specific cognitive strategies and skills to replace these beliefs with more appropriate positive ideation and coping responses. This is often accompanied by strategies to increase pain control and self-efficacy through biofeedback, hypnosis, relaxation, stress-management, and attention diversion (Hanson & Gerber, 1990; Philips, 1988; Turk et al., 1983; Turner & Chapman, 1982). While applications of these cognitive-behavioral techniques with some brain-injured patients may be limited because of compromised cognitive functioning, adaptation in the form of increased structure and concretization puts many of these techniques within useful clinical reach of this group.

The general consensus seems to be that the majority of pain patients who are willing to comply with these kinds of treatments improve to a considerable extent and maintain improvement at follow-up (Benjamin, 1989). However, for some patients, psychodynamic and personality issues may complicate the implementation of a straightforward pain management approach, and in such cases, more intensive psychotherapeutic intervention may be needed, either as a supplement or as a primary treatment modality.

Psychotherapy of the Chronic Pain Patient

Given the wide interest in personality variables contributing to the chronic pain syndrome, there are surprisingly few published studies dealing with the psychodynamically oriented treatment of chronic pain. The general consensus from recent reviews is that, while psychotherapeutic experience may be helpful in understanding the process the "psychogenic" pain development, patients with these disorders are generally regarded as unsuitable for sustained psychotherapy, and treatment approaches are usually limited to information, explanation, and support (Benjamin, 1989; Kellner, 1986). Indeed, one gets the impression from reading the clinical accounts of their interactions with such patients, that many therapists find them irritating, frustrating, and distasteful to work with.

Nevertheless, just as some clinicians are beginning to appreciate the role of psychodynamically oriented psychotherapy in the comprehensive treatment of brain-injured patients (Cicerone, 1989; Lewis & Rosenberg, 1990; Miller, 1990d, 1991a, 1991d; Small, 1980; see Chapter 3), this approach likewise has promise for treating pain patients—with or without brain injury. Indeed, for many such patients, it may be the only effective alternative after the clinician has exhausted all the quick-fix behavioral and cognitive techniques.

Dorsel (1989) argues that the first essential step in psychotherapy for chronic pain is bringing any underlying *psychological* pain into awareness, affirming its significance, and encouraging the patient to accept issues that have been the source of some considerable stress in his life. This requires that the therapeutic environment provide a safe and acceptable outlet for the verbal, as opposed to the somatic, expression of pain.

This first step lays the groundwork for the important second step of teaching the patient new outlets for, and techniques for managing, somatic pain. The patient must learn through guided and monitored practice how to express his emotions appropriately, how to act assertively, how to relax and cope with stress, how to communicate effectively in family and other social situations, and how to develop himself academically, occupationally, and recreationally as necessary for his overall well-being. Often a group setting can facilitate this.

In fact, for some patients I have found social skills training in a group setting to be an important therapeutic adjunct to more traditional psychotherapeutic modalities. These groups teach and reinforce such skills as how to communicate with other people, how to make oneself understood through words instead of emotional outbursts, and even how to have "fun." Such approaches have been adapted for brain injury (Prigatano et al., 1986), chronic pain (Hanson & Gerber, 1990), and alcohol dependence (Monti et al., 1989). Group therapy is not necessarily appropriate for everyone, though, and clinicians should use their judgment.

In my experience, patients with uncomplicated pain syndromes often respond relatively quickly to a course of behavioral medicine (biofeedback, relaxation, hypnosis), coping skills training, and short-term psychotherapy. As with brain injury, simple explanation and reassurance by a knowledgeable therapist should not be underrated, since a surprising number of pain patients, despite having been repeatedly examined and clucked over by a battalion of specialists, have never had one of these clinicians take the time to sit down and actually explain just what the physical and psychological nature of the pain problem actually is. Again, as with many brain-injured patients, "Why didn't my surgeon/neurologist/orthopedist/internist/physical therapist/rehab counselor tell me that?" is a typical refrain of the pain patient. In fact, Prigatano et al. (1986) specifically recommend providing brain-injured patients with some form of explicit explanatory model to help them understand what has happened to them and what they can expect. No less should apply to an accompanying chronic pain problem.

Unfortunately, while some clinicians are quick to apply a diagnosis of psychogenic pain or hysteria to the patient's chart, they seem to chicken out when it comes to actually confronting the patient and his family with this diagnostic formulation. Often, a vague, evasive answer is provided: "We're still considering some possibilities"; "We haven't come up with anything definitive as yet"; "We'll watch it for a while"; and so on. Not surprisingly, this fills the patient and family with even greater anxiety as to what mysterious pathological entity is being missed or neglected. This may lead to increased symptom hypervigilance, suspicion of clinical authorities, and doctor-shopping—another vicious cycle.

For those chronic pain patients whose conditions are refractory to the more conservative approaches, Coen and Sarno (1989) recommend a different strategy. To begin with, the therapist must project a sense of resolute confidence that the pain is psychologically derived and is self-limited—although I have found this easier to accomplish with "pure" pain syndromes than where the pain complicates a coexisting brain injury. In the latter case, verbal interventions will have to be tailored to the individual patient's level of comprehension and, in addition, the strict differentiation between organic and psychogenic symptoms is more difficult to make.

Operating from a psychodynamic perspective, Coen and Sarno (1989) recommend that the patient be clearly confronted with his intolerance and fear of his own wishes and feelings. The more severe the case, the more imperative it is that the patient's hypervigilance and character rigidity be interpreted immediately. He should be shown his extraordinary watchfulness over his bodily functioning, behavior, feelings, and wishes. He should be made aware of how strongly he believes that anything negative in him makes him unacceptable. He should be informed that his pain will not disappear until he is able to stop scrutinizing his physical symptoms and stop believing that he can be worthwhile only if he is all good.

The therapist should encourage the patient to question the rigidity of his internal standards and relax his adherence to those standards. Empathic explanation and beginning psychotherapeutic work on why the patient has had to be so afraid of not being good enough to be wanted will help to lessen his intense self-scrutiny, hypervigilance, guardedness, and panic. That, say Coen and Sarno (1989), is usually sufficient for the pain to resolve. In effect, the capacity to tolerate one's own affective life seems to preclude the development and maintenance of a psychosocially dysfunctional chronic pain syndrome.

If any kind of general statement in this regard can be made, I would say that dealing with anger, dependency/control issues, and inability to directly and verbally express emotion are elements of virtually all extended courses of psychotherapy for chronic pain. Hard-driving achievement-oriented types may be reduced to clinging, whining, shadows of their former selves if the compulsive striving has been used characterologically as a defense against feelings of inner vulnerability and worthlessness. Other patients may view the caretaker's response to their pain as a "test" of the latter's loyalty and devotion, or use the pain as a weapon to punish the caretaker for having failed to meet their needs in the past. Still others may be trying to prove how wronged and wounded they've been by the injury.

One kind of patient resistance strategy I've noted is playing the brain injury and the pain off of one another. As discussed in Chapter 3, Cicerone (1989) notes that brain-injured patients may freely acknowledge their physical symptoms, but deny any cognitive, behavioral, or emotional dysfunction. This may be because physical problems are perceived as more removed from the person's core sense of self, and thus less psychologically threatening. I have seen a number of cases where a brain-injured patient attributed all of his problems in adjustment to intractable pain: "If only my pain were cured, I could function all right."

Cicerone (1989) recommends treating the brain-injured patient similarly to the characterologically "fragile" patient described by Pine (1985). Many chronic pain patients also fit this description: weak ego integration, unstable relationships, and poor emotional modulation—similar to the *primitive personality* described by Robbins (1989) (see Chapter 12). This, of course, underscores one of the most important principles of psychotherapy for different "syndromes." In all such cases, what we are treating is the whole person who is reacting to particularly distressful life circumstance in his or her most characterologically adaptive way (Miller, 1992a, 1992b, in press e).

Pain Clinics and Pain "Packages"

Most coordinated programs for chronic pain involve a treatment "package," the underlying philosophy of which is based on the concept of rehabilitation to overcome disability and restore function, despite the acceptable continuation of at least some pain. The quest for a specific physical cause leading to a specific "cure," which can be administered to the passively recipient patient is discouraged, and the patient is urged to take increasing responsibility for his or her progress—this kind of model will be familiar to physical therapists. Most pain treatment packages rely on some combination of operant and cognitive-behavioral approaches (Benjamin, 1989; Hanson & Gerber, 1990; Philips, 1988).

Components of many pain treatment packages include the following (Benjamin, 1989; Hanson & Gerber, 1990; Philips, 1988; Turk et al., 1983):

1. The identification of specific behavioral goals, such as return to previous or new domestic, employment, or recreational activities.
2. Some sort of signed contract specifying treatment offered and accepted, and mutual commitments.
3. Operant-based activity programs to increase appropriate behaviors and reduce inappropriate "pain behaviors," such as verbal complaints, inactivity, and inappropriate use of physical treatments.
4. Exercise and increased activity levels.
5. Liaison with other involved agencies—medical, vocational, social service—to establish a consistent approach.
6. Marital and/or family therapy to ensure consistency in reinforcement schedules and to resolve associated problems in relationships.
7. Cognitive-behavioral strategies to identify and replace inappropriate thoughts about pain.
8. Relaxation training, sometimes with biofeedback and/or hypnosis, to provide a sense of self-control and mastery over pain.
9. Problem-solving, communication skills, assertiveness training, and social skills training.
10. Medication monitoring, with the goal typically being the reduc-

tion and eventual elimination of unnecessary pain medication, especially narcotics.

11. Individual psychotherapy where indicated.

With regard to outcome, the overriding impression seems to be that these "packages" lead to worthwhile improvements for the majority of patients who comply with them (Benjamin, 1989; Miller, in press b, in press c).

Less clear is the relative effectiveness of inpatient pain clinics vs. outpatient treatment. Many British pain specialists, who typically see patients in low-cost outpatient clinics within a socialized health care system, are openly critical of their American counterparts who seem to prefer pricey, for-profit, private hospital settings — a similar situation exists in the head injury and substance abuse rehab fields (see Chapters 2 and 6). There does not seem to be any evidence that, overall, one form of pain treatment facility is superior to the other or, indeed, that either does a better job than office-based treatment by a skilled therapist or private practice group. In addition to economic incentives, patient selection factors may play a role in who goes where for pain treatment (Tunks, 1990). Patients referred to specialty clinics tend to have a greater prevalence of psychosocial adjustment problems than those who remain in the care of community, private practice clinicians (Crook et al., 1986; Kleinknecht et al., 1987). As with brain injury, the most "difficult" pain patients who cannot be handled at home or in the community are the ones who get dumped at the door of the local institutional treatment facility — assuming they can afford it.

POSTTRAUMATIC HEADACHE

Headache is such a ubiquitous complaint after brain injury that it warrants separate coverage. Much of this section focuses on Bennett's (1988) work with posttraumatic headache, with my own comments added where applicable.

Assessment of Posttraumatic Headache

Most clinicians have observed that chronic, recurrent headache commonly follows traumatic head injury. Interestingly, it is seen more often in individuals who have experienced minor head trauma than in those more seriously injured, and I suspect that this is due to a masking effect of more severe symptoms in major head injury, especially in the early stages. Many posttraumatic patients who initially present only with headaches are found, under careful neuropsychological evaluation, to be concurrently suffering from verbal and communicative disorders, deficits in information processing and reaction time, memory difficulties, problems with perception, impaired concept formation, and impaired reasoning ability (Alves et al., 1986).

Bennett (1988) has grouped posttraumatic headache into five main classifications:

1. Steady Pressure with Caplike Distribution   This is the most common and persistent variety of headache after traumatic head injury. It often occurs along with other headache types and is most commonly referred to circumscribed areas not involving the actual site of the injury. The pain is typically described as a deep tenderness in the neck or shoulder region and can be induced by pressure to the sensitive areas. Intensity varies from mild to severe and the pain can recur for many years postinjury. It is usually made worse by effort, stress, coughing, stooping, or turning of the head. During severe episodes the patient may experience sensations of spinning, dizziness, or sensitivity to light. The syndrome may lead to overall functional incapacitation.

These headaches are associated with persistent and sustained muscle contraction in the head, neck, upper back, and shoulders. The usual treatment is with muscle relaxants, analgesics, tricyclic antidepressants, heat, and massage; however, the syndrome is often resistent to treatment. I have found specific EMG biofeedback of involved sites to be effective for some patients. A few patients have responded well to a combination of relaxation training and hypnosis.

2. Circumscribed Superficial Tenderness Around the Impact Site   This consists of circumscribed, relatively superficial tenderness of the scalp at the injury site and is often, but not always, associated with a visible or palpable scar. The pain usually consists of spontaneous aching at the impact site and may be precipitated by even light pressure, such as that from a hairbrush or hatband. It is usually described as moderate in intensity, typically resolves within a year, and appears to be related to injury of the scalp vasculature.

3. Episodic, Unilateral Aching or Throbbing Pain   These are described as aching, throbbing or pounding headaches, usually unilateral, and typically occurring in attacks of relatively short duration. This type of headache may represent an intensification of, or overlap with, the type 1 headache described above. It is most commonly referred to the temporal region of the head, but also occurs in frontal, occipital, or postauricular (behind the ear) regions as well. The intensity ranges from mild to severe and is increased by effort, coughing, bending, or lying down. Although typically beginning unilaterally, the headache often becomes generalized; I have seen at least two patients who have described the onset as sudden and intense — "like a crash of thunder and lightning," as one put it. The headaches often begin in the morning or are present upon awakening, may persist throughout the day, and are often accompanied by loss of appetite, nausea, and vomiting.

The pain is not relieved by heat or massage, but ice packs, cold compresses, narcotic analgesics, and sometimes ergotamine tartrate provide relief. These headaches appear to be vascular in nature, related to painful distention of cranial arteries, and are more commonly seen in patients with personal or family histories of migraine — indeed, it may represent the precipitation of a vascular headache syndrome in patients already at risk.

4. Episodic, Unilateral, Frontotemporal Pain with Ipsilateral Mydriasis and Hyperhydrosis   This headache type is associated with anterior neck injuries caused by cervical whiplash. The pain is experienced episodically, usually two to 12 per month, is unilateral and frontotemporal in distribution, and is accompanied by ipsilateral mydriasis (pupillary dilation) and facial hyperhydrosis (sweating). When the pain subsides the patient is left with ipsilateral miosis (pupillary constriction) and ptosis (eyelid drooping). The pain does not respond to ergotamine, but may respond to prophylactic treatment with propranolol. It appears to represent a localized autonomic nervous system dysfunction, probably related to Horner's syndrome.

5. Pain in the Superior Temporal Region   This is an intermittent, recurrent, relatively steady pain in the region of the temples or just above. It may be unilateral or bilateral, is typically characterized as feeling like a band extending from temple to temple, and is often accompanied by jaw popping during chewing. This syndrome may be related to temporomandibular joint (TMJ) dysfunction due to the injury. The most likely scenario is an auto accident that results in the person striking the windshield or dashboard. The impact may displace or injure a healthy temporomandibular joint, or exacerbate ongoing TMJ degeneration that was in progress premorbidly.

Causes, Mechanisms, and Vicious Cycles

As Bennett (1988) points out, posttraumatic headache vividly illustrates the interaction among the autonomic nervous system, the cerebrovascular system, elevated levels of muscle tension, and emotional factors. Muscle tension levels are commonly elevated in the head, neck, shoulders, and upper back regions after trauma, although this is typically not evaluated in diagnostic studies. In addition, high emotional arousal is frequently present in these patients and such arousal increases activity in the sympathetic nervous system. Prolonged, excessive sympathetic activity can in turn exacerbate pain levels by increasing perception of the intensity of stimuli related to pain. These physical and emotional factors can create a vicious cycle in which pain becomes a stressor, eliciting emotional (anger, frustration) and physical (increased muscle tension) factors that then produce more pain. The longer this cycle persists, the more difficult it is to break.

Treatment of Posttraumatic Headache

As with pain syndromes generally, a variety of treatment approaches may be applied to posttraumatic headache. In studying the treatment preferences of headache patients vs. doctors, Packard (1979) found that physicians ranked medication higher than did the patients. The patients gave their highest rankings to the need for information about the causes of their headaches and the need for relief from pain. This indicates to Bennett (1988) that education must be an integral part of any headache treatment plan. Indeed, explanation and education is an important part of all comprehensive pain programs (Hanson & Gerber, 1990; Philips, 1988), and patient empowerment through information has been stressed throughout the present book.

Bennett (1988) typically begins by explaining to the patient the nature of the vicious cycle of headache pain. Headache patients, like pain patients generally, often have a misconception—an almost magical expectation—that their medication is supposed to completely alleviate the pain and make them feel pretty good overall. It is thus often disappointing for them to learn that a certain amount of pain must be tolerated and dealt with actively, rather than passively eliminated.

According to Hanson and Gerber (1990), pain patients often harbor similar illusions about the magical properties of biofeedback, relaxation, and other behavioral medicine techniques, expecting these to act like quick fixes they can easily and automatically turn on and off at will—like getting a shot or popping a pill—to relieve any pain or discomfort. This, of course, may represent the relative intolerance of painful feelings, somatic or psychic, that characterizes many patients in the head injury/chronic pain/substance abuse/personality disorder cluster (Miller, 1989b, 1990a, 1990c, 1992a, 1992, in press a).

Bennett (1988) endorses Bakal's (1982) headache program for brain injury patients, which I too have found useful in many cases, inasmuch as it represents the specific application to headache of a number of general pain management techniques (see also Hanson & Gerber, 1990; Philips, 1988). While Bakal utilizes EMG biofeedback as an integral part of his program, Bennett focuses more on attention diversion and thought management techniques.

The patient being taught *attention diversion* learns that we normally only focus on one thing at a time, and we ordinarily can use our volition to attend to whatever we want. Thus, we can influence what we are attending to by shifting our attention from one aspect of our environment to another, internal or external. It is difficult, if not impossible, therefore, to stop focusing on one's pain unless one shifts attention to something else. Within this general framework, the patient is provided with a number of attention diversion strategies to learn. They are initially practiced during headache-free periods and later applied to episodes of significant headache discomfort.

Thought management involves helping the patient control negative and/ or catastrophic headache-related thoughts, feelings, and reactions. The patient is encouraged to understand that distressing cognitions not only increase the pain experienced, but they also interfere with the ability to cope effectively with the headache pain. These thought patterns can be identified and modified. The patient learns that the process of "negative talking" can be reversed, and training is given in how to accomplish this.

First, the patient is told to be alert to those times when he or she is experiencing distressing feelings and thoughts. Second, the patient learns to use these distressing thoughts as a signal to start making positive self-statements. Third, the patient learns to actively replace the distressing cognitions with positive, coping-oriented statements. In order to demonstrate this process, the patient is provided with a list of positive statements to be used during different stages of the headache episode. The patient is encouraged to develop his or her own statements as well. Again, this intervention is over-practiced during headache-free periods before being implemented during periods of active headache.

Since many patients are on high doses of multiple medications, I try, where possible, and with the cooperation of the patient's prescribing physician, to encourage the patient to titrate down the medication dosages as increasing behavioral control of headache pain is achieved. Some patients are able to accomplish at least some reduction of medication, and in a few cases, narcotic pain medication can be gradually eliminated entirely, and the patient maintained only on necessary doses of prophylactic medication like propranolol. However, some patients resolutely refuse to give up their pain medication; here behavioral pain management techniques may at least foster some sense of control or help keep the dosages from getting out of hand. Sometimes, just keeping the pills in a drawer, knowing they're there if and when he needs them, is enough to give the patient the psychic leeway to handle a pain episode using nondrug techniques. As noted above, where relatively straightforward behavioral medicine techniques fail to appreciably affect the pain syndrome, more in-depth psychotherapy may be called for.

In this respect, more generally, the most important question will turn out to be not which treatment is most effective, but which kinds of treatments work best for which kinds of pain patients with which kinds of pain disorders. For the present, I agree with Benjamin's (1989) recommendation for an eclectic and empirical approach to the psychological treatment of chronic pain: Use what is known to work, but be flexible in individual cases. As in the field of brain injury, further research should focus on determining the most effective treatments for different kinds of pain syndromes, patient characteristics, and goals, and to identify the effective components of treatment and the common elements of various effective strategies. In addition, we should study those pain sufferers and brain injury survivors who are coping well, and who therefore manage to stay *out* of the pain clinics, rehab centers, and private offices. Lessons from such success stories may yield valuable clues to improving our treatment of those patients who remain in distress.

PART IV

Special Populations

CHAPTER 8

Young Minds:
The Brain-Injured Child
and Adolescent

AS UNFORTUNATE AS BRAIN INJURY may be for an adult, we feel a special sense of tragedy when a child is injured, since the prospect of arrested potential and curtailed chances for a happy, productive life seems all the more poignant the earlier it occurs. Children are, after all, in the minds of most adults, the most "innocent" of victims. Even within the brain injury field, rather less is known about pediatric brain injury than about adult brain syndromes. This chapter will examine the main features of child and adolescent brain injury and make some recommendations for treatment and management.

DEMOGRAPHICS OF
PEDIATRIC BRAIN INJURY

Lehr (1990) notes that in infancy, excluding birth-related injuries, most traumatic brain injuries are caused by falls or child abuse. The preschool-age period is the next highest risk period, second only after adolescence. The primary causes of injuries in this age group are still related to falls, but an increasing number are now sustained in pedestrian accidents as children begin to venture away from their homes. The school-age years are one of the lowest in terms of incidence of head injury when compared to the rates in the infancy, preschool, and adolescent years, and motor vehicle accidents continue to cause most of the severe injuries in this age group, including those in which children are either passengers or pedestrians. Sports-related injuries increase during this period, with many accidents involving bicycles, skateboards, and baseball bats.

The incidence of head injury, which remains relatively stable throughout childhood, increases dramatically in adolescence. The number of severe injuries in the 15- to 19-year old range equals that of all the previous 14 years combined. Since most injuries in adolescence are related to motor vehicles, either as the driver or passenger, it is not surprising that this increase occurs when adolescents are getting their drivers' licenses and spending much of their time in cars. Many adolescents also experiment with drugs and alcohol, which, as discussed in Chapter 6, are often implicated in motor vehicle and other accidents that produce brain injury.

RISK FACTORS FOR
CHILDHOOD TRAUMATIC BRAIN INJURY

As in the case of adults, some children are more likely to sustain traumatic brain injuries than others. According to Butler and Golding (1986), boys have more accidents than girls and are more likely to have repeated accidents. Moreover, children with more than one accident are more likely to be described as disobedient, destructive, hyperactive, and prone to fighting with other children. They are more likely to have somatic complaints related to their head injuries, to suffer sleep disturbances, and to bite their nails. Their mothers are more likely to be younger, employed, heavy smokers, and to live in urban areas. Similarly, Klonoff (1971; Klonoff et al., 1984) has found an increased incidence of childhood head injuries to be associated with marital instability, lower occupational status of the father, and living in congested, lower-income residences. Factors in this study that were apparently unrelated to increased head injury incidence were hyperactivity, mental deficiency, preexisting brain damage, emotional disturbance, and developmental anomalies.

Rutter (1980; Rutter et al., 1980) has discovered intriguing differences between children who sustain mild head injuries compared to those suffering more severe injuries. Subjects with mild head injuries are more likely to be described as less intelligent, behaviorally deviant, and more likely to behave in reckless and impulsive ways that lead to accidents. At the time of the accident, the children sustaining mild head injuries are more likely to be engaging in prohibited activity and to suffer falls, reckless sports injuries, and injuries sustained in fights. The children in the more severe head-injured group are more likely to sustain these injuries in traffic accidents. As noted in Chapters 5 and 6, impulsive thrill-seeking behavior is highly associated with the likelihood of traumatic brain injury — apparently, the kinds of injuries sustained in this group tend to be milder than those that are more purely "accidental."

EFFECTS OF CHILDHOOD BRAIN INJURY

The pathophysiological aspects of pediatric brain injury have been considered in Chapter 1. This section will deal with the effects on personality and behavior.

General Effects

Citing Teuber and Rudel (1962), Lehr (1990) points out that there are three possible patterns of occurrence of functional deficits, depending on the nature of the injury and the age at which it was sustained. First, deficits may be apparent soon after injury and then later disappear. This is attributed to one part of the brain that is not yet committed to the function it usually performs being able to take over or compensate for a damaged part. The drawback of this form of recovery is that it may lead to atypical neural connections, poor survival mechanisms, and deficits in a different area as parts of the brain are subsequently not available for the function they eventually should perform. In addition, this "neural compensation" model is still controversial.

Second, there may be deficits related to general effects of injury that are apparent at all ages, such as slowing of reaction time, less efficient processing of language and other information, less adequate storage of information, and greater fatigue. According to the neural compensation hypothesis, this may be the price paid for takeover of function by a less direct, less competent neural substrate than the one genetically specified.

Third, deficits may not appear right after injury but may gradually become apparent after a delay. This can occur in a variety of ways. The damaged brain structure or system itself may not be functionally mature and not utilized at the time injury occurs. However, when it is expected to be viable, but is not able to support complex functioning, deficits are readily apparent. Other systems may also be able to mediate the functions of the damaged area at least to a degree, but when functional requirements become more complex and demanding, their limitations may become noticeable.

Cognitive Sequelae

Dalby and Obrzut's (1991) analysis of cognitive functioning in children and adolescents with closed traumatic head injury leads them to draw the following conclusions:

1. A relationship exists between Glasgow Coma Scale score, clinically observed coma, posttraumatic amnesia, and cognitive deficits.
2. The effects of brain trauma in this young group tend to be more marked with respect to visuospatial and visuomotor skills as opposed to verbal skills.
3. Cognitive sequelae may occur with localized as well as generalized brain lesions, but is more likely to occur with the most extensive local lesions.
4. Intellectual impairment is most frequent following generalized damage, but may also occur as a result of severe localized damage.
5. Long-term storage and retrieval deficits are frequent following severe brain injury in children and adolescents.
6. The child's age at the time of injury has little effect on the pattern of cognitive deficit.

Behavioral, Psychosocial, and Emotional Sequelae

Black et al. (1969) found the most common behavior disturbances exhibited by children with head injury to include overactivity and hyperkinesis, impulsive disobedience at home and school, explosive outbursts of anger and irritability, delinquency, stealing, cruelty and destructiveness, deficient anger control, sleep disturbances, and problems with appetite. However, more recently, Brown et al. (1981) found only socially inappropriate behavior significantly more common in behavior disorders attributable to head injury. The issues relating to causality of behavior disorders in childhood brain injury are probably similar to those described for adults in Chapter 5.

According to Dalby and Obrzut (1991), behaviors exhibited frequently by brain-injured children, albeit falling just short of statistical significance in controlled studies, include overeating, overtalkativeness, bedwetting, general slowness, and stuttering. Posttraumatic headache is rarely prolonged, but is more pronounced and frequent the older the child is at the time of injury. Dizziness is even rarer among childhood posttraumatic sequelae. These authors argue that, unless the brain-injured child has shown maladjustment prior to the injury, psychological disturbances such as nightmares, tension, and hysterical features rarely occur.

Perrott et al. (1991) investigated the long-term neurobehavioral recovery of a group of children who had sustained moderate to severe head injuries, compared to a sibling comparison group composed of brothers and sisters of the brain-injured children. A comprehensive battery of intellectual, academic, and neuropsychological tests revealed relatively few differences between the groups. Very little residual cognitive impairment was observed in the brain-injured group as a whole. Thus, cognitive recovery appears to have been relatively complete for most of the brain-injured children.

These optimistic findings did not, however, extend to behavioral and psychosocial domains. Parents reported significantly more behavioral problems for the brain-injured children than for sibling controls. In addition, both parents and teachers rated the brain-injured group lower in academic performance. The presence of difficulties in school performance was further confirmed by the fact that about half of the school-age brain-injured children had repeated a grade. Moreover, these school problems did not appear to be related to limited academic skills per se, because the brain-injured children performed at average levels on tests of academic achievement. Problems therefore seemed to be due more to difficulty in skill application or to behavioral aspects of school performance not assessed in formal tests of academic aptitude.

Information obtained from the parents also suggested that the brain-injured children were experiencing more difficulties in adapting to the demands of everyday living and imposing greater stress on the parent-child relationship, compared to their brothers and sisters. Brain-injured children placed greater demands on their parents and tended to be more active and distractible than their siblings. Approximately one-half of the parents interviewed indicated that they were still experiencing stressed family relationships, which they attributed directly to their child's brain injury. Two of the mothers reported that the stress they were experiencing in caring for the brain-injured child was almost intolerable, and this stress was visibly apparent on clinical interview.

Bergland and Thomas (1991) have extensively studied the reactions of adolescents to brain injury. Such adolescents tend to view themselves as different persons, to be painfully aware of their physical, cognitive, emotional, and behavioral changes, as well as their loss of abilities. This often results in sharply compromised academic and extracurricular opportunities, not to mention long-term career goals. Also notable are impaired social relationships with friends, stress and disappointment in the family, and progressively diminished social support as the novelty of their problem wears off within their social circles and/or they become increasingly difficult to deal with. Emotional life may then come to be dominated by crushed self-esteem, conflict, and guilt.

One particular problem cited by this study is that professionals in schools and private facilities were perceived as overwhelming, frustrating, insensitive, and condescending. Of particular concern was the use of jargon and terminology unfamiliar to the nonprofessional. Some professionals were perceived as lacking in the ability to offer hope, unwilling to admit a lack of knowledge, or unable to provide realistic services. Parents also perceived some people in the community as well-meaning in their intentions, but irritating with their insensitivity, including "a lot of free advice that was totally unrealistic."

"Positive" Effects of Brain Injury in Children and Adolescents

Psychosocial and emotional changes after brain injury are not always perceived as negative by family members of the young patient (Lehr, 1990). For children and adolescents who have had a history of preinjury behavioral control difficulties and who experience a constriction of affect and behavior after injury, these changes may be welcomed by their families who may hardly hope for a "recovery" of preinjury incorrigibility. Conversely, children and adolescents who were considerably shy or withdrawn before injury may enjoy the experience of disinhibition. Their families may also prefer to have their previously quiet children and adolescents act in a more outgoing way both with themselves and with other people.

I have personally observed the first reaction pattern, but can't recall ever encountering the second. My observation has been that postinjury disinhibition is usually not experienced as "enjoyable" by either patient or family. If anything, the child is frequently frightened and discouraged by his or her own loss of control. As noted in Chapter 2, a similar phenomenon of "positive" personality change after brain injury has been reported for some brain-injured adults. In such cases, I wonder how carefully the patient's own feelings and perceptions of this experience have been probed by the investigators, as opposed to relying on family's and others' reports.

Risk Factors for Psychosocial Sequelae of Pediatric Brain Injury

According to Lehr (1990), those children who have been functioning well psychosocially before the injury are less likely to develop new disorders in this area after injury than those who were experiencing premorbid psychosocial problems — again, this pattern is a familiar one in adults with brain injury (Chapter 5). However, even premorbidly well-functioning pediatric patients may still be at increased risk for developing problems after brain injury. Lehr cites a study by Rutter et al. (1983) showing that one-fourth of children with a history of normal preinjury adjustment developed a new psychiatric disorder by one year after head injury, but one-half with difficulties before injury did so. Lehr (1990) notes that, as a consequence of the sometimes rapid early recovery and improvement in cognitive functioning, the brain-injured child or adolescent is able to realize more fully the impact of injury and thus react emotionally to these felt changes.

Segalowitz and Brown (1991) surveyed a large sample of high school adolescents and found that reported mild head injury was almost ten times as common as the two to three percent high school rate suggested by hospital administration records. Despite the widespread notion that mild head injury is generally benign, these investigators found a significant correlation between reported head injury and hyperactivity, stuttering, mixed handedness, and dislike of mathematics. It is doubtful, argue the authors, that children who are more likely to take risks that lead to serious brain injury with unconsciousness are more likely to dislike mathematics more readily than other school subjects, including science, to have mixed hand preference, and, in a smaller number of cases, in boys, to develop speech-related or hyperactive characteristic, and, in girls, depressive characteristics. Thus, they posit a causal connection between brain injury and these subsequent disabilities.

However, demographic and clinical studies do point out an association between hyperactivity and learning disabilities on the one hand and impulsive acting-out (mainly in boys) and depression (mainly in girls) on the other (Bellak, 1979; Borland, 1979; Buskirk, 1992; Cantwell, 1979; Huessy et al., 1979; Leichtman, 1992a, 1992b; Miller, 1987, 1988b; Nathan, 1992; Wender, 1979). And as we have noted in Chapters 5 and 6, impulsivity is a prime risk factor for traumatic brain injury in adults. Once again, the chicken-and-egg issues encountered throughout this volume make their appearance, this time in the case of pediatric brain injury.

Inherent in such conceptualizations, however, is the danger of "blaming the victim" for a brain injury, and perhaps overfocusing on premorbid characteristics to the neglect of injury-produced changes in personality in behavior—although, as I've noted in previous chapters, the opposite is usually more likely to occur. Questions about causation of cognitive and behavioral deficits may also become a forensic issue (see Chapter 10). Therefore, it is useful to consider a recent study by Donders (1992), which assessed the premorbid adjustment of a large group of six- to 16-year-old children with traumatic brain injury by means of standardized rating forms completed by parents and teachers.

Results showed that only 11% of the children were identified by their parents as having behavioral and social adjustment deficits prior to injury. The average premorbid adjustment of children who sustained their brain injuries in high-risk situations was not significantly different from that of children who were injured in low-risk situations, although there was a statistically nonsignificant trend for more children with mild-moderate injuries to show premorbid behavioral disturbances than children with severe injuries. This might suggest that a certain degree of premorbid impulsivity may be associated with increased risk-taking that puts the child in danger of more frequent, but less potentially damaging injuries (e.g., falls, fights) than purely accidental, but more serious injuries (e.g., passenger in an auto accident).

In any event, this study seems to contradict some previous notions of the universally impulsive, premorbidly behavior-disordered "at-risk" child, although a few cases—I've seen a number of them—do fit the stereotype. Clearly, more empirical research and competent case-study conceptualizations are needed in this area, and clinicians are urged to take special care in examining both current behavior and premorbid history, including family history, in working up their cases.

The Role of Frontal Lobe Injury

Recall from previous chapters that many of the cognitive and psychosocial sequelae of brain injury in adults have been attributed to frontal lobe damage, insofar as these difficulties involve impairment of judgment, impulse control, and emotional stability. Similar issues may be raised as to the role of frontal lobe damage in the psychosocial sequelae of childhood brain injury.

Filley et al. (1987) found that discrete frontal lobe injury or clinical evidence of diffuse axonal injury was implicated in persistent emotional sequelae in children and adolescents after severe brain injury. Two deficit patterns were identified. One was characterized by overarousal, including inattentiveness, irritability, hyperactivity, impulsiveness, inappropriate behavior, and aggressiveness. The other pattern involved underarousal demonstrated through apathy, poor motivation, and social withdrawal. Note that this description is similar to the one given by Blumer and Benson (1975) to distinguish a "pseudopsychopathic" syndrome caused by orbitomedial frontal lobe damage from a "pseudodepressed" syndrome caused by dorsolateral frontal lobe damage.

Grattan and Eslinger (1991) have compared frontal lobe syndromes in children and adults. According to these authors, the major barriers to normal growth, adaptation, and development after adult frontal lobe damage may reflect a combination of self-regulatory and cognitive factors. These include: (1) a preference for structured settings where the patient may rely on overlearned and routine behaviors; (2) lack of ability to abstract themes and engage in perspective-taking; (3) difficulties with planning, goal-setting, self-monitoring, and assessing programs toward goal attainment; and (4) impairment in integrating temporally disparate information. These deficits hinder reflective, insightful perspective-taking and planning abilities necessary for such processes as reminiscence, reappraisal, prioritization, and the historical integration of life experiences. Such patients studied by the authors show a stagnant sense of personal history, meaningfulness, and creative growth.

The traditional conceptualization of frontal lobe injury in children vs. adults is that, in children, the acquisition of cognitive and psychosocial skills is often arrested following frontal lobe injury, while frontal lobe damage in adulthood involves primarily the dissolution of previously acquired skills and abilities. Grattan and Eslinger (1991) argue that, inasmuch as frontal lobe development typically continues well into the fourth decade and possibly beyond, in younger adults, too, progression to mature cognitive and psychosocial development may be fully or partially arrested. In the psychosocial domain there may be a similar pattern of consequences in childhood frontal lobe injury, that is, certain types of cognitive impairment may underlie and contribute to social and emotional disability. There may be a delayed onset of adaptive skill maturation, and a progressive disparity between expected adult development and actual development. Thus, it appears that children and adults with frontal lobe lesions may suffer both dissolution and impaired acquisition in selected domains of behavior.

FAMILY AND SOCIAL ISSUES

As important as the family is to the adjustment of the brain-injured adult (Chapter 4), it is all the more vital in contributing to the psychosocial outcome of the brain-injured child.

The Family

From Lehr's (1990) clinical experience, as well as from the literature as a whole, if a child or adolescent has a history of significant psychiatric disorder before injury, these preexisting difficulties are likely to reemerge with recovery. Often, both the family and the treatment team are hopeful that this will not occur and may become quite resistant to the possibility. Brain injury recovery can be seen as a second chance for both the parents and their child or adolescent, something that will "knock some sense" into the patient's head. For the severely injured child or adolescent, these hopes are sustained through early and middle stages of recovery when the patient is somewhat docile and tractable, but are often dashed in the later stages with reemergence of preinjury personality and behavior, which may even be exacerbated. When this happens, the family can become very angry and feel "betrayed" by their brain-injured child or adolescent for becoming worse rather than better (see also Chapter 4).

Some reactions of family members can be very difficult for professionals to deal with constructively. Family members may insist, despite severe brain injury and obvious deficits, that their child or adolescent is no different than before injury. They may focus on the similarities to preinjury behavior and personality with scant attention to changes after injury. Hospital, rehabilitation, and school personnel may become frustrated in trying to plan for the child in the face of the parents' denial of deficits and may feel that the child's parents cannot be trusted to manage the child safely at home.

However, according to Brooks (1991), much of what may be thoughtlessly dismissed as "denial" by clinicians may in some cases really represent the expectable response of family members who are exhausted, lacking in knowledge of medicine or psychology, distressed, and just unable to hear any more bad news, and who therefore simply don't seem to be able to process the unwelcome negative information given by the clinical staff.

As discussed in Chapter 4, while some rehab personnel complain that families "sabotage" or "don't cooperate with" home practice assignments, we really can't expect the patient's family to turn their home into a boot camp. Overprotection, Brooks (1991) notes, can play a major role in undermining the work of therapeutic staff as the brain-injured child achieves high levels of functional competence while in active rehabilitation, only to lose many of these gains upon going home. It is easy to blame family members in this situation, but in truth they may have little alternative but to do things for the injured person (dressing, washing, etc.), rather than spending the time necessary to supervise, prompt, and cue—not to mention engaging in pitched battles with the resistant child or adolescent. Family members are torn between duties to the patient and to other noninjured family members, a point that rehab staff may forget or ignore, resulting in blaming the family or labeling them as uncooperative or overprotective. In fact, the family may simply have no option but to behave in ways that staff view as overprotective. Also, I'd point out, at the end of a hard frustrating day, the clinic staff can go home. Burnt-out family members enjoy no such refuge. Still, the sensitive clinician must try to encourage the family to support their child's move toward independence.

Lehr (1990) recommends that the clinician spend some time with family members in gathering a comprehensive picture of the child or adolescent before the injury as one means of trying to clarify real changes in behavior that are related to the injury. This can also help bridge the gulf that occurs when family and professionals each emphasize what they know best, for example, the family's knowledge about their child's preinjury functioning and the professional's expertise about brain injury effects. Also, allowing the family time to become more fully aware of the extent and characteristics of psychosocial changes after injury can relieve some of the tension between family and professionals. However, this usually does not occur until after discharge from the acute-care or rehab facility. As the family becomes more cognizant of the child's deficits, it is important for professionals not to react to this awareness in an I-told-you-so manner and thus further distance the family when they may be most in need of support and services.

It is clear, Brooks (1991) points out, that families of brain-injured children face all the problems of other brain-injured families, including anger, denial, etc., plus others that relate specifically to issues of dependency, protection, and caring for the noninjured siblings. Children are dependent on parents even without an injury, and head trauma considerably increases that dependency. Part of the work of the clinician is to facilitate independence as well as social and educational reintegration, and the combination of very natural parental overprotection and posttraumatic behavioral and cognitive changes in the injured child tends to inhibit normal maturational development and social experiences.

Related to the issue of dependency is that of protection. The child who has become disinhibited and socially fearless is now at increased risk for social and sexual exploitation, as well as for harming others, and the parents face the challenging dilemma of fostering independence and recovery, while at the same time providing control and structure to maintain safety.

Parents

Brooks (1991) notes that, despite a consistent trend in the literature that mothers of injured sons cope better than wives of injured husbands (Rosenbaum & Najeson, 1976; Thomsen, 1974, 1984), little actual evidence can be found to support this (Peters et al., 1990), and unequivocally negative findings have been reported (Brooks et al., 1987; Livingston, 1987— see Chapter 4). The common argument is that one of the main features of posttraumatic behavior change in the patient is childishness or other regressive reactions, and these are considered to be more difficult for a wife to deal with as they represent a new feature for her, whereas the mother has previously dealt with them in her child. For one, the problem is a total role shift (spouse changing from partner to caretaker), while for the other it is a role reentry (from parent back to parent).

Although it may be less common with parents of children than with spouses or parents of adults, the former, says Lehr (1990), sometimes have the reaction that the brain-injured child is not "their child" after injury. When this reaction occurs in extreme form, it can be quite devastating for both the parent and the child. In such exceptional cases, the child's emotional and behavioral control deficits may be attributed to such circumstances as getting blood transfusions from a bad person or to the devil getting into the victim, although I have only seen such frankly delusional reactions in rare cases where premorbid psychotic tendencies in a parent could be documented. However, clinicians should be sensitive to cultural variations.

Siblings

According to Lehr (1990), siblings may have felt responsible for the injury to their brother or sister, especially if they were taking care of them or were with them at the time of the accident. Even younger siblings may feel guilty about the circumstances of injury if they were aware of what their older brother or sister was doing, for example, drinking and/or driving dangerously "behind their parents' back." In addition, as noted in Chapter 4, parents may blame uninjured siblings, especially if older, for not "looking out for" the brain-injured child.

After a brain injury, the relationships among siblings can shift significantly. A younger, noninjured brother or sister may be expected or may be eager to take on the responsibilities and privileges of an older sibling. However, with recovery or improvement, the injured sibling is not likely to tolerate this usurping of rights. Changes in psychosocial functioning after injury are likely to be very apparent and often quite confusing to the brain-injured child's or adolescent's brother or sister. Jealousy and reawakened rivalry may lead to behavioral regression in the uninjured sibling, inducing one parent to exclaim, "First I had two mature children, then I had one child and one baby, now I have two babies." Siblings may react with significant anger and a heart-felt wish that their family return to the way it was before the injury, blaming their brain-injured sibling for "wrecking the family" (Brooks, 1991; Lehr, 1990).

Nonetheless, Brooks (1991) points out, the uninjured sibling can sometimes become a potent source of help and support for the patient, and stability for the family. In my experience, this usually happens in one of two ways. In the best case, one or more brothers or sisters adopts the role of protector, looking out for the injured sibling at school and in the neighborhood, helping with homework and household tasks, and generally just "being there" for the injured sibling. One 13-year-old boy told me that he "wouldn't have made it" if not for the help and support of his older sister.

A less salutory, albeit stabilizing, role is played by a sibling when that child begins to act-out, get depressed, or flunk in school and so becomes the "identified patient" in the family, taking some of the heat off the brain-injured sibling. This was the case in the family with "two babies" mentioned earlier. Family therapists will recognize the almost uncanny knack of certain children to discern how splitting a finite quantum of parental anxiety between two children may serve to dissipate some of its explosive energy that would otherwise fracture the family's fragile equilibrium if it were directed in only one direction.

Friends

Lehr (1990) cites two primary features of altered friendships after child and adolescent brain injury. One concerns the changes in the individual child or adolescent that interfere with the ability to maintain and initiate friendships. The other involves the perceptions and experiences of the other children and adolescents, that is, what it is like for them to have a friend who has had traumatic brain injury.

Whereas for adults, especially men, work role disruptions constitute a prime source of extrafamilial interpersonal stress after brain injury, for brain-injured children and adolescents, the impact of loss of friends is often most apparent in their play or leisure activities. Instead of riding bicycles, playing ball, attending Scout meetings, going to the movies, or just hanging out with other kids, the brain-injured child may be left to solitary pursuits such as watching television, reading, or playing computer games (Lehr, 1990). One observation I've made is that many children seem to be more able than adults to tolerate loss of ability, i.e., in playing sports or computer games, if surrounded by supportive friends. Perhaps brain-injured kids are less into "pride" than their grown-up counterparts — although adolescents may be exquisitely sensitive.

PSYCHOTHERAPEUTIC CONSIDERATIONS

In my experience, the psychotherapy of brain-injured children relies less on the application of any unique "techniques" than on the therapist providing a stable relationship object for both patient and family. Certainly, many of the same principles of therapy apply to children, especially adolescents, as to adults, e.g., dealing with posttraumatic headaches, substance abuse, behavioral control of aggression, and attending to rage, anxiety, depression, and confusion, as described in previous chapters. Some children may be especially sensitive to the post-traumatic psychological stress aspect of traumatic brain injury, displaying nightmares, panic episodes, and bizarre disturbances of behavior; this must be explicitly addressed where appropriate (Leichtman, 1992a, 1992b; Miller, 1993b). What is crucial in virtually every case, however, is the therapist's providing a reality anchor that both the child and the family can grab onto when either is feeling submerged and on the verge of drowning.

I usually like to meet twice a week, once with the child him- or herself, and once with the whole family. The format is flexible, and sessions may involve patient and parents, patient and siblings, just siblings, or any combination that is clinically indicated. Even the scheduling may be flexible: When the therapeutic relationship has stabilized, the child and family are permitted, even encouraged, to skip sessions if they truly (and realistically) feel they can "handle things" on their own. As with psychotherapy of brain-injured adults, after a time, the therapeutic sessions typically become more and more spaced out, and eventually they may be scheduled on an as-needed basis. In some cases, however, the child and/or family may need more extensive therapeutic work.

Sometimes the parents drop out soon after the first session, content to let the therapist "take over" the treatment and, indeed, to serve as a surrogate parent. This is a delicate role for many therapists, but one that may be essential for many children, and especially adolescents, if they are to maintain any kind of adaptive attachment to a supportive adult—the parents may just be too stressed-out or burnt-out. Be prepared, however, for splitting, sabotage, and all the other game-playing that family therapists are familiar with. An interesting observation I've made is that siblings of brain-injured youngsters are often more therapeutically helpful than parents, providing more accurate histories than parents and participating more readily in the treatment process. Perhaps these siblings perceive the therapy as "involving" them to a greater extent than do the parents—however, each family is different (see also Chapter 4).

The general principle seems to be to let the child and family know that there is somewhere to turn when things get too rough to handle on their own—indeed, this is one of the main functions of almost all types of psychotherapy. Most of the time, the therapist's role will involve trying to keep the family functioning as a cohesive and mutually supportive unit, but in some cases, the therapist may have to "take sides" and become the child's staunch ally and advocate. Almost nowhere else is the therapist's optimal blend of clinical skill and interpersonal sensitivity more important.

CHAPTER 9

The "Other" Brain Injuries: Stroke and Brain Tumor

THE EMPHASIS OF THIS BOOK reflects the emphasis of the general literature on the psychosocial aspects of organic brain syndromes—that is, heavily weighted toward traumatic brain injury. However, "brain injury" in the commonly understood sense can occur from other sources as well. The two next most frequently seen types in psychotherapeutic practice are stroke and brain tumor (Miller, 1991d), and this chapter will address these two syndromes.

STROKE

Demographics

Stroke is the leading neurologic disorder in the United States, affecting 400,000 people a year and killing about 160,000 of them. Stroke is the third leading cause of death, after heart attack and cancer, and about one-third of stroke victims are under age 65. However, the life expectancy of patients after stroke is increasing, and both overall incidence and death rates have been steadily declining over the last two decades (Clark et al., 1985).

Kinds of Strokes

A stroke, or *cerebrovascular accident*, occurs when the blood supply to a part of the brain is interrupted for more than a few minutes, resulting in the death of neurons. There are several major types of strokes. A *thrombo-*

sis results from obstruction to blood flow through an artery due to the build-up of atherosclerotic plaque. A piece of this plaque may break off and become lodged in the narrower part of the artery downstream. In an *embolism*, a blood clot, fat globule, or other mass gets trapped in the lumen of the artery, often already narrowed by atherosclerosis, which, again, obstructs blood flow. A cerebral *hemorrhage* involves a rupture of the blood vessel wall. As a result, not only does blood supply get diverted from its destination in the brain, but the leakage of blood into the brain cavity causes problems of its own, including pressure effects and metabolic disturbances. An *aneurysm* is a thin-walled outpouching of a segment of blood vessel that is especially prone to hemorrhages because of its fragility.

Some strokes are preceded by one or more *transient ischemic attacks*, or TIAs, which are brief, stroke-like blockages of blood supply that resolve quickly enough to avoid permanent damage. These often presage more serious—i.e., more permanent—strokes to come, and their occurrence should spur prompt medical attention.

Clinical and Neuropsychological Features

The particular symptomatology of stroke in any given case depends upon which brain structures and systems are affected. In fact, much of our knowledge of regional cerebral localization of function comes from the study of stroke syndromes—the so-called "stroke model" of neuroanatomy familiar to neurologists and neuropsychologists. Brain damage due to stroke may produce a wide variety of cognitive, emotional, and personality disturbances (Joseph, 1990; Lishman, 1978; Miller, 1990f), and the following are some of the main types (see also Chapter 1).

When motor areas of the brain are affected, limbs and other regions of the body musculature become weak or paralyzed; correspondingly, injury to visual, auditory, or somatosensory areas causes impairment in those modalities. Limbs not actually immobilized may suffer from higher-order disorders of coordination and motor planning, the *apraxias*. *Agnosias* are disturbances of higher-order perception, such as being unable to recognize or discern the meaning of sounds, sights, objects, or people that can otherwise be clearly received through the intact sense organs.

Damage to language areas, which, for most people, are in the left hemisphere, produces one or more types of *aphasia* involving deficits in speaking, writing, reading, or understanding the speech of others. In receptive aphasia, paranoia may develop around the patient's lack of verbal comprehension, while expressive aphasia may be accompanied by an agitated depression punctuated by explosive outbursts. Damage to the right hemisphere may produce deficits in either expressing or comprehending the emotional tone of communication—the *aprosodias* (Ross, 1981; Ross & Rush, 1981; Ross et al., 1981)—which may present clinically as a flat, apathetic, depressive-like syndrome.

Memory disorders may involve short- or long-term memory, verbal or visuospatial memory, remembering events or remembering skills, and so on. Damage to the frontal lobes may produce impairment of abstraction, judgment, and behavioral self-regulation. Left hemisphere damage in general tends to differentially affect verbal, analytic, and mathematical functions, while right hemisphere damage is more likely to impair visuospatial, musical, and some types of emotional functioning.

As a rough clinical rule, left hemisphere damage tends to produce depressive-dysphoric emotional syndromes, while right hemisphere damage results in more manic-euphoric presentations, sometimes including unawareness or denial of disability. In general, depression is the most common emotional disorder following stroke, occurring in up to 50% of stroke patients during the acute stroke period and in an additional 30% over the next two years. Severity of depression may range from mild to severe (Sweet et al., 1992).

Aside from lateralized and focal effects, generalized effects of brain damage include fatigue, concentration deficits, orientation problems, and sometimes difficulty controlling emotions and behavior.

Psychotherapeutic Issues in Stroke

Although it is difficult to separate organic from reactive components, almost all stroke patients experience a variety of psychological responses to their disability. The main types of reactions and the psychotherapeutic issues surrounding them are presented below. This section is adapted mainly from the work of Bucher et al. (1984), Oradei and Waite (1974), Watzlawick and Coyne (1980), and my own clinical observations.

Grief   Grief, or even a sense of bereavement, is a common reaction, both to the patient's loss of body function and to the resulting diminished independence. In some cases, patients' reactions to their strokes may be similar to that seen in actual bereavement or terminal illness, showing the stages of denial, anger, depression, and eventual acceptance.

Especially in the early stages, a pervasive mood of helplessness is typically seen, the patient sometimes waiting for or expecting the clinician to "do something" or "make me better." Psychotherapy may be rejected because "What's it going to do to fix my stroke?" In such cases, the therapist should make it as clear as possible that the purpose of the session is for the patient to express whatever is on his or her mind, not necessarily to "fix" anything—or worse, to "psychoanalyze" the patient.

Fear   As rapport with the therapist develops, the stroke patient may begin to pour forth what seems like an endless torrent of anxiety, despair, and feelings of helplessness. Common themes include fear of further disability from additional strokes, as well as loss of control over the patient's life. Patients are concerned that they will no longer be useful to their families. Younger patients worry mainly about sexual dysfunction and inability to work, while older patients are more concerned that they will be a burden to their families who will then dump them in a nursing home.

Many of these issues are best dealt with in the course of family therapy. However, individual psychotherapy may be the only place the patient is able to vent his or her fears, or to ask questions that would make other members of the family uncomfortable. In fact, the privacy of the individual psychotherapy session may be one of the rare settings where the patient can speak to a clinician without some family member or other caretaker hovering nearby.

Anger and Resentment   "I worked hard all my life, put three kids through college; now I should be entitled to a few years of easy retirement, and then this shit happens," is how one stroke patient put it, expressing the sentiment of many. Strokes—the name is apt—tend to strike just when people are either at the fulfillment stages of their careers or at the phase of retirement when the children have settled on their own and there is finally enough money and peace of mind to enjoy all those things that were put off for decades in expectation of better times to come. Naturally enough, the post-stroke patient feels cheated—and, typically, so does the spouse who now suddenly finds him- or herself saddled with an onerous caretaking responsibility instead of having a recreation partner in long-awaited retirement bliss.

Angry outbursts may have an organic basis, the *catastrophic reaction* to frustration seen in many cases of brain injury. This tends to occur more commonly with left hemisphere strokes, particularly those that produce expressive aphasic syndromes, and also with some kinds of frontal lobe damage. However, it may occur with brain injury of any type. In addition, impaired brain functioning may serve to weaken normal inhibitory control over, or lower the threshold for, angry behavior produced in large part by the understandable frustration and confusion of living with an altered mind and body.

Anger and resentment may be felt toward nonimpaired relatives, friends, clinicians, and health care personnel. The patient may envy and resent the youth and health of a younger therapist who "couldn't possibly understand" what the patient is going through. This resentment may manifest itself in the form of resistance to psychotherapy and to treatment efforts in general. Anger at staff and others may also represent feelings of displaced hopelessness, especially when the patient feels he is not making sufficient progress toward recovery. In patient support groups, anger at fellow group members may be seen if those members are perceived as "not trying hard enough"; in many cases it is clear that this represents projection of the accusing patient's own guilt and self-loathing at not working hard enough or getting better fast enough.

Some of this anger may be directed at home health care personnel, who may take the rap for the patient's inability to manage affairs as before. Nothing the poor aide can do is right, and there are always complaints and recriminations. The house isn't clean enough, the food not cooked enough, the bath not warm enough, responses not quick enough; communication problems compound the difficulty. Here, the issue is obviously the displaced frustration the patient feels with his or her own disabilities, combined in many cases with organically diminished impulse control, setting the stage for frequent angry outbursts.

Unrealistic Expectations   Early in recovery, often while still in the hospital, many patients will talk about their plans for discharge and beyond in startlingly unrealistic terms. This is typically a reaction to fears and uncertainties about the unknown future, and many patients become depressed and discouraged when the reality of slow, painstaking, and typically incomplete recovery has to be faced, along with the realization that a complete "cure" will probably never occur. As patients face these issues, there occurs some reworking of their grieving over lost independence, as sometimes shown by a reversion to denial of illness and tearful depression over their loss.

Usually, it is best at this stage to avoid confrontational approaches; there will be plenty of opportunities down the road for the patient to "face reality." While not reinforcing blatantly unrealistic expectations, the therapist can gently clarify certain facts about strokes and functional recovery. A workable way of handling these issues at this stage is not to force any information on the patient but to answer the patient's questions as honestly and forthrightly, albeit encouragingly, as possible. Comments should be ego-supportive and encourage self-reliance in those areas of functioning where this is realistic. Patients may need help in identifying new methods of coping with their current situation, and alternative ways of dealing with stress.

Information and "Reasons"   One way of getting a handle on a situation—of getting *control* in a very fundamental, personal sense—is to acquire information about it. It is the rare psychotherapy session or support group meeting that does not include at least a few questions about the nature of stroke, its causes, course, possible functional outcomes, and so on. In some cases, this kind of abstract, detached fact-finding may be a way of avoiding discussion of emotional issues—the defense of intellectualization familiar to psychotherapists. Not that this is necessarily counterproductive—far from it: In many cases, skirting the edges of a recovery issue in an emotionally detached way is a first step toward entering and navigating the stormier emotional terrain.

However, in many cases, basic lack of knowledge is just that: lack of knowledge. A distressingly high number of stroke and other brain-injured patients have never been given a clear picture of what to expect by their physicians, hospital, or rehab staff. Sometimes this is due to clinicians' hedging to avoid "upsetting" the patient; often it results from clinicians' lack of tact or communication skills, or their own emotional difficulties and inhibitions. In any case, it may actually reflect a certain degree of courage for the patient to ask for information, since to pose the question, after all, is to risk the possibility of a disappointing answer. Being ready to ask such questions and to deal with the information may be a sign of therapeutic progress.

A possible downside of such information-seeking is the tendency for some stroke patients to hold themselves responsible for causing or predisposing the stroke. There is a need to find a "reason" for why such a terrible thing could have happened to them, and believing that one has caused something by one's own actions at least puts some of the control back into one's own hands. "Overwork" is often cited by patients as a precipitating factor, which presumably is a more socially acceptable cause of cerebrovascular disease than, say, smoking, poor diet, or other indications of self-indulgence or laxity in personal health care. In fact, there is some evidence that experiencing severely threatening life events often precedes stroke onset, even controlling for standard risk factors (House et al., 1990), and general "stress" is sometimes identified by patients as a cause.

Interestingly, having a hereditary predisposition to stroke—ostensibly among the most self-exonerating of explanations—is often vehemently resisted by patients, apparently because it implies something wholly out of control. Probing deeper, the therapist may find that control over the causes of stroke may be linked with fantasies of being able to control the outcome. In this regard, patients sometimes hold themselves responsible for not recovering faster. There is a tendency to believe that "if you just put your mind to it, you can do it," and guilt and depression may ensue when such an attitude does not speedily lead to miraculous improvement. Early in recovery, the clinician may observe roller-coaster cycles of alternating high striving vs. frustrated giving-up. Sadly, this sometimes resolves into a steady state of depressed resignation where the patient just "throws in the towel." The issue of realistic goals is of obvious importance here.

Family Reactions   The ups and downs of stroke patients' expectations and aspirations for recovery often apply to their families as well. Spouse and children may start out being quite hopeful and encouraging, only to fall back on increasingly manipulative and coercive strategies to motivate the patient when he fails to make sufficient "progress." This fuels the patient's self-view as a failure, causing him to become increasingly hostile and depressed, which saps motivation still further, leading to another of the many vicious cycles seen in recovery from brain injury.

At such times of travail, the family may capitulate out of desperation and despair, and begin doing things for the patient that he could well do for himself. There is sometimes an undercurrent of hostility on the family's part, in that little is expected of the patient and he is deliberately treated "like a baby." If the patient shows glimmerings of effort on his own behalf, hope is renewed, expectations may be set too high, and the crash soon comes again. This cycle of hope and demoralization is repeated, with growing resentment and resistance on the patient's part, and increasing frustration and bitterness by the family. While some of the patient's limitations may be self-imposed, the spouse may capitulate as well. Going out to eat, visiting friends, and so on, become less a recreation and more a burden on the caretaker, and finally it just becomes easier to stay home.

To break this cycle of optimism and demoralization, family members can be encouraged to think about some very small but specific change that they might be able to bring about in the patient's behavior. The targeted change need not be—indeed, at first probably should not be—a chore, but rather an everyday activity that the patient once liked, but has ceased to engage in. As in most aspects of recovery from brain injury, the process of small steps coalescing into bigger and longer strides is what tends to produce optimum progress in the functional, cognitive, emotional, and behavioral spheres.

BRAIN TUMOR

Demographics

The yearly incidence of primary brain tumors (see below) in the United States is 20,500; for secondary brain tumors, 20,700. Primary malignant brain tumors are the second most common cause of cancer death in children and young adults up to age 34, and the third most common cause of cancer death in males aged 35–54 (American Brain Tumor Association, 1992).

Kinds of Brain Tumors

Primary vs. Secondary   *Primary brain tumors* arise from the substance of the brain itself, usually the supportive glial cells or other nonneural brain structures and tissues. Primary brain tumors may be benign or malignant (see below) and are more likely to occur singly. *Secondary brain tumors* are malignant and have spread to the brain from cancer sites in other parts of the body. The most common cancers of origin are lung cancer, melanoma, breast cancer in women, and prostate cancer in men. Secondary brain tumors may involve multiple sites within the brain, and there may also be coexisting spread of tumors to other body areas, e.g., bone or liver.

Malignant vs. Benign   The term *malignant* literally means "evil." Malignant brain tumors are histologically cancerous: Like any other cancer, they involve cells that replicate and proliferate in an uncontrolled fashion and have a tendency to metastasize, i.e., spread to other sites. *Benign* brain tumors are not cancerous and do not metastasize. However, since the skull is a nonelastic enclosed space, even a relatively small, histologically benign brain tumor can exert deadly effects if it grows quickly and compresses vital brain structures—this is sometimes called "malignant by location." Conversely, some very slow-growing benign tumors, such as meningiomas, may attain quite a large size before producing symptoms, especially if they begin growing in so-called "silent areas"—i.e., nonsensory, nonmotor regions—of the brain.

Malignant primary brain tumors are assigned different gradings, 1 to 4, depending on degree of malignancy, defined as proportion of undifferentiated cells within the tumor. Grade 1 tumors are relatively slow-growing and generally do not metastasize, while grade 3 and 4 tumors tend to metastasize and are more rapidly fatal. Some tumors, however, may start out as relatively benign and increase in malignancy and metastatic potential over time.

Clinical and Neuropsychological Features

Specific vs. Generalized Effects   A brain tumor may exert focal effects when it impinges on a fairly localized brain structure or pathway, and one may then observe any of the focal symptoms familiar to clinicians from the study of stroke and focal head trauma patients: aphasias, apraxias, agnosias, amnesias, sensory, motor, cognitive, and emotional changes. Sometimes one of these focal signs is the first evidence of the tumor.

The most important generalized effect of a brain tumor is increased intracranial pressure. As mentioned, the brain lives within the hard, enclosed case of the skull; anything that starts growing will compress what is already there. Signs of increased intracranial pressure may include dizziness, fatigue, drowsiness, concentration difficulties, nausea, vomiting, and headache. The latter is usually of a dull, steady type, and often worse on rising in the morning. More severe effects of intracranial pressure include herniation of brain membranes, brainstem compression, coma, and death.

Seizures   Many brain tumors, often in otherwise asymptomatic patients, announce their presence dramatically in the form of seizures. Seizures may be caused by focal or generalized pressure on neural structures, or by metabolic disturbances, or both. Seizures may be of various types, grand mal, petit mal, focal, or psychomotor. The presence of seizures, or their frequency or type, is not necessarily an index of the severity of the tumor, but seizures often require anticonvulsive treatment so that they don't cause further damage on their own.

Surgery, Medication, Radiation   The outcome of brain surgery to remove all or part of a brain tumor is determined by several factors — most importantly, where the tumor is and what it is. Small, well-defined, noninvasive tumors that lie close to the dorsolateral (top and sides) surfaces of the brain are generally the easiest to get at, to get all of, and to involve the least amount of damage to surrounding brain structures. The deeper the tumor, the closer it is to the base of the brain, the more it impinges on, wraps around, and intermingles with vital brain structures, the less promising the surgical outcome.

From the brain's point of view, surgery is just another kind of brain damage, and the neural tissue reacts as it would to any other type of injury. There is the possibility of seizure development, vascular changes, and metabolic reactions to the surgical trauma. A period of prophylactic anticonvulsant treatment is standard after brain surgery, as may be the use of other medications, such as steroids and antidiuretics, to reduce swelling. These drugs, not to mention chemotherapy and radiotherapy, may exert effects on cognitive functioning, along with the effects of the tumor itself and the surgery to remove it. In particular, some patients report a period of fatigue and impaired concentration following a course of radiation treatment. In some cases, where the tumor cannot be gotten at surgically, chemo- and radiotherapy may be the treatments of choice.

Psychotherapeutic Issues in Brain Tumor

In contrast to the burgeoning literature on psychotherapy of traumatic brain injury, and the admittedly sparse, but at least extant, psychotherapy literature on stroke patients, I was unable to locate even a single reference dealing with this topic as it applies specifically to brain tumor patients. Hence, virtually all of what follows comes from my own experience in dealing with cases of this type, as well as clinically justifiable extrapolations from the psychotherapy literature on head injury and stroke.

The Brain Tumor Patient   As we've seen, certain brain syndromes have their own demographics. For the most part, strokes tend to affect an older population and both sexes fairly equally, while traumatic head injury typically singles out young men. In stroke, many of the cognitive and emotional sequelae can be attributed to focal damage, upon which is superimposed the person's psychological response to his disability. In the head injury population, posttraumatic behavioral and psychosocial difficulties are as likely to represent a continuation or intensification of premorbid personality and behavioral patterns as they are to be due to the effects of the brain injury itself (see Chapters 2, 5, 6, and 7).

But brain tumors cut across most demographic lines — not surprising, considering the sheer variety and causes of brain tumors. Age distribution tends to be bimodal, with peaks in childhood and middle/older age, but many young adults are affected. Gender distribution across tumor types is about equal. Brain tumor patients represent a cross-section of the so-called "normal" population, including all socioeconomic, ethnic, and cultural groups. There is no evidence for an increased prevalence of premorbid psychopathology, personality disorder, substance abuse, or psychosocial dysfunction; indeed, there does not appear to be a higher rate of health or medical problems as a whole, except where secondary brain tumors have spread from preexisting metastatic disease.

Some preliminary research just starting to come in (Taphoorn et al., 1992) suggests that, for patients with low-grade gliomas, one year after radiation treatment, no serious focal deficits are found on neuropsychological testing, although concentration and memory deficits are present. In addition, most patients in this study reported depression, anger, fatigue, tension, or lack of vigor.

In general, the way the person has characteristically adjusted to serious life events will determine his or her psychological reaction to brain tumor, and this necessarily has some important consequences for psychotherapeutic treatment (Miller, 1991d).

Fear and Uncertainty   Patients with malignant brain tumors have a double burden: They have an organic brain syndrome affecting their ability to think, take care of themselves, relate to other people, and generally enjoy their prior quality of life—and they also have cancer. Even histologically benign tumors can sometimes recur and may require additional surgery with all of its attendant risks and discomforts. And so, for many of these patients, the future may be quite uncertain.

Traumatic head injury is usually a one-shot deal, as long as the person henceforth avoids the common risk factors for recurrence, such as drunk driving, aggressive fighting, impulsive chance-taking, and so on. As noted earlier in this chapter, many stroke patients are preoccupied by the possibility of further damage. However, while having had one stroke does place a person at a somewhat higher risk for future strokes, it by no means guarantees them, and many stroke patients recover adequately without major additional cerebrovascular disease.

But everybody fears cancer because, while the outlook continues to improve, the statistics are still fairly grim. In support groups, I find that there tends to form an almost unconscious division between the "brain-damaged-but-over-with" constituency, e.g., those who have had their surgery for benign meningiomas or acoustic neuromas and are now just living with the aftereffects, and the "brain-damaged-with-life-threatening-illness" group who must fear the future as well as adjust to the present. Although many of the challenges of life with a brain syndrome are common to all patients, those in the second group, like cancer patients generally, tend to be preoccupied with issues of living and dying, and less concerned with cognitive and motility deficits, except insofar as exacerbations or improvements signify changes in the course of the disease.

Therapy thus becomes similar to that with other patients suffering from life-threatening disease. Straightening out priorities, finishing unfinished business, dealing with grief, loss, rage, and depression are all components of helping these patients.

In many malignant brain tumor patients, I have observed an interesting parallel in reaction patterns to patients with Alzheimer's disease. Both groups seem to have two sets of mortal concerns, a sort of double existential timetable: one concerns dying, as would be expected, but another kind of question concerns how long the patient will continue to have "intact faculties," be "in their right minds," be competent, sane, and so on. Both groups voice concern about becoming a "vegetable" before they die. As a clinical observation, most brain tumor patients, even many of those with massive infiltration and multiple sites, seem to retain their core personalities and identities until close to the very end; cognitive and personality disintegration seems much more a characteristic of the degenerative nature of Alzheimer's disease than of the external assault inflicted by tumors on an otherwise healthy brain.

Causes and Reasons   Unlike heart disease or lung cancer — or traumatic head injury, for that matter — where there is at least some putative relationship between an individual's behavior or lifestyle and the risk for disease (poor diet, lack of exercise, smoking, drunk driving, etc.), in most cases of brain tumor, there is no ready explanation, no "reason." This has two sides. On the one hand, guilt or responsibility for causing the illness is usually not an issue. On the other hand, there is no sense of control, nothing the individual feels he or she can do to directly affect the course of the illness, other than being an informed medical consumer who acts intelligently in his or her own best interest.

While obviously not responsible for *getting* the brain tumor, many patients anguish over not *finding* it earlier. A common fantasy is that if only they had run to the doctor at the very first headache or dizzy spell or transient feeling of fatigue, insisted on a full neurodiagnostic workup, and sought second, third, and umpteenth opinions in the early stages when their doctors told them there was no detectable disease, then maybe they could have "caught" the tumor in time. Patients castigate themselves over the normal denial we all use to dismiss vague symptoms and avoid seeing doctors until the condition gets too uncomfortable or persists too long to ignore.

Guilty feelings for neglecting the brain tumor in the early stages may be ragefully projected onto the family for not noticing the patient's early symptoms, not taking the patient's early complaints seriously enough, and so on. Patients are often understandably frightened of going to a doctor and facing the possibility of having a serious illness diagnosed. They therefore may rely psychologically on the spouse or parents or even children to provide the motivation for them, to play the "bad cop" chiding the patient to seek medical counsel, so that the patient can use his or her own psychological energies in the service of denial — the "good cop" who says don't worry, it's the family that's making me go for this stupid checkup, what a bunch of worry-warts, everything's really okay, but I'll see the doc just to humor them, etc. In some cases, however, family denial may in fact be a true impediment to seeking help in the early and even later stages (see below).

Family Reactions, Family Support   As in other cases of serious brain injury or illness, family reaction patterns will vary according to a host of factors. For the most part, I find somewhat more family support and less overtly psychopathological or dysfunctional family reactions with brain tumor patients than with traumatic head injury patients. Perhaps this reflects demographics: As we've seen, head injury patients tend to be a preselected group in terms of risk for other kinds of psychosocial maladjustment (Bond, 1984; Miller, 1989b; Oddy, 1984 — see Chapters 2, 5, and 6), while brain tumor patients are more representative of the "normal" population.

Two particular traps that families of brain tumor patients tend to fall into are denial and overprotectiveness. Spouses and especially parents understandably have tremendous difficulty accepting that their loved one may be seriously ill. If there are no overt signs of impairment, but the patient suspects he or she is just "not right," families may pooh-pooh the patient's attempt to seek medical confirmation. This is not infrequently abetted by physicians themselves who may minimize or dismiss vague complaints.

When the tumor is finally discovered, extreme resentment at the obfuscatory attitudes, comments, and actions of the family may be expressed by the patient: "Damn it, I knew there was something wrong with me; why didn't you believe me and back me up?" Worse, this family denial may extend over the course of treatment and recovery: "You had the surgery, the tumor's out, so what do you mean you still feel lousy? C'mon — snap out of it!"

The other extreme is family overprotectiveness. In these cases, the patient now wants to stop being a "patient," but the family is so used to "taking care of" him or her, that this caretaking role is hard to give up. More than once, I've observed otherwise supportive families sabotage a patient's attempts at independence, usually out of their own psychological need to maintain a certain stable, if dysfunctional, family homeostasis. It is in these cases that the entire clinical armamentarium of family therapy skills and techniques must be brought to bear. In some instances, such intervention can have a profound effect not just on the patient's, but the whole family's quality of life. In most cases, more modest gains may be expected, but, as with brain injury treatment as a whole, "modest" is often enough to turn the course from disaster to opportunity.

PART V

The Road Ahead

CHAPTER 10

Matters of Justice:
Brain Injury, Recovery,
Compensation, and the Law

LIFE AFTER BRAIN INJURY frequently extends beyond the clinic and the family, and into the courtroom, the workplace, and the world at large. A number of recent reviews have dealt with the relationship of neuropsychology to the law (Doerr & Carlin, 1991; Dywan et al., 1991; Golden & Strider, 1986). The present chapter considers those aspects of forensic neuropsychology that are likely to have an impact on the clinical treatment of brain-injured patients.

NEUROPSYCHOLOGY AND THE LAW

The frequency with which traumatic brain injury seems to interface with the legal system should not be surprising. Each year in the United States two million head injuries occur in motor vehicle accidents alone, with a new injury occurring about every 16 seconds. The annual direct and indirect costs of traumatic brain injury are 25 billion dollars a year, and accidental head injuries result in 35,000 lost man-years of productive labor. Since most head injuries that occur in motor vehicle accidents and many that occur at the worksite are perceived to be someone's "fault," lawsuits are common and are a big business for personal-injury attorneys (Varney, 1990).

THE NEUROPSYCHOLOGY EXPERT WITNESS

Many therapists working with brain-injured patients may also be neuro-psychologists who have evaluated the patient at some point in the treatment. Of these, a number may find themselves involved in court cases regarding their patient. The following is not intended as a comprehensive tutorial in psychological testimony, but rather to acquaint the reader with some basic realities of forensic neuropsychology (Miller, 1990b, 1992c, 1992e).

To begin with, the proper role of the expert witness in court proceedings is that of an advocate for the facts as discovered through evaluation of the attorney's client and any pertinent records. To effectively represent the truth about a client requires a working knowledge of the current literature, procedures, and tests used to evaluate brain-injured patients. The burden of demonstrating the extent of disability rests with experts who are knowledgeable about the unique sequelae of traumatic brain injury (Berry, 1990; Rosenthal & Kaplan, 1986).

Other Experts

Neuropsychological expert testimony must give credence and value to other experts' testimony, while at the same time reserving the right to disagree with any questionable conclusions. If one remembers to separate the person from the statement they are making, the effective expert witness can help the judge and jury distinguish the "objective facts" from another expert's "opinion" (Berry, 1990).

Golden (1986) points out that, although many physicians may denigrate psychological testing, there is an impressive body of empirical research that supports the use of standardized measures in making clinical assessments with far greater reliability and accuracy than the use of intuitive opinion based on qualitative factors, as in the standard neurologic or psychiatric examination. Indeed, research suggests that different examiners often reach quite different results when given the same facts. In the final analysis, the psychologist is much better off emphasizing that which is uniquely the province and strength of psychology, rather than pretending to be an oddly and poorly trained neurologist.

With standardized testing, Golden (1986) argues, one can argue that the neuropsychologist not only does what the neurologist does in terms of observation and clinical history-taking, but in addition, adds the extra accuracy and power of standardized testing. When the two are integrated effectively, complementing one another so one can explain both how the neurologist reached his or her conclusion and why the neuropsychologist is disagreeing, this provides a powerful impression. Such integrative testimony helps give the juror a logical reason why the experts disagree. Thus, the juror need not choose one expert over another but rather can, in effect, "agree" with both while accepting the neuropsychologist's conclusions.

Aurich (1990) points out that the standard medical exam is concerned primarily with assessing common neurological deficits after brain injury, such as partial or complete paralysis, changes in a person's gross motor skills such as his gait, and gross sensory deficits. This type of exam is not sensitive to the neuropsychological deficits so often observed in brain-injured patients. A patient may exhibit few, if any, sensory-motor neurologic symptoms but may manifest a host of cognitive and personality problems that can only be adequately assessed through a comprehensive neuropsychological evaluation. Indeed, this is precisely why physicians refer their patients for a neuropsychological workup in the first place. Paradoxically, these cognitive deficits can make the patient a particularly poor historian and testifier on his own behalf, from the point of view of the attorney's case (Parker, 1988).

My own experience has involved facing off against psychiatrists more often than neurologists, since a greater number of the latter seem to appreciate the nature and value of neuropsychological assessment—indeed, many such referrals come from neurologists—and also tend to see themselves as less in a general turf battle with psychologists than do psychiatrists. However, in Chapter 1, I have criticized an overreliance on psychometric tests.

The Reluctant Witness

Sometimes you needn't go out of your way to seek involvement in forensic psychology—the legal system may find you whether you like it or not. This is especially true for therapists treating brain-injured patients, many of whom will be involved in legal proceedings at one point or another.

An increasingly common dilemma has cropped up for therapists and other health care professionals who may not have directly been involved in the neuropsychological evaluation of the patient, but are now seeing the patient in psychotherapy. Here, an attorney for the defendant in a patient's legal action requests information from, or a face-to-face meeting with, the clinician to discuss a patient's condition (Rambo & Cohen, 1990). Traditionally, defense attorneys did not request such a meeting, and the courts did not permit defense counsel to contact the patient's treating physician except by subpoena or court order to obtain the physician's records, or by other formal legal proceedings. It was only the patient's own attorney who had access to, and the opportunity to engage in, informal meetings and discussions with the patient's health care provider.

However, customary practice by defense attorneys has changed, and the law is being challenged on this issue. Although such contact has tradition-ally occurred in medical malpractice cases, where the defense counsel makes such a request of a subsequent treating physician, it is foreseeable that in the future other clinicians, psychotherapists included, will be contacted to "discuss" a patient's case with counsel representing someone the patient has sued. In my experience, the caller either lays on the flattery ("Doctor, you're such a recognized expert, your opinion would be most valuable. . . . ") or else tries to be evasive about which side of the case he or she is representing.

Technically, such contact is termed *ex parte* communication because it occurs outside the presence of, and without the knowledge of, the patient, the patient's attorney, or the court. In the context of *ex parte* communica-tion by a clinician with defense counsel, various courts have disagreed as to the propriety of *ex parte* interviews, and the rulings may vary from region to region. Even where permitted, however, if the statements made by the clinician are not "pertinent and material" to the case at hand, that clinician could be subject to liability for defamation or for breach of confidentiality. The safest course recommended by Rambo and Cohen (1990) is to refuse *ex parte* communications with defense counsel and insist that contact with such counsel occur only through sanctioned court proceedings and in re-sponse to subpoenas or court orders.

And sometimes the subpoena does come—right in your face. Blau (1984) notes that psychotherapists per se are rarely called to testify as experts, although in the case of treating neuropsychologists, the same clinician may have evaluated the patient as well as be doing the therapy. Where a psycho-therapist is subpoenaed, says Blau, it is usually as a "treating doctor" or one who may have information as to some aspect of the case at hand.

Some attorneys will approach a psychotherapist during the discovery phase of a trial, complete with subpoena, and insist on examining all of the therapist's records. Being served with a subpoena can be quite an intimidat-ing experience the first time around. The attorney may schedule a deposi-tion during which the psychotherapist will be subjected to probing ques-tions concerning the client's character, past behavior, and personal secrets. The therapist himself may be grilled relentlessly in an attempt to get him to contradict himself and thus impeach his testimony. Psychotherapists can be overwhelmed by such an authoritarian and adversarial approach and reveal information about their patient that the therapist is actually under no legal compulsion to divulge. In such cases, the psychotherapist may then be guilty of breach of privilege and subject to various criminal, civil, or ethical charges — not the most pleasant situation for either therapist or patient.

When faced with a subpoena for the records of a patient, Blau (1984) recommends that the psychotherapist do the following:

1. Contact the patient. Tell him you have been subpoenaed, and suggest that he contact his attorney as soon as possible. Request permission to call the patient's attorney to discuss the subpoena and the anticipated deposition or trial. Ask the patient to provide a written document that includes permissions or restrictions expressed by the patient. Some clinicians have the patient fill out and sign a separate Release of Information Form for attorneys, aside from the one he or she completed on intake to allow them to talk to other clinicians.
2. Contact the patient's attorney. Ask the attorney to forward a copy of the most current statutes on privileged communication for psychotherapists. Actually, this may not be too realistic, as busy attorneys typically ignore requests for anything that does not serve their immediate purpose. In such cases, you may have to dig up the information yourself.
3. Review the record thoroughly. Discuss this review with the patient and the patient's attorney, preferably in a joint session if the patient agrees.
4. Review the current status regarding privileged communication for psychotherapists before complying with the subpoena, forwarding records, or testifying at a deposition or trial. I would add that if you haven't done so already, get permission to talk to other clinicians who may evaluated and treated the patient. Use a separate Release of Information Form, or update any such forms in the record.

THE MALINGERING/SOMATIZING PATIENT: CLINICAL-FORENSIC ISSUES

One of the main points of contention in personal-injury cases involving brain-injured patients is the extent to which the deficits found on evaluation, and purported to be caused by the injury in question, are in fact "real." Individuals seeking monetary compensation, judicial vengeance on the alleged perpetrator of their injury, and/or legally and socially sanctioned validation of their victimhood have ample reason to play up their disability. As discussed throughout this book, pure "impairment" almost never occurs in a psychosocial vacuum. Yet clinical complexity may collide with the cut-and-dried legal view of damages and compensation, and it is here that the problem of the patient/plaintiff who "makes up" symptoms and deficits becomes prominent.

Malingering: Clinical and Demographic Aspects

Traditionally, it has often been presumed that when there are no visible signs of significant tissue damage, persisting complaints and other symptoms dependent on a subjective report represent a psychogenic reaction to the trauma or an exacerbation of a previous neurotic condition (Guttman, 1946; H. Miller, 1961). The popular clinical conceptualization has come to view this behavior as directly or indirectly motivated by a desire to recover monetary damages through litigation, and the symptoms are commonly held to mysteriously vanish when the case is settled: This has sometimes disparagingly been called the "green treatment." Significantly, however, there is a great deal of correspondence across patients in the type and nature of their complaints (Fantie & Kolb, 1991)—unusual if each patient were inventing his own syndrome. Common symptoms include frequent headaches, dizzy spells, greater susceptibility to fatigue, memory deficits, decreased ability to concentrate, increased irritability, anxiety, insomnia, undue concern about bodily function, and hypersensitivity to both light and noise—a collection of symptoms characteristic of the postconcussion syndrome (see Chapter 2).

Perhaps the most common diagnostic mistake is to assert a diagnosis on the basis of a lack of objective evidence. It does not follow that if no measurable brain damage or dysfunction can be detected, then the problem must therefore be psychological. Similarly, a history of psychological problems in the presence of nonsignificant neuropsychological findings does not automatically mean there is no organic basis. Some neuropsychologists go so far as to assert that negative results on neuropsychological testing ipso facto signal malingering or a factitious disorder. We and our procedures are not perfect, however, and the evaluator as expert witness cannot and should not presume that lack of findings in one area presupposes a diagnosis in the other (Berry, 1990).

Some defense neuropsychologists try to have it both ways, arguing for malingering if most neuropsychological test results are negative, and then using this as a basis for arguing that the few positive findings that do occur must be due to "faking bad." Yet sometimes this is exactly what happens:

patients who are intact in most areas may have genuine impairment in some other areas, which they then exaggerate to the point of clinical unbelievability, thus leading the examiner to doubt the integrity of the entire test protocol. This is why the clinician's expertise and experience is crucial in discerning the correct meaning of otherwise ambiguously interpretable findings.

As discussed in Chapter 2, a head injury is typically termed "minor" when the loss of consciousness or period of posttraumatic amnesia is brief. In most cases, there is nothing resembling a medical emergency, that is, there is no life-and-death crisis. However, as a result of abrasions to orbital frontal and medial temporal brain regions, a so-called minor head trauma can have far-reaching neuropsychiatric consequences. For many, the term "postconcussion syndrome" has become a pejorative term denoting a patient with an apparently minor head injury who makes a variety of vague neurological and psychological complaints (e.g., headache, depression, paresthesias) and has pending litigation. The common wisdom is that these symptoms are brought on by the stress of being involved in litigation, possibly with some supplementary coaching by attorneys, and that these would magically vanish if the patient would simply discontinue the lawsuit (Varney, 1990).

Many compensation cases arise from accidents that occur at the worksite. The commonly reported composite profile of the injured worker is someone who is blue collar, carries out medium to heavy exertion work, has limited reading and arithmetic skills, most often has musculoskeletal injuries, falls in the age group from early 30's to early 50's, and is most frequently a married man (van der Kolk & Stewart, 1988). Research has demonstrated that many factors contribute to difficulty in returning to work, including lack of transferable skills, reduced exertional limits, inability to emotionally cope with the disability, chronic pain, sexual dysfunction, and financial disincentives (van der Kolk & van der Kolk, 1990).

Frank Malingering

Clinical views of malingering usually take one of two forms, what I like to call a "conservative" view, which advocates the highest level of clinical circumspection, and a "liberal" view, which gives patients with as-yet medically undocumented pathology the benefit of the doubt with regard to honesty of self-report, i.e., innocent until proven faking. Clinicians' standings on this suspicion barometer usually reflect the kinds of settings they work in and the patients they treat. Those accustomed to dealing with well-motivated, cooperative, and interpersonally engaging patients tend to take these patients at face value, while those clinicians whose caseloads include large numbers of compensation claims that are fabricated and/or embellished come to adopt a more cautious, if not cynical, attitude.

One apparent representative of the "conservative" view is Binder (1992), who defines malingering as the intentional production of symptoms for the purpose of obtaining an external reward, such as financial compensation, dodging military duty, or avoidance of punishment for criminal behavior. The incidence of malingering differs across settings and populations, with incidence estimates ranging from one to 50% (Resnick, 1988). It may be less common in severe traumatic brain injury patients who have no trouble proving disability than in so-called mild head trauma patients—indeed, earlier, Binder (1986) argued strenuously for the legitimacy of many post-concussion symptoms (see Chapter 2).

Presently, Binder (1992) notes that mental health clinicians sometimes seem reluctant to make a diagnosis of malingering that implies that symptoms are exaggerated or totally factitious and induced by a desire to obtain money or other reward. Yet, at least one survey (McMordie, 1988) has revealed that most psychologists and neurosurgeons believe that financial incentives play a role in the postconcussion syndrome. Many clinicians, Binder points out, fail to appreciate the reinforcing value to many people of gaining money through clever deception rather than through "honest" work. Although mental health professionals—most coming from, and being inculcated with, solid middle class values—tend to regard work as a noble enterprise, not all people share these values, particularly those in lower-status, unfulfilling occupations (see also Baumeister, 1991). Some people do things for money that are far more unpleasant and demeaning than malingering. For such people, sustaining a financially compensable injury is perceived as equivalent to winning the lottery, and only a fool would fail to milk the system for all it's worth.

There are several reasons, says Binder (1992), for the relative infrequency of a diagnosis of malingering in many clinical settings. Perhaps mental health professionals find it difficult to be skeptical and therapeutic at the same time. Or skepticism may have translated into "acceptable" functional diagnoses such as depression or conversion reaction rather than malingering. Clinicians who diagnose malingering sometimes are considered callous, mercenary, and countertherapeutic. A related consideration, not mentioned by Binder, is that there is no billing code for malingering per se, but there are for depression, somatoform disorder, and other treatable psychiatric diagnoses. The private, for-profit, inpatient treatment facilities that employ many of the clinicians making these diagnoses often convey subtly, but very clearly, exactly what these clinicians are expected to find.

Perhaps some clinicians avoid the diagnosis out of concern for a negative reaction from a colleague or referral source, including attorneys. Or they may fear the wrath of patients. Binder (1992) cites Parker's (1979) report of an Australian patient who expressed his grievance against having his back pain diagnosed as malingering by going on a killing spree, murdering two orthopedic surgeons and wounding a third, before committing suicide. At best, some dubious posthumous satisfaction might be gotten from the finding on autopsy that no organic back pathology was found, thereby justifying the functional diagnosis. Less dramatic, but just as scary, is the prospect of professional negligence lawsuits brought by patients financially damaged or just angered by a diagnosis of malingering.

The best method of avoiding the outrage of colleagues and patients alike, says Binder (1992), is to minimize diagnostic errors. The only sensible procedure, he argues, is for the clinician to consider the possibility of malingering in every patient who has any monetary or other external incentive for faking on a neuropsychological exam. Malingerers, Binder asserts, are often cunning and experienced deceivers who have much to lose if they are detected. Consequently, they take great pains to avoid discovery.

Binder (1992) delineates a number of causal and/or contributory factors to malingering, the most important of which for our present clinical and psychotherapeutic purposes are those related to premorbid personality. In histrionic personality, inattention to detail and disdain for facts are characteristic. Among other features, narcissistic patients have feelings of entitlement, exploit others, and often feel that they do not have to play by the rules governing society as a whole. Pathological lying, or *pseudologica fantastica*, in persons with borderline personality may result from poor tolerance of the anxiety caused by telling the truth, poor self-esteem, or poor impulse control. The anger and tendency toward defensive projection of the borderline personality lead to blaming others for actions for which the patient is responsible. It is difficult to determine if these fabrications and fantasies result from delusional thinking or a desire to deceive — or some combination of both (see also Chapter 12). These patients may falsely claim that clinicians seen previously have diagnosed disorders that serve some ulterior purpose; for example, claiming a pain syndrome or anxiety disorder to get narcotics or benzodiazepines. Indeed, two disorders that are almost universally associated with deception, antisocial personality disorder and substance abuse, greatly increase the likelihood of malingering (see Chapters 5, 6, and 7).

In his review, Binder (1992) provides some suggestions and useful clinical instruments for practicing neuropsychologists, which are beyond the scope of the present chapter. As a psychotherapeutic issue, however, evidence of malingering needs to be forthrightly, if sensitively, addressed. Exhortatory confrontations are less effective than attempts to delicately discern what the patient fears he will lose if he does not maintain the image of cognitive and functional impairment. Many of the principles of treating factitious cognitive disorders are similar to those for chronic pain discussed in Chapter 7. As in those cases, the clinician must be prepared to appropriately deal with refractory cases where the chronic impairment syndrome is less a therapeutically addressable psychodynamic issue, but rather a case of the patient's calculated unwillingness to give up the complaint because there is simply so much to gain from the pretense. Sometimes, opportunity just beats recovery, and, despite all the clinical and judicial checks and balances, a disconcertingly large number of malingerers do manage to bilk the system. Unfortunately, the wrath of the authorities may then come down on the poor heads of "innocent" plaintiffs seeking legitimate compensation — part of the larger problem of justice in the adversarial tort trial system.

"True" Symptoms and Their Implications

Fantie and Kolb (1991) — apparent exponents of the more "liberal" camp of malingering theorists — question the assumption that litigation is responsible for the persistence of complaints, even in patients with active lawsuits. Is it not just as likely, they ask, to expect that those people whose discomfort and deficits are, in fact, persistent and disabling will be more likely to adopt legal recourse when available and less likely to be deterred or discouraged by the effort and time investment required to win a court battle? Some law firms are even beginning to address the issue of legal malpractice actions against attorneys who settled claims without sufficiently taking into account the potentially dire implications resultant from "mild" head injuries (see Chapter 2).

Faced with frequent disbelief and sometimes outright hostility and ridicule, the mild head injury patient with a postconcussion syndrome may be rather defensive by the umpteenth clinical or forensic examination because no one seems to believe that his complaints represent more than a "functional overlay" or "compensation neurosis" (Varney, 1990). For similar reasons, the spouses and parents of patients with so-called minor head injuries can be quite abrasive and argumentative, and in many such cases this attitude has developed from the manner in which medical professionals have treated the case. When a loved one appears clearly impaired to a relative, and multiple physicians and psychologists have pronounced to the contrary, the natural reaction is to become defensive (Miller, 1991b; Varney, 1990 — see Chapter 4).

In many such cases, an apparently irate relative can become rather cooperative and serve as a valuable source of corroborative information if treated with a bit of extra deference and consideration (Varney, 1990). Indeed, I have been impressed by how simply conveying to relatives that the clinician is "on their side" can transform them from stonewalling adversaries to informative collaborators. However, a number of patients and relatives have been burnt once too often by clinicians who play at this kind of "bonding" in an insincere, patronizing way, and they may react at first by an increase in bilious resistance. A subset of such relatives may be fundamentally unreachable, partly due to medical mistreatment, partly because of their own issues.

Compounding the problem is the fact that some clinicians, out of their own ignorance or skewed theoretical biases, may purvey information that is frankly wrong. For example, a patient who had suffered a ruptured aneurysm with resulting temporary global anterograde amnesia was told sometime later by his inpatient therapist that his memory loss for the events surrounding his injury was due to psychodynamic repression of the painful psychological trauma of the event, stemming from re-evoked childhood feelings of loss of control. Needless to say, such an erroneous misdiagnosis is at best clinically irresponsible and at worst constitutes malpractice — not to mention damaging the credibility of nonmedical clinicians who work with the brain-injured. (Mark Twain: "It ain't what you don't know that gets you; it's what you know that ain't so.")

Hartlage (1991) provides an account of the major implications that "mild" head injury can have in terms of job performance and psychosocial adjustment (see also Chapter 2). In the cognitive domain, a brain injury to a person of average intelligence that lowers IQ by less than ten points could disqualify that person from about 6,000 job categories, including many that have projected high growth rates over the next decade. Inasmuch as the U.S. Department of Labor has identified a total of about 24,000 job categories, approximately one-fourth of this patient's job opportunities would be precluded by his "minor" IQ loss. Professional people, those with advanced degrees, and people whose preinjury developmental levels and accomplishments were well above average may have lowered ability levels following minor head injury and still appear to be "normal" in terms of intelligence, knowledge, or ability level. The types of mental abilities most impaired by minor head injury are often not detected by the traditional mental status examination by a neurologist or psychiatrist, or even by standard neuropsychological testing.

Memory deficits, admittedly very common sequelae of mild head injury, are often underestimated with respect to their vocational implications. According to Lees-Haley (1987), a 10% loss of memory is rated as mild, but employees like teachers or paralegal secretaries who forget 10% of what they read in an eight-hour work day may be in 100% trouble. Similarly, attention and concentration deficits can be especially limiting to workers in settings where such requirements are part of the job, for example, paramedics or bookkeepers. Workers who have to maintain more than one set of instructions or ideas, such as nurses, secretaries, foremen, or police officers, may find themselves unable to tolerate distractions from one task or idea, and thus be unable to perform their prior work at an acceptable level, even though their postinjury IQ is still sufficiently high as to suggest their "potential" for doing such work. Even workers with only one set of instructions or tasks, such as inspectors or production workers in assembly, packaging, or machine operation may be unable to maintain necessary levels of attention over an eight-hour day on a sustained basis. Additionally, fatigue that accompanies brain injury often exacerbates any of the other problems.

Emotional and psychosocial factors may also impede return to work in individuals with mild brain injury, even when their cognitive abilities are relatively unaffected (Weddell et al., 1980). Many of the common posttraumatic changes in personality and behavior, such as apathy, impaired initiative, inability to plan and carry out behavioral sequences, and low frustration tolerance, are incompatible with success in the workplace (Fantie & Kolb, 1991).

Following injury, according to self- and relatives' reports, many patients become more absentminded, agitated, angry, confused, depressed, easily upset, forgetful, impatient, irritable, shaky, short-tempered, slow, tense, tired, afraid, discouraged, disagreeable, distractible, temperamental, thoughtless, and unhappy. They become less calm, cheerful, contented, energetic, enthusiastic, good-natured, happy, and strong (Hartlage, 1991). This has obvious implications for almost any kind of employment.

Other common, personality-related sequelae, such as defective social judgment, childishness, egocentricity, and irritability not only affect potential employability but have a tendency to disrupt other aspects of the patient's social life as well. In addition to the downgrade in vocational status, many patients do not resume their leisure activities or reestablish their social contacts to the same extent as before the injury. Rehabilitation programs and therapy should not be directed solely toward returning the patient to work but also must consider helping to restore leisure activities and social relations for an overall improved quality of life (Fantie & Kolb, 1991; Oddy & Humphrey, 1980). The issue of quality of life will be discussed further in the next chapter—for now, the forensically involved clinician should be aware that such job and lifestyle factors may enter into the determination of damage awards in personal-injury and compensation cases.

"Organic" vs. "Psychological" — Again

According to Varney (1990), many of the complaints offered by postconcussion syndrome patients may refer to symptoms of depression and/or partial complex seizures. Symptoms of depression can include dysphoria, anergia, insomnia, crying spells, memory difficulties, poor concentration, physical aches and pains, enhanced pain sensitivity, poor appetite, low sex drive, irritability, loss of interest, and social withdrawal. Symptoms of partial complex seizures can include paresthesias, anesthesias, headache, photophobia, nausea, abrupt mood shifts, memory gaps, episodic confusion, episodic irritability, episodic anxiety, episodic tinnitus, occasional speech difficulty, déjà vu, jamais vu, "odd" bodily sensations, episodic suicidal inclinations, olfactory hallucinations, and intrusive thoughts about the accident. Not only are these symptoms "real," but they are potentially treatable with antidepressant or anticonvulsant medication.

Of course, it's usually not that simple. As Cullum et al. (1991) point out, "psychological" and "neurophysiological" events occur on a continuum. Certain phenomena that are traditionally regarded as "mental" can have measurable physiological and neuropsychological correlates. Examples include conditioning of the EEG alpha rhythm, as well as the physiological changes that can occur in hypnosis and other suggestible states. This suggests that whereas some of the variation in neuropsychological performance in conversion, dissociative, and even some malingering cases might reflect unconscious or partially voluntary motivation to appear "impaired," there may also be subtle alterations in central nervous system functioning that are by-products or correlates of such hysterical states (see Parker, 1990; Miller, 1993b; also see Miller, 1990f, 1991f for an in-depth treatment of the mind-brain-body issue). Needless to say, these complexities are often difficult to boil down to a level that will help a judge or juror determine the presence of damages and the size of any resultant award.

Research on Patients Involved in Litigation

Studies can be found that either challenge or support the established clinical wisdom that pending or ongoing litigation results in increased complaints. Merskey and Woodforde (1972) divided a series of postconcussion patients into two groups: one composed of subjects who had either no claims or claims that had already been settled, and the other group made up of those whose cases were still before the court. The quality and quantity of subjective symptoms reported by both groups were found to be comparable. Rimel et al. (1981) reported that pending litigation had a negligible effect, if any, on the level of adjustment achieved by traumatic head injury patients, thereby contradicting the suggestion that litigants characteristically delay their progress by fraudulently producing additional complications.

Van der Kolk and van der Kolk (1990) surveyed a group of injured patients involved in litigation an average of three years postinjury to determine their current medical and vocational status. Twenty percent of the sample were currently employed. High rates of chronic pain and depression were found among those with poor postinjury work records. Most of the sample was on medication, reported physical limitations as the main barrier to employment, had not been involved in therapeutic or vocational counseling, had performed medium or heavy exertion work prior to injury, and had not received adequate vocational or educational assistance. The authors concluded that early and intensive nonmedical psychosocial rehabilitation services could have increased vocational success.

Binder et al. (1991) studied a group of patients after resolution of lawsuits and found that most subjects eventually had substantial remission of their psychological symptoms. Factors associated with better outcome of psychological symptoms after an accident and the resulting litigation included a longer time after resolution of the litigation and a shorter time between injury and litigation. One hypothesis is that the stress of the litigation process itself maintains or exacerbates psychological symptoms. If the plaintiff has had a shorter time to endure the stress of litigation, the outcome is better. In addition, as more time passes after litigation is finalized, the plaintiff has more time to recover from the psychological stress of the accident and the litigation. It is interesting that the important factor is not the amount of time after injury but rather the amount of time relative to the settlement of the lawsuit. Plaintiffs who had the most psychological symptoms after their injuries had the worst outcome on follow-up. Hence, severity of the plaintiff's initial psychological symptoms appears to be a risk factor in terms of the likelihood of having a poor outcome.

Legal matters after brain injury often merge with other aspects of long-term adjustment, and it is to these that we now turn.

CHAPTER 11

Back to the Future: Long-Term Outcome, Support Groups, and Quality of Life

THROUGHOUT THIS BOOK, the function and purposes of psychotherapy have been conceived broadly, as reaching far beyond the therapy session and extending into family, social, legal, and recreational domains. This chapter will explore this wider role of the psychotherapist in facilitating the brain-injured patient's transition back to the real world, and in finding a comfortable place in it.

BACK TO WORK: PSYCHOTHERAPEUTIC AND REALITY ISSUES

For most young and middle-aged American males, and a growing number of women, work provides one of the fundamental sources of meaning in life (Baumeister, 1991). Consequently, the loss of ability to work can have a demoralizing effect on the brain-injured patient—professionals reading this book should take a moment to contemplate their own anticipated reactions to having their chosen vocation cruelly and suddenly snatched from them by adversity. Even where there is no complicating litigation, and where the patient genuinely wants to get back to work, problems may arise.

Cognitive Factors: Facing Reality

In many cases, the difficulty is due to altered cognitive status. Lam et al. (1991) divided a sample of posttraumatic brain injury patients into competitively employed, marginally employed, and unemployed groups. They found that higher cognitive functioning was associated with better vocational outcome. Specifically, the competitively employed were more intact on measures of visuospatial reasoning, visuospatial memory, and distractibility. Full Scale IQs and weekly wages were significantly correlated. The unemployed and marginally employed groups did not significantly differ from one another on cognitive status. Thus, patients with higher cognitive functioning, better visuospatial memory, and less distractibility were more likely to be back at work and to earn more money.

One potential complication is the fact that a number of brain-injured patients *think* they can go back to their old jobs when they really can't. Parker (1987) has examined many patients who were unaware of deficits represented by an estimated loss of as much as 30 IQ points. Some of these patients had been highly paid professionals or executives who pluckily returned to previous activities, only to find themselves plagued by headaches, memory problems, poor coordination, fatigue, and/or inability to concentrate.

The brain-injured worker may perceive that he retains the individual skills to perform his job, but be less aware of his inability to consistently integrate, apply, and generalize existing skills. He often fails to appreciate the nature of his deficits and the realistic options for return to work. Instead, vocational aspirations are often determined by intact memories of premorbid, often high-level, capacities. The result is that he has great difficulty setting realistic vocational goals or accepting the need for vocational rehabilitation activities that he finds uninteresting or less than challenging to his premorbid sense of self.

Following head trauma, older, vocationally established adults often persist fruitlessly in attempting to return to their previous level of work, while younger adults, cut off from exploring the full range of vocational options, may be unintentionally undercut by well-meaning family members who push for the attainment of long hoped-for, but now clearly unrealistic, goals. Worse, the vocational adjustment expectations placed on those who appear "intact" are typically high, but in marked contrast with their actual reduced capacities (Kay & Silver, 1988).

We know that brain-injured patients who show remarkable cognitive strengths and practical skills may nonetheless be unable to integrate those strengths and skills appropriately into ongoing behavior—recall the pattern of the frontal lobe patient. They may fail to generalize and to apply their knowledge from one situation to another, may be unable to generate problem-solving strategies appropriate to the particular situation—especially if it is unstructured, deviates from the familiar, or is fraught with anxiety—or may be unable to step back from a situation to think abstractly about it and the available options.

Such patients, while they may score in the average range or above on standard intelligence and cognitive tests and may look "on paper" like ideal candidates for a particular work situation, may nevertheless be severely impaired in their on-the-job functional work skills. They may actually do best in repetitive job situations in which task demands don't change and active problem-solving or application of strategies to new situations is not required. Conversely, patients with specific cognitive impairments, e.g., in language or perception, may show good abstraction and problem-solving skills and do much better on jobs requiring flexibility of thinking, as long as it avoids their primary area of deficit (Kay & Silver, 1988).

Because most jobs involve a number of many repetitive functions, many brain-injured patients can continue to work on the basis of prior knowledge, although some kinds of brain damage result in an inability to retrieve former information and skills. However, loss of "intelligence" means, in part, less ability to learn new ideas and function in new situations. Individuals who suffer IQ loss may therefore be passed over for promotions in their occupations or fail to cope with organizational changes. The illusion of intact vocational capacity may be further sustained if the patient retains social skills and other nonintellective characteristics (Parker, 1987).

Often, clinicians rely on neuropsychological testing to delineate a pattern of cognitive strengths and weaknesses that will be prognostic for a patient's return to work. However, as discussed in Chapter 1, there are limits to what neuropsychological evaluation can reliably predict. Neuropsychological tests attempt to directly measure abstract thinking, problem-solving, and concept formation. However, assessment of a patient's ability to integrate information in a useful manner and to generate learning across situations often depends on the examiner's clinical skill in observing behavior and in inferring capacities across test situations. The more specific the rehab counselor or jobsite supervisor can be about what information is needed, and the more the neuropsychologist is aware of what vocational questions need answering, the more focused and valuable the neuropsychological evaluation will be.

Back on the Job: Some Strategies

How, then, can the clinician help prepare the brain-injured employee for return to work? According to Kay and Silver (1988), the dual goals of prevocational preparation are awareness and accommodation. *Awareness* involves the recognition of the nature, extent, and impact of one's residual strengths and limitations and the acceptance of these limitations for how one lives one's life. This process is essentially a psychological one and involves, in most cases, a changed sense of self that is necessary for a positive rehabilitation outcome. It is here that the psychotherapist may make the largest contribution. The goal of *accommodation* involves the remediation of existing cognitive and behavioral deficits, or compensation through modification of both environment and habitat for deficits that cannot be remediated. Failure to recognize the brain-injured patient's need to go through this often long and difficult prevocational process is, say Kay and Silver, the single most important reason why traditional vocational programs fail with these patients.

QUALITY OF LIFE

As vital as one's job or career may be to a sense of accomplishment or even identity, for most people there is more to life than work. More importantly, for many individuals work shades over into other aspects of daily living that give life its overall meaning (Baumeister, 1991; Heath & Heath, 1991). Brain injury can have an impact on these non-work life areas, too.

Cognitive Factors

Klonoff et al. (1986) examined predictors and indicators of quality of life in a group of closed head injury patients two to four years postinjury. Lower education, frontal lobe damage, and seizure disorders were associated with poorer overall quality of life. The strongest predictors were degree of motor dysfunction related to those aspects of quality of life that involve activities of daily living and social role functioning, such as performance in the work and home settings. Those patients with residual motor dysfunction reported more impaired self-care, decreased mobility, difficulty in getting around, problems swallowing food, and difficulty articulating speech. The degree of motor disability also appeared to influence social role functioning, as those patients with motor slowing reported increased dysfunction in the work and home settings. Apparently, independence and mobility are important factors in postinjury adjustment.

Psychological Factors

Dougherty (1991) has reviewed some of the important values implicit in the broad field of rehabilitation, and many of these insights correspond to my own experiences with brain-injured patients in particular.

Happiness Since fully "curing" the patient is rarely a realistic goal, much of the work of rehabilitation involves an implicit commitment to fostering as happy a life as possible. Accordingly, the goals of rehabilitative care are maintaining, enhancing, restoring, and compensating for disabling conditions; promoting the highest possible quality of life; and integrating the patient into his or her family, community, job, or vocation. These goals are particular ways of trying to maximize patients' physical and psychological well-being.

As noted in previous chapters, rehabilitation patients are not always grateful for the care they receive. They sometimes resent their caregivers for the demands they impose and for being free of disabilities themselves. They may become depressed, suicidal, or otherwise "unmotivated." Families, too, live with feelings of anger, guilt, anxiety, helplessness, and hatred directed toward the patient, health care providers, third-party payers — even themselves. As discussed in Chapter 4, families can make all the difference in whether or not there is a successful outcome. On the other hand, families are being asked to bear extraordinary care burdens and to sacrifice opportunities for recreation, socialization, career advancement, etc. Providers of care, both professionals and families, face the constant threat of burnout when the buoyancy of therapeutic optimism gives way to feelings of powerlessness, apathy, lowered self-esteem, and resentment of the patient for "ruining the family's life." This necessarily means less happiness for all concerned.

Fairness This mainly involves issues of patient selection. Clinical factors, especially diagnosis and prognosis, properly play key roles in the decision of who gets the full array of available and appropriate treatments, but, Dougherty (1991) notes, so do a number of nonclinical factors. These include potential for benefit, likely burden on rehabilitation resources, age of the patient, ability to learn, geographic and emotional availability of family support, social situation, vocational background and objectives, probable disposition at discharge, degree of patient responsibility for the disability, patient attitude, and potential quality of life.

Don't forget ability to pay. The truly worst off — persons with disabilities who are also poor and un- or underinsured — are least likely to be selected for rehabilitation, especially by the high-tech, high-priced, private, for-profit rehab centers (a similar situation exists in the addictions treatment field—see Peele, 1989). In these facilities, there may at times be a conflict of interest between patient and insurance company. Third-party payers' interests in limiting benefits and costly services or in "forcing" a speedy return to work may conflict with the wishes of the patient and even with his or her best medical interests. The demands of business may take precedence over concerns to deliver optimal human services.

Finally, rarely are potential rehab patients aware of the factors that determine a decision to accept or reject them for a particular program—in essence, they are kept in the dark about the factors that determine their fates. Dougherty (1991) urges that rehab professionals become active in advocating for a more equitable health care delivery system, but I wonder how many clinicians are prepared to rock the boat or put their careers on the line for the sake of fairness.

Freedom   In rehabilitation and other health care facilities, Dougherty (1991) points out, patients are routinely required to sign a consent for surgery or even medication but are typically not consulted with regard to physical therapy or vocational training. After trauma, or when there is disfigurement, loss of a limb, or inability to speak, a patient may be depressed or in denial about his or her disability. In these cases, families and health care professionals may feel justified in imposing rehabilitation without consent or even in the face of outright patient refusal. In such cases, traditional medical paternalism has strong appeal, and the justification is often prospective: "We know what's best for you"; "Someday you'll thank us for this." A similar situation exists in addictions treatment facilities and in inpatient psychiatric settings where patients also tend to be infantalized and deprived of basic decision-making rights about their own welfare. Even patients in medical hospitals have experienced this stripping away of autonomy. "Patienthood" of any type is typically not an empowering role.

Legal Rights and Guardianship

This brings us back to the legal aspect of rehabilitation and postinjury care. Dougherty (1991) makes the strong point that providers may be at legal risk in situations where treatment is judged to have been improperly imposed or consent improperly obtained. A patient who is legally competent and yet is not offered a choice about rehabilitation, or whose choice is coerced, may have grounds to sue for battery. A lawsuit might also arise out of a treatment provider's good-faith decision to rely on a family member's proxy consent in the case of presumed patient incompetence if that family member has not been designated by statute or court order to be the legal proxy decision-maker. In either case—and this is probably more terrifying to treatment facilities than even lawsuits—a patient or his insurer might successfully refuse to pay for rehabilitation already received on the grounds that no legally proper consent was given for it (Banja, 1986).

Among other things, the need for treatment decision-making renders the issue of legal guardianship very important. In the case of brain injury, this has been explicitly addressed by Anderson and Feary (1989), who point out that most brain injury patients do not maintain a steady level of cognitive or emotional functioning throughout their rehabilitation course. Unlike most mentally retarded and many mentally ill persons, for whom issues of guardianship more commonly arise, significant improvements in the mental status of the traumatic brain injury patient can occur over a period of months to years, often resulting in a return to competency—if competency had in fact been lost. Unfortunately, the legal institution of guardianship, i.e., the appointment by the court of one individual to make decisions regarding another's person and property, presumes a steady state of incompetency as well as the presence of mental illness or mental retardation.

Typically, the assumption is made that once a person is deemed incompetent and made a ward of the guardian, he or she is likely to remain so, and the burden is upon the ward to bring the case back to court to have the guardianship terminated. Further, guardianships in many states are plenary, i.e., conferring all power over person and property to the guardian and leaving none to the ward; these arrangements are also usually without time limits. Because the guardian will be held legally and morally responsible for any harm resulting from the ward's risk-taking, the guardian has an understandable desire to control the situation—this aside from all the other family control issues discussed in Chapter 4. This is hardly a situation designed to foster the brain-injured patient's growth toward competency and autonomy. Despite even the most well-meaning desire of family and treatment providers to protect the patient from risk, Anderson and Feary (1989) note, the patient can only progress toward independence if he is allowed to take responsibility for making decisions and accept the risks of failure that such responsibility implies.

Anderson and Feary (1989) suggest that a procedure more in keeping with rehabilitation goals would not allow plenary guardianships without a limitation on their duration. Moreover, guardianships would be narrowly tailored to allow the guardian only limited powers that are tied explicitly to proven incompetencies. The guardianship would be effective for 90 days or some other period that the court deems appropriate in light of the patient's projected progress in rehabilitation. Significantly, if the guardianship were about to expire, the burden would be upon the guardian to renew it and not upon the patient, or ward, to have it vacated. To date, the clinical and legal issues of guardianship for brain-injured patients are only beginning to be adequately addressed.

SUPPORT GROUPS

Sometimes the best help is self-help, and the best therapy involves helping others. Support groups fill an important role in the rehabilitation and resocialization of the brain-injured patient, as the number and popularity of such groups attest. I refer all my brain injury patients and their families to appropriate support groups, and I consider support group participation an integral part of brain injury rehabilitation for both patient and clinician.

Research on Brain Injury Support Groups

Whitehouse and Carey (1991) undertook a survey that helps clarify some of the characteristics of individuals who seek out and participate in a brain injury family support group. To begin with, they report that "parents, rather than spouses, tended to continue their participation in the support group for extended periods of time. Nevertheless, previous research [see Chapter 4] suggests that spouses report significantly more distress than parents of persons with head injury" (p. 28). Whitehouse and Carey suggest several possible explanations for this apparent paradox.

"First, spouses may be less well prepared than parents to adjust to and accept a potentially lifelong caregiving role with the injured patient." Inasmuch as going to support groups confirms this caregiver role, such groups may be shunned. "Second, issues of major importance to spouses of brain injury survivors may not lend themselves as readily to being aired in a group context. For example, spouses' concerns regarding intimacy and sexuality . . . may be considered too personal to share with a group. . . . Third, . . . different problems are associated with specific family relationships." I have also observed that conflicts between parents and children are often regarded as more socially acceptable than between husband and wife. A vicious cycle discouraging spouse participation may therefore develop. As Whitehouse and Carey comment, "since parents comprise a significant proportion of the group's membership their concerns may dominate group meetings; by default, spouse concerns may not be adequately addressed or are dealt with too infrequently" (p. 28). So fewer of them come, and they come in less often.

Another, somewhat counterintuitive finding of Whitehouse and Carey's study was that "family members with higher functioning survivors tended to be involved in the support group for longer periods of time. . . . Perhaps the greater mobility of higher functioning survivors and their increased interaction with the community outside the family causes their families to face greater and/or more varied challenges in adapting to the survivor's post-brain injury behavioral repertoire" (p. 29). I have also noted that since patients with greater impairment usually need more intensive and extensive care, families who finally get a night off may want to do anything but go to a support group to hear other people talk about incapacity and caretaking.

In addition, the study found that "when the survivor lives with the family, as opposed to outside the home, family support group attendance also tends to be more sustained. The support group may provide a useful problem-solving forum for particular issues that arise from intensive daily contact with the survivor" (p. 29).

Whitehouse and Carey continue: "The vast majority of group members listed specific aspects of survivor adjustment as being highest in priority among brain injury educational topics to be discussed in regular group meetings. Newer members, however, were more likely to be interested in topics concerned with the cognitive and behavioral changes that the survivor might be expected to exhibit, many of which are quite subtle and understandably perplexing to those new to head injury. In addition, discussion of family adjustment issues was given greater priority by newer members of the group. This may reflect the increased distress of families having recently experienced a traumatic event involving a loved one or the struggle to cope with the additional stressors associated with new responsibilities and role changes in providing for the recovery of a post-acute brain-injured survivor. Presumably, more veteran members of the group have weathered these experiences and have less demanding adjustment needs. . . . Among the topics of greatest interest to newer members of the group was legal information relevant to brain injury. Given the pattern of interests associated with the length of the family's experience with head injury, it would seem that the value of support group participation is increased by encouraging more experienced members to serve as resources for the group.

"Finally, with regard to the preferred format of family support meetings, the survey identified a general preference for increased sharing time. On the other hand, the desire to retain a somewhat structured agenda and the opportunity for educational lectures by professionals in brain injury rehabilitation were also important features of the meetings for many members. Clearly, a brain injury family support group is expected to address a multiplicity of needs. This seems to be best accomplished with a judicious balance of experience-sharing with peer support and education tailored to be responsive to the many concerns of group members" (Whitehouse & Carey, 1991, p. 29). Although this study dealt with a support group for families, most support groups involve the patients themselves as primary participants. In many areas, existing groups will be available for patients to join. However, sometimes the only way to have a support group is to start one. Using sources such as Whitehouse and Carey's (1991) research and my own and others' experiences (Miller, 1992d), the following suggestions are offered.

Functions of a Support Group

Support   This is probably the most obvious function. Just knowing that others have gone through the same experience, that they've endured it, lived through it, surpassed it, can have a powerful effect on the brain injury survivor and no less on caretaking family members. Sharing "war stories," crying and laughing together, and helping each other over the rough spots in recovery are all support functions of this kind of group.

Information   A recurrent theme of this book is that brain injury patients and their families must act as informed consumers in the health care marketplace. Support groups provide a valuable resource for pooling information about treatment options, local doctors and facilities, community support servies, and general advances in the treatment of brain injury and other brain syndromes. In every support group I've been affiliated with, there have invariably been at least one or two members whose courses of recovery were dramatically affected by access to information obtained from other group members — information that had been available nowhere else. In a few cases, lives have been saved or extended.

Advocacy   A local support group can become a force to be reckoned with, both in the community and nationally. Involvement in local government, local sponsorship of national conventions, and other activities give the brain injury patient and his family a sense of having a larger stake in the welfare of the community and of society as a whole.

Support vs. Therapy   Technically, a support group should not be run as a therapy group. The latter is usually conceived as being more intensely challenging to the individual members' defenses with the goal of fostering greater psychodynamic insight into each member's personality functioning and dealings with life. Support groups, by contrast, are more concerned with building up, rather than tearing down, defenses and more focused on here-and-now concerns rather than "deep" issues.

In practice, the distinction between therapy and support becomes blurred as group members may confront one another's maladaptive coping strategies or attempt to break up the logjams of denial or self-pity as only a concerned friend who has actually been through the experience can. Still, the goal is usually to find short-term, practical solutions, rather than to analyze intrapsychic conflicts or dysfunctional interpersonal behavior patterns. This support function should not necessarily be equated with molly-coddling or "there-there" handholding, however, and many support group meetings can get quite hot and heavy as patients and families challenge one another or vigorously disagree on various issues. The role of the facilitator is important here, as will be further discussed below.

**Forming a Support Group:
Some Guidelines**

Assess the Need   Find out how many people in your community would attend the support group on a regular basis, because regular attendance is crucial. Generally, I find that most groups have a core of faithful members who make each and every meeting a priority. But if sufficient interest cannot be sustained, the group will fizzle out.

Put Someone in Charge   A president or other senior member(s) should be elected, or self-appointed if need be. His or her job is to oversee the functions and running of the group. Usually one or two particularly enthusiastic group members will volunteer for this position. This is the person who coordinates many of the steps to be described below, who outreaches new members, keeps membership records, follows up on members who've missed meetings, and usually lends his or her business or home phone number and mailing address to the cause.

Enlist a Facilitator(s)   This is usually a professional who can serve the dual role of question answerer and group session structurer. The facilitator keeps the group on target, prevents it from degenerating into a bull session or coffee klatch, may present minilectures on select topics, answers technical questions, and generally serves as the "resident expert." With larger groups and/or where part of the group is spent in individual subsessions (see below), more than one facilitator may be useful. As the facilitator's role is quite important, be sure to enlist someone who can make the necessary regular time commitment.

Invite Guest Speakers   From time to time, it is useful to have experts in the community volunteer to present information or coordinate discussions on select topics, e.g., medication, special rehab techniques, vocational issues, etc. Volunteer speakers I've enlisted have included pharmacists, rehab counselors, vocational counselors, neurosurgical nurses, and home health care representatives — even some neurologists and neurosurgeons may occasionally be pressed into service to donate one evening to such an extracurricular, nonprofit activity. Many private facilities will be only too glad to send a speaker to plug their hospital or rehab center, and the group member scheduling the presentation should do some preliminary screening to ensure that the topic covered is what the group wants to hear, not just a sales job by the marketing rep. As a rule, these programs should be supplementary to the main functions of the group meetings, otherwise you may end up with a lecture series rather than a support group.

Secure a Location   You can't have a support group meeting without a place to meet. A little local research will usually yield a number of places that will volunteer a room for 90 minutes, once or twice a month. In fact, many rehab facilities or hospitals make a practice of sponsoring support groups and may even supply coffee and other amenities. Often, the facilitator you work with can help track down appropriate meeting places.

Hook Up to Larger Networks   Virtually every major neurologic or other medical disorder has a national organization that serves it. This includes head injury, brain tumor, stroke, epilepsy, multiple sclerosis, Tourette syndrome, Alzheimer's disease, Parkinson's disease, and many others. In addition, most organizations have state and/or regional branch associations you can contact. Don't reinvent the wheel: These larger organizations will usually be quite happy to provide materials and advice you can use in setting up your local support group.

Get the Word Out   This means publicity. At first, word-of-mouth will probably attract the core group of initial members. After a few meetings, when it looks as if the meeting will be a regular event, notices can be sent out to hospitals, doctor's offices, rehab facilities, and so on, describing the group and giving the dates and times. Ads in local newspapers are important, and many papers devote a page or two a week for community events of this sort. Also consider local cable TV "bulletin boards."

If a hospital or rehab center is sponsoring your group, they may offer some of their own marketing skills, mailing lists, and other services to help attract prospective members. They may also lend audiovisual materials, provide speakers, and so on. The only potential drawback of this kind of institutional enmeshment I've encountered is the tendency for some of these places to treat the support groups they sponsor as marketing tools for their facility and to make that their top priority. So at first, you may have to make a decision to forgo a little autonomy as a tradeoff for support. If the institution becomes too intrusive, the members themselves will usually balk and the necessary changes in venue or terms of agreement can be made.

In general, any way you can get the word out will help attract prospective group members. After a while, the name and nature of your group will hopefully saturate itself into the local network and referrals to the group will become regular. What typically happens is that you get a kind of "revolving core group" of members who show up at every meeting, supplemented by a larger population of more sporadic attendees.

Structure of the Meetings

There is no one "right" way to structure a support group meeting; however, certain formats seem to work better than others. The following recommendations have evolved out of my own experiences and the experiences of other support group facilitators.

Assume a 90-minute time framework. The first five or ten minutes is devoted to introductions by each of the members. Where everybody already knows everybody, this is usually limited to reminding one another of names. New members get extra time to tell their story. Patients and caregivers make their own introductions where feasible.

The next 20 or 30 minutes is devoted to information and news, much of the kind described above. Members are encouraged to clip stories from newspapers or health newsletters, to recount relevant TV news shows they've seen or lectures they've attended, and to share accounts of personal experiences with new treatments or new local clinicians or facilities. Questions may be fired off at the facilitator, and a general discussion of the topic usually ensues. Sometimes, the popular media provides material for discussion: The movie, *Regarding Henry* served as the focus of passionate discourse in one support group meeting. Where you schedule a guest speaker, give him or her this time slot: 20 minutes to make the presentation, then another 10 minutes for questions and answers.

The bulk of the meeting then divides the group into separate patient and family support subgroups, where each constituency can express, among their "true" peers, the things that they might never otherwise be able to say in front of their loved one. To encourage sharing and support, the ground rule is: What's said in the room stays in the room. Anger, resentment,

grief, and fear are the main feelings that come welling up in such an emotionally safe environment, and most families and patients are grateful for
the opportunity to ventilate and work through these issues that they may
have been sitting on for years. Note: in choosing a facility for the meetings,
consider having two rooms, or a room with an adequate divider.

The last few minutes of the meeting has the whole group reconvene and
raise any last-minute questions and/or plan the next group agenda. An
informal meet-and-greet then ensues with members and facilitators throng-
ing around the room, while others begin to leave. Any one-on-one questions, individual telephone number exchanging, date-making for extra-
group get-togethers, etc., take place at this final stage. In this regard, an
important function of the group occurs outside the group meetings and
members are encouraged to keep in contact with each other between meetings.

In sum, participation in a properly run support group is one of the
greatest contributions that the neuropsychologically trained mental health
professional can make to brain injury patients and their families. I urge
clinicians to devote some of their time to this important and rewarding
enterprise.

PART VI

Broader Implications

CHAPTER 12

Cognitive Rehabilitation, Cognitive Therapy, and Cognitive Style: Lessons for All Psychotherapy

PRACTICING CLINICIANS sometimes encounter patients whose psychopathologies don't seem to fit traditional psychodynamic models or whose courses of treatment don't seem to follow traditional psychotherapeutic rules. Often, these patients are diagnosed as "atypical" borderline, schizoid, narcissistic or other personality disorders and relegated to "supportive" therapy. At the same time, clinicians treating brain-injured patients are frequently struck by the efforts these supposedly concrete and otherwise cognitively impaired patients make to understand and cope with their altered worlds through the barriers imposed by damage to the brain.

In the rehab clinic, most brain-injured patients participate in some form of *cognitive rehabilitation*: in effect, training the patient to use intact cognitive modalities to compensate for impaired functions. For example, a patient with visuospatial impairment may be taught verbal strategies for learning his way around unfamiliar places, or a memory-impaired patient may be trained to structure activities hierarchically so that each event acts as a cue for the next one. Patients with deficits in judgement and impaired insight into their own behavior present a particular challenge because the very brain systems that coordinate the other cognitive functions — *ego functions* in the parlance of psychoanalytic theory (Hartmann, 1939) — have been impaired.

It is just these ego functions that seem to be deficient in many of the personality-disordered patients who present for psychotherapy. Previously

215

intact ego functions that in one patient have been damaged by injury or disease may have never adequately developed in another patient. The clinical presentations might resemble one another, although the causes differ. But the effective psychotherapeutic approaches used in both cases may involve similar strategies and dynamics. It is this potentially fruitful psychotherapeutic interchange between neurocognition and psychodynamics that this final, somewhat more theoretical, chapter will explore. Specifically, what lessons can the general psychotherapist learn from the treatment of brain-injured patients that are applicable to the larger population of psychotherapy patients?

THE ORGANIC PERSONALITY

As discussed throughout this book, there are many variations of the clinical picture seen after brain injury, depending on the type and location of the lesion, as well as preexisting cognitive and personality traits (see Dimond, 1980; Hecaen & Albert, 1978; Joseph, 1990; Miller, 1990f for comprehensive reviews). However, certain behavioral commonalities are typically found in patients with different kinds of brain damage. Probably one of the best descriptions of the *organic personality* as a unitary, composite, clinical entity comes from the early work of Kurt Goldstein (1952). Goldstein conceived of brain damage as impairing the patient's ability to make the necessary adaptations to his or her world in the service of discharging tensions and satisfying needs—what psychodynamically minded clinicians would call adaptive ego functions (Hartmann, 1939; Pine, 1990).

Thus, some organically impaired patients are unable to tolerate even small changes in environment or routine; others cannot sustain close relationships because this usually involves tolerating some degree of frustration of immediate needs; they may appear overly demanding, clingy, or "childish." Still others can't bear the loss of function caused by the brain damage, such as the ability to express themselves through language, to process information as efficiently as they used to, or to perform tasks they had been accustomed to doing.

Many such patients learn to achieve a kind of fragile equilibrium, wherein their range of activities in different environments is self-constrained to the level that their altered cognitive capacities allow. This often requires nothing less than a redefinition of the self and self-image—difficult enough for, say, a newly physically disabled person with an otherwise intact brain; a colossal undertaking for someone in whom, aside from any other bodily infirmities, his or her cerebral adaptive psychological capacities have been reduced by the injury or illness.

Aside from, or in addition to, focal deficits such as aphasias, aprosodias, apraxias, agnosias, and amnesias, many of the difficulties experienced by the brain-injured patient were ascribed by Goldstein to what he called a *loss of the abstract attitude* (Goldstein & Scheerer, 1941). This is found most often in individuals with focal frontal lobe damage, but also is seen with many other kinds of focal or generalized brain damage — not surprising, Goldstein pointed out, since the frontal lobes constitute about one-third of the human brain volume, so sufficient impact pretty much anywhere in the cranial cavity is bound to affect this area to some degree (see Chapter 1).

It is the abstract attitude, said Goldstein, that enables a person to detach his ego from the outer world or inner experiences; to assume a particular mental set; to account to himself for his own behavior and to verbalize that account; to shift reflectively from one aspect of a situation to another; to hold several aspects of a situation or problem in mind simultaneously; to grasp the essentials of a given whole, to break up a given whole into parts, and to isolate and synthesize those parts; to abstract common properties of a thing reflectively and to form hierarchic concepts; to plan ahead ideationally, to assume an attitude towards the "mere possible," and to think or perform symbolically.

Later, Luria (1973, 1980), in his now-classic studies on the neuropsychology of cognition, outlined the stages ordinarily involved in what we regard as mature, productive thought. First, there must exist a task or problem for which there is no instinctual or automatically habitual solution. Next, there must be some motivation for solving that problem. Further, the person must be able to restrain impulsive responding and be capable of investigating and analyzing the features of the problem. Out of many possible alternative courses of action, the individual must select those few that are judged to be most appropriate, sequence the action correctly, then put the plan into action and, finally, evaluate the results against the original goal.

Other modern neuropsychologists have similarly conceptualized reasoning and problem-solving as the most complex of all intellectual functions, requiring a number of intact emotional and cognitive abilities. These include adequate levels of motivation and attention; the restraining of impulsive tendencies; the ability to organize, categorize, and shift responses; the productive use of feedback to modify behavior; and the capacity to evaluate final performance (Ben-Yishay & Diller, 1983; Goldstein & Levin, 1987).

When the adaptive capacity of the individual breaks down — which may happen frequently in the early stages of recovery from brain injury — the clinician may observe what Goldstein (1952) characterized as the *catastrophic reaction*. Expressions of this behavior may range from the frankly explosive—the patient screams, curses, lashes out, throws things—to more subtle and therefore more easily overlooked manifestations, such as passive withdrawal, regression, hostility to staff or to other patients and family, sullen refusal to cooperate with activities, or failure to participate in self-care.

Over time, said Goldstein (1952), the brain-injured patient begins to develop *protective mechanisms* in order to forestall anxiety, frustration, and the catastrophic reaction. Examples of this include denial of deficit and withdrawal from demanding and frustrating activities. The latter frequently plays havoc with the rehabilitation staff, who may not understand why the patient "doesn't want to get better," little appreciating what a blow to self-esteem and self-image each little failure and struggle entails.

Obsessive-compulsive behavior may develop as the patient tries to achieve maximal control over a delimited aspect of his or her environment. An inability to fully comprehend the requirements of the social milieu may lead to a variety of immature or inappropriate behaviors. The need to discharge tension immediately may be expressed in impulsive, angry, and entitled demands to food, drink, sex, and so on. The concreteness associated with neurocognitive impairment may lead to a coarsening of thought, feelings, and behavior. A frequent report by relatives and other observers is that the patient seems to have "lost his sense of humor." Inasmuch as the all but the grossest, slapstick-type forms of humor depend on some degree of abstraction, generalization, and sensitivity to innuendo, the cognitively concrete brain-injured patient simply doesn't "get" most jokes (see Chapter 2).

More recently, Lewis and Rosenberg (1990), drawing on their experience with traumatic head injury patients, have presented a characterization of the organic personality that comes close to the one purveyed earlier by Goldstein (1952). Brain-injured patients, in this account, must struggle with high levels of anxiety at the same time that their capacity to tolerate painful emotions of any type has been reduced. Heightened affective arousal, coupled with reduced tolerance of affect, is a perfect set-up for the appearance of catastrophic reactions and other maladaptive responses. By virtue of the neurologic dysfunction and resultant cognitive deficits, the patient is less adept at smoothly integrating raw feeling with refined perceptual apprehension and cognitive understanding.

The brain injury has thus created a condition Lewis et al. (1983) call *cortical vulnerability*. These individuals tolerate emotion poorly because the brain injury has deprived them of the capacity to sufficiently titrate and modulate emotion, to make it comprehensible and manageable. This may be exacerbated by a tendency to actively avoid thinking about, or "dwelling on," painful feelings, thereby precluding the development of adaptive coping—an attitude often abetted by well-meaning persons seeking to avoid "upsetting" the patient.

THE PRIMITIVE PERSONALITY

Freud (1915, 1923) originally proposed that the transformation of primitive instinctual impulses into consciously acceptable substitutive drive-derivatives involves the utilization of cognitive processes such as symbolization and language. The purpose of thinking, said Freud, is to permit the ego to achieve a delay of motor discharge, to serve as a kind of "experimental action," which allows for the exploration of behavioral alternatives with far less effort and painful consequence than would be required for the real-world testing of these different options.

But especially in his later writings, Freud chose to focus on the role of instinct in personality developmental, deemphasizing the cognitive model-building he had begun in his earlier work (see Miller, 1991f for a comprehensive account). It fell to the ego-psychologists, exemplified by Hartmann (1939), to stress the importance of what they regarded as constitutionally given mental endowments and apparatuses for psychological development—such faculties as memory, perception, attention, and intelligence. According to Hartmann, these basic human cognitive apparatuses constitute a core of adaptive psychological functioning that is relatively independent of instinctual conflict, what he called the *conflict-free ego sphere*. These cognitive apparatuses also influence the form of, or preference for, different ways of handling conflict—that is, they are the prerequisites for, and the underpinnings of, defense.

Hartmann (1939) proposed that evolution leads to increasing independence of the organism from its environment so that reactions that originally occurred in relation to the external world are progressively displaced to the interior of the organism, that is, to a mental domain. In order to achieve a certain adaptation to, and mastery of, the world, a person need not test every possible response and observe every possible reaction. Rather, he or she can think about consequences, anticipate outcomes, and create contingency plans of alternative means-end possibilities, which Hartmann collectively described as the process of *internalization*. Accordingly, Hartmann spoke of *ego autonomy* as involving the relative freedom of the ego or self from blind obedience to instinctual emotional and motivational demands, as well as from a dependency on immediate environmental reinforcement for each action and plan.

The term *cognitive style* was introduced by Klein (1954, 1958) to refer to the arrangement of general regulatory or control structures in each person's psyche. These cognitive controls, Klein argued, may have a basis in the types of constitutional givens suggested by Hartmann (1939) and may contribute to the direction that personality development follows. For example, a highly verbal or rational person might express his particular neurosis by endless talking, writing, or analyzing, while someone with a more emotional and imagistic cognitive style might more impulsively, graphically, even creatively, express his or her inner conflicts. In this conceptualization, cognition is as much a shaper of personality as is passion.

Gardner et al. (1959) assessed the psychodynamic profiles of a group of patients, using such standard projective tests as the Rorschach, and compared the results with the subjects' performance on a large battery of cognitive tests measuring concentration, memory, conceptualization, speed of mental processing, and so on—what today we would probably call "neuropsychological" tests. Based on their results, the investigators delineated what they termed the *cognitive control principles* that underlie certain personality types. For example, some people's style of thinking involves a leveling-out of memories and experiences, others a sharpening of focus on what they perceive and remember. Some people can pick out the relevant features of a task and perform with great accuracy, albeit at a relatively slow and deliberate pace; others zip through the task, but make many clumsy errors. Some tend to see the similarities among things, others are more sensitive to differences. Some can use the power of logical analysis flexibly to deal with unexpected changes in form or routine; others get stuck in a rut or try to twist the situation in the direction of their own preconceptions.

These types of cognitive style characteristics were found to be associated with different patterns of psychodynamic defense. Congealing memories and perceptions together in an undifferentiated melange sets the stage for repression: It is difficult to recall any particular piece of information if it was processed only hazily to begin with and has subsequently become mixed up with other material. On the other hand, rationalization—the defensive tendency to find logical, acceptable "reasons" for things—is abetted by a more focused and concentrated cognitive style that teases out unessential details and makes those the subject of obsessive preoccupation, while ignoring the important overall context.

Shapiro (1965) used the term "style" in his conceptualization of *neurotic styles*: characteristic neurotic modes of functioning that are built around each person's characterological pattern or style of perception, thought, and action. According to this view, symptoms or prominent pathological personality traits regularly appear in the context of attitudes, interests, intellectual inclinations and endowments, and even vocational aptitudes and social affinities with which the given symptom or trait seems to have a certain consistency. Thus, neurosis is not simply the result of instinctually driven, intrapsychic conflict superimposed on a tabula rasa personality. Rather, the form that the neurotic expression of conflict takes is strongly determined by how that person perceives the world, thinks about it, reacts emotionally to it, and behaves in it—that is, by how his or her own set of constitutional cognitive traits is arrayed in the psyche. Shapiro identified four main neurotic styles, the obsessive-compulsive, the paranoid, the hysterical, and the impulsive.

More recently, Shapiro (1989) has asserted that the neurotic person is "estranged from himself" to the extent that his maladaptive or neurotic cognitive style contributes to the obfuscation of his own motivations and interpretations of external reality. The sense of self as an autonomous actor, rather than *re*actor, is vitiated, and a consequence of this neurotic self-estrangement is a reversion to an egocentric reactiveness. When one does not recognize the existence of one's own interest in a figure or situation, the polarity, or distance, between oneself and that figure or situation is impaired. That figure or situation is no longer an object of consideration, but a trigger of immediate egocentric reaction.

In these circumstances—reminiscent of Goldstein's descriptions of the concreteness and catastrophic reaction of brain-injured patients—the personality reacts quasi-reflexively to dispel or forestall anxiety, prompted by the incipient psychical discomfort produced by sensations or awareness of the self that threaten the all-too brittle and fragile stability of the personality structure. Hence, there is also, more or less continuously, a degree of distortion of self-awareness producing the characteristic self-deception associated with the neurotic personality. To preserve psychological stability, the person reflexively shakes off painful thoughts and feelings like a bronco throwing its rider.

Robbins (1989) has provided a conceptualization of the *primitive personality*, under which he subsumes the borderline, narcissistic, paranoid, and schizoid personality types. Other writers have also included the impulsive and hysterical personalities in this category (Begun, 1976; Masterson, 1988; Millon, 1981, 1990; Shapiro, 1965). The key feature of primitive personalities is the fundamentally compromised, often self-destructive, existences these individuals characteristically lead.

Robbins (1989) delineates three basic clinical characteristics of primitive personalities. The first is described as an *absence of personality integration*. Primitive personalities are dominated by self-contradictory thinking, at one moment gripped by emotionally extreme ideas and positions, which stand in contrast to equally extreme, but opposite, ideas the patient has held at other times. The second characteristic is *sensorimotor-affective thinking*, a form of cognition and emotion which is undifferentiated from raw perception and nonreflective action. Like infants—or, we may add, organic patients—primitive personalities tend to be immersed in their immediate interpersonal surroundings. They misconstrue their cognitive-affective conceptualizations of others, and experience strong urges to impulsively act toward these persons in a possessive, controlling, destructive, or distancing manner. Finally, primitive personalities suffer from an *inability to identify and sustain core emotions*. They are unable to recognize and own feelings, longings, and impulses more than transiently, or to institute appropriate behavioral adaptations. The inability to form and sustain affect-representations leads them to emote with little restraint or control.

And frequently they rage. Rage as the predominant emotional response, according to Robbins (1989), stems from two factors: first, an enactment of sensorimotor-affective thinking in lieu of stable mental representation and reflective awareness; and second, lack of integration with other, more stable segments of the personality. Thus, the primitive personality is strikingly deficient in the capacity to experience and express anger appropriately. Similarly, the fragile support structure of the personality permits little breadth of emotional experience, and many clinicians have commented on the humorlessness, the fundamental cheerlessness, of primitive personalities. An appreciation of humorous irony requires some capacity for cognitive-affective detachment, a quality that is noticeably lacking in many impulsive, narcissistic, or borderline individuals—as it is in many organic patients.

These fundamental trait characteristics of primitive personalities are, according to Robbins (1989), responsible for three derivative characteristics. The first of these is *pathological symbiotic adaptation*, the experience of inconstant and inaccurate interpersonal boundaries that, in some cases, may have a delusional quality. The second characteristic is *global destructiveness to self and others*, which may be overt—such as self-mutilation, suicidal behavior, dissipatory substance abuse, ruined careers, and shattered relationships—or more subtle, emerging only during psychotherapy, when the patient subjects his own and the therapist's thoughts and feelings to ridicule and devaluation. The third derivative characteristic of primitive personalities is an *absence of self- and object-constancy, with chronic disorientation*. This describes the ongoing sense of emotional-existential uneasiness that seems to be the natural mental state of the primitive personality, and that probably stems from his or her lack of self- and object-constancy and unawareness of feelings and needs.

The above considerations explain why, when we see patients with combined personality-neurobehavioral syndromes, the chicken-and-egg issues of which "comes first," the personality disorder or the organic cognitive impairment, frequently becomes difficult to disentangle (see, for example, Chapters 5, 6, and 7). This is because a primitive personality organization may actually predispose the individual to incurring traumatic brain injury, as well as shape the clinical expression of that injury in ways that may be mistakenly attributed to the effect of the brain damage itself.

As discussed in previous chapters, many of the standard neuropsychological and personality profiles after head injury may relate more to premorbid cognitive style than to acquired brain injury effects — recall, for example, the whole issue of "frontal lobe" impairment in traumatic brain injury patients with premorbid antisocial, substance abusing, somatizing, or psychiatric histories. Many of these would certainly fit the description of primitive personalities.

PSYCHOTHERAPY, PERSONALITY, AND COGNITIVE STYLE

Chapters 2 and 3 described the cognitive rehabilitation and psychotherapy approaches most useful in the treatment of brain-injured patients. If the neuropsychodynamic line between organic and primitive personality patients is frequently a fluid one, then the kinds of psychotherapeutic techniques used in the treatment of nonorganic psychotherapy patients may share some fundamental characteristics with the psychotherapeutic principles described for brain-injured patients in this book.

According to Erickson and Burton (1986), the kind of cognitive impairment relevant to overall rehabilitation of psychiatric and other psychotherapy patients seldom consists of the severe, discrete deficits usually associated with focal brain damage, such as aphasias, apraxias, or sensory defects. Rather, they typically represent more general deficiencies in higher-level complex processes such as attention and concentration, learning and memory, psychomotor speed, and problem-solving. Such deficiencies are not only found among brain-injured and chronic psychiatric patients, but may also occur with normal aging, various personality disorders, and substance abuse.

Robbins (1989) points out the difficulty frequently encountered by clinicians in forming a therapeutic working alliance with primitive personalities. This is because such patients characteristically lack the capacity for self- and object-constancy, are unable to sustain a sense of pleasure in relationships, and tend to form pathological symbiotic adaptations in which one party is exploited as the "possession" of the other.

Work with primitive personalities often involves dealing with what some therapists have called *pseudoinsight*, repetitive sequences of apparent insight and understanding, followed by seemingly total forgetting. Interactions that, at the time of their occurrence, may have been viewed as meaningful and relevant seem to vanish from the patient's memory, as if they never took place — similar, as we have noted, to the problems of therapeutic continuity experienced by patients with organic memory disturbances and conceptual deficits. What accounts for these discouraging cycles in the case of primitive personalities, says Robbins (1989), is their characteristic lack of integration, absence of self- or object-constancy, global destructiveness, and inability to represent and sustain affect experiences — again, reminiscent of the problems in adaptation experienced by organic frontal lobe patients.

Many clinicians, including Masterson (1988) and Robbins (1989), have noted the overall refractoriness of primitive personalities to accepting and utilizing interpretations in general. If a patient has no internally experienced emotional referent for the emotions the therapist perceives, and lacks the capacity to hold in mind and contrast the conflictual representations implied by contradiction that the therapist observes, he or she may feel misunderstood or criticized, rather than enlightened by the therapist's interpretive comments — similar to Lewis and Rosenberg's (1990) characterization of psychotherapy as a "burden" to brain-injured patients (see Chapter 3).

Accordingly, Robbins (1989) argues, developmental-ontogenetic interpretations are a particularly futile enterprise, as the past is just not relevant to primitive personalities. Such individuals lack meaningful affective representations of childhood interactions with important figures, and their sensorimotor-affective thinking is oriented toward the present — however misperceived and misinterpreted — and toward action, rather than reflection. For the same reason, they cannot contain and verbalize emotionally meaningful fantasies for analytic introspection, but regularly engage in what is often labeled "acting-out," a maladaptive strategy, as we've seen, also exhibited by many organic patients.

In a similar vein, Shapiro (1965) has described the striking lack of memory consolidation shown by many patients with hysterical cognitive styles, which I (Miller, 1984a, 1986–87, 1990f) have attempted to relate to the neuropsychological differences between episodic and sematic memory processing, and to the attentional-emotional shifts produced by interactions among the brain's reticular formation, limbic system, and the right cerebral hemisphere. Shapiro also notes the characteristic leap-to-action shown by those with impulsive cognitive styles, which, in turn, may have its neuropsychodynamic basis in a deficient use of left-hemisphere inner speech (Vygotsky, 1962) to modulate frontal lobe control over behavior (Joseph, 1982, 1990; Miller, 1987, 1988a, 1988b, 1990a, 1991c).

Thus, in the treatment of the primitive personality, it is necessary to interpret and work through the cognitive and affective deficits before analysis of content or meaning is possible. The foundations of this approach exist in the work of Hartmann (1939) on the adaptive functions of the ego, which has been further explored by Gardner et al. (1959), Klein (1954), and Shapiro (1965) in their researches into cognitive controls, cognitive styles, and personality; this has been the subject of my ongoing project of neuro-psychodynamic reformulation and synthesis (Miller, 1986a, 1988c, 1989a, 1990f, 1991c, 1991f, 1992a).

Robbins (1989) proposes a cognitively oriented psychoanalytic technique to treat primitive personalities, the elements of which may sound familiar from the modalities of psychotherapy and cognitive rehabilitation of brain-injured patients discussed in this book. Robbins' technique requires a process of clarification and interpretation directed more toward these patients' unusual cognitive processes and affective deficits than toward their putative unconscious conflicts and defenses. Such cognitively oriented psychodynamic psychotherapy first addresses the question of *how* the patient constructs meaning from his or her experience, and only secondarily explores *what* that meaning might be. Rather than uncovering conflict, the emphasis of psychotherapy with primitive personalities, says Robbins (1989), should be an educative one—we might say a rehabilitative one. For these individuals, analysis of cognition and affect occupies the central position that analysis of conflict and defense occupies in the treatment of other, more cognitively and dynamically integrated patients.

According to Shapiro (1989), the neurotic patient's problem is not a matter of a specific repressed conflict or memory, but a relatively stable distortion of the personality, a constitutional—or, we might say, "organic"—trait variable. This means that substantial change can be achieved only slowly and probably incompletely. Fundamental to all psychotherapy that relies on self-understanding or insight to achieve its results is the concept of an infringement on the individual's autonomy by his own unconscious wishes, or at least by that which is dissociated from his sense of what he is and what he wants. Accordingly, says Shapiro, the goal of psychotherapy should be to reduce or eliminate the distress and disability that are a consequence of the neurotic person's reaction against himself. Psychotherapy aims, in other words, to reduce self-estrangement, to bring the person into contact with himself—to reclaim a shattered self.

The raising of consciousness of a previously unacknowledged and unarticulated feeling or aim, says Shapiro (1989), allows symptomatic behavior that had been experienced passively to now be incorporated as one's own, as purposeful and active. Pressure is changed to purpose, and the person becomes, at least temporarily, more purposeful, more completely integrated. Knowing what one truly wants increases the deliberateness of action and allows for a fuller contemplation of actions and their goals. The effect of articulating such kinds of subjective experience is that the sense of self is sharpened and, at the same time, the polarity, the reflective distance, between the self and the external object or situation of interest is increased.

In some cases, an external agency, i.e., the therapist, intervenes and initiates what cannot be initiated spontaneously by the patient, namely the articulation that would otherwise be reflexively avoided. The therapist's action frequently meets with discomfort, confusion, objection, or temporizing on the patient's part. But once past these forms of resistance, what has been unassimilable as a vague, unarticulated sensation now increasingly becomes at least partially assimilable as an articulated feeling, aim, or idea. It is not catharsis, says Shapiro (1989), but the articulation of subjective experience, that is the normal therapeutic value of talking—just as it is, we have observed, in the case with many organic patients where verbal psychotherapy plays the role of clarifying internal thoughts and feeling states through the medium of an outside agency, the therapist.

According to Beck et al. (1990), individuals diagnosed as having personality disorders tend to show certain patterns of behavior that are hypertrophied, or overdeveloped, and other patterns that are underdeveloped. The deficient features are frequently the counterparts of the strong features. Similarly, the characteristics of the neurotic personality have generally been described in terms of labels such as "immature" or "childish," i.e., emotional lability, exaggerated responses to rejection or failure, unrealistically low or high concept of self, and intense egocentricity.

Reminiscent of the conceptual and behavioral perseveration and stereotypy seen in patients with organic brain damage, individuals with personality disorders are characterized by Beck et al. (1990) as carrying out the same repetitive behaviors in different kinds of situations. The typical maladaptive schemas in personality disorders are evoked across many or even most circumstances, have a compulsive quality, and are less easy to control or modify than are their counterparts in other people. Any situation that has a bearing on the content of their maladaptive schemas will activate those schemas in preference to more adaptive ones. For the most part, these patterns are self-defeating in terms of these individuals' important goals. In sum, the dysfunctional attitudes and behaviors of patients with personality disorders are overgeneralized, inflexible, imperative, and resistant to change.

Accordingly, say Beck et al. (1990)—coming, as these authors are, from a psychodynamically tinged cognitive therapy framework—the choice of a particular therapeutic option is based on the goals and the conceptualization of the individual case. The first option is called *schematic restructuring*, which involves tearing down the old psychical structures in a stepwise fashion and building new structures in their place. This has traditionally been the goal of psychodynamically oriented therapies.

However, not all dysfunctional schemas can be restructured. Therefore, the second possibility on the change continuum is *schematic modification*. This involves smaller relative changes in the basic manner of responding to the world, such as changing a paranoid personality's relevant schemas regarding trust into less mistrustful and suspicious beliefs, and inducing the patient to provisionally trust some people in some situations and then evaluate the results.

The third possibility is *schematic reinterpretation*. Here, the goal is to help the patient to understand and reinterpret his or her lifestyle and schemas in more functional ways. For example, if a narcissistic person wants to be looked up to and respected, earning a title or promotion at work is one way he or she could meet the desire for status without being driven by compulsive beliefs regarding the value of prestige.

According to Tankle (1988), impulsive patients may sometimes be encouraged to approach more structured and delimited tasks in a slower and more systematic manner. This suggests that the individual has the capability to perform adequately on problem-solving tasks when the impulsiveness is externally controlled by increased structure — just the kind of phenomenon observed in cognitive rehabilitation with brain-injured, especially frontal lobe-damaged, patients. The treatment can then be focused on developing the structure of the individual's daily activities to reduce the impact of the impulsiveness, rather than trying to directly rehabilitate problem-solving ability.

Self-talk is a strategy often used in cognitive rehabilitation with brain-injured patients to foster the transition from externally-directed to self-directed, but not yet sufficiently internalized, behavior. This usually begins with the therapist verbally guiding the patient through activities, and progressively encouraging the patient to do this verbal guiding himself, first overtly, or out loud, and later as a more internal process. More generally, Zastrow's (1988) conceptualization of cognitive therapy asserts that many psychiatric patients' discomforting emotions and ineffective actions primarily arise from self-talk that is negative or irrational. It follows that any therapeutic technique that is successful in changing emotions or actions must facilitate self-talk that is more rational and positive.

Strupp's (1989) view is that therapists should rarely confront or challenge patients. Rather, major attention should be paid to communications that convey understanding of the patient's subjective world, primarily feelings that occur in the present. What is often helpful is for the therapist, at appropriate times, to put into words his or her tentative understanding of a pattern that emerges from within the patient-therapist interaction, and to relate it to what the patient is currently struggling with in his or her daily life, thereby also stimulating the patient's curiosity and collaboration. In short, Strupp suggests that interpretations be given sparingly, and that, as far as possible, they minimize the likelihood of power struggles. Formulations should be parsimonious and stay close to the patient's current understanding and affective experience. There should always be a minimum of inference and speculation, and the emphasis should be on empathic understanding, which includes the patient's collaboration with the therapist.

Similar to Shapiro's (1989) conceptualization of neurotic character — and certainly the case with most kinds of brain injury — *cure*, Strupp (1989) asserts, is a term that should probably be stricken from the therapeutic vocabulary. What can be realistically expected in most cases are: (1) improvements in interpersonal functioning; (2) increases in self-esteem; (3) greater interest in living, energy, and satisfaction; (4) a greater sense of mastery and competence; and (5) significant diminution of the symptoms or problems that brought the patient to therapy.

CONCLUSIONS: CONTINUITY AND DICHOTOMY, UNITY AND DIVERSITY

The kind of therapeutic approach discussed above may turn off many therapists who are annealed to more classically psychodynamic models of personality, psychopathology, and psychotherapy. Although perhaps dichotomizing things a bit too sharply, Guze (1988) discusses two current, popular views of psychotherapy. One of these, the *etiological* view, is based on the premise that the psychotherapeutic process provides a basis for laying bare the complex driving forces responsible for the patient's condition, and that such an approach is the only legitimate way of understanding and treating the disorder. This, of course, is the view of psychotherapy held by classical psychoanalysis and its derivatives. The problem, says Guze, is that since the success of the treatment depends on the validity of the model, if the etiological hypotheses are flawed, the justification for the psychotherapy is undermined.

The second approach to psychotherapy described by Guze (1988) is the *rehabilitative* view, which approaches the patient's disorder without any obligatory assumptions about etiology, although it may involve careful assessment of the patient's psychological functioning. That is, the patient's symptoms, personality, attitudes, emotions, perceptions, strengths, weaknesses, expectations, and relationships are all evaluated, but without assuming any etiological hypothesis concerning the presenting disorder. The aim is to help the patient understand him- or herself better and, with the aid of the therapist, function more effectively, with less discomfort and less disability, even if there occurs little "insight" as to why the patient's problems began or how the patient's personality developed. A clinical analogy would be to physical therapy, or physical rehabilitation, which is indicated for a wide variety of orthopedic, neurologic, and other diseases. This form of treatment is nonspecific in that it does not necessarily deal with putative causal conditions or pathogenetic factors. It takes into consideration age, strength, personality, previous skills, etc., in an attempt to foster recovery or improvement in physical disability, but its practitioners need not accept any particular theory of etiology to account for the syndromes they treat.

Probably, effective psychotherapy combines elements of both the etiological and the rehabilitative approaches, in different proportions for different types of patients and problems. Indeed, as discussed throughout this book, for brain-injured patients there is no clear line where "cognitive rehabilitation" ends and "psychotherapy" begins; each contributes to the other. And even in traditional psychotherapy, teaching the patient to think more clearly is typically either an overt or implicit goal, whether the therapist believes it occurs through direct training or as a side benefit of unsnaggling the knots of psychic conflict.

We may conclude that what psychotherapy with organic patients and those with "functional" disorders of personality share in common is, first, an emphasis on shoring up the fragile ego structure, the sense of self — indeed, the patient's core identity — before trying to explicate and resolve dynamic-conflictual issues. Elsewhere (Miller, 1988c, 1990f, 1991c), I have argued that this sense of integrated identity, or ego-autonomy, is itself built upon the neuropsychodynamic building blocks of thought, feeling, and action. In some cases, the self has been shattered by acquired brain injury; in others, it never fully developed due in part to the vagaries of individual early experience, but also in some measure to neurodevelopmental processes that we are only beginning to understand (Miller, 1990f). In all cases, however, it requires our sharpest clinical and empathic skills to evaluate and treat these challenging patients, and our efforts must respectfully bow to diversity even as we breathlessly pursue unity.

References

Abbot, M. W., & Gregson, R. A. M. (1981). Cognitive dysfunction in the prediction of relapse in alcoholics. *Journal of Studies on Alcohol, 42*, 230–243.

Ackerly, S. S. (1964). A case of paranatal bilateral frontal lobe defect observed for 30 years. In J. M. Warren & K. Akert (Eds.), *The frontal granular cortex and behavior*. New York: McGraw-Hill.

Adamec, R. E., & Stark-Adamec, C. (1983). Limbic kindling and animal behavior: Implications for human psychopathology associated with complex partial seizures. *Biological Psychiatry, 18*, 269–293.

Adams, R. D., & Victor, M. (1977). *Principles of neurology*. New York: McGraw-Hill.

Adler, A. (1945). Mental symptoms following head injury. *Archives of Neurology and Psychiatry, 53*, 34–43.

Allen, J. G., Colson, D. B., & Coyne, L. (1988). Organic brain dysfunction and behavioral dyscontrol in difficult-to-treat psychiatric hospital patients. *Integrative Psychiatry, 6*, 120–130.

Alterman, A. I., & Tarter, R. E. (1985). Relationship between familial alcoholism and head injury. *Journal of Studies on Alcohol, 46*, 256–258.

Alves, E. M., Colohan, A. R. T., O'Leary, T. J., Rimel, R. W., & Jane, J. A. (1986). Understanding post-traumatic symptoms after minor head injury. *Journal of Head Trauma Rehabilitation, 1*, 1–12.

Amaducci, L. A., Fratiglioni, L., & Rocca, W. A. (1986). Risk factors for clinically diagnosed Alzheimer's disease: A case-controlled study of an Italian population. *Neurology, 36*, 922–931.

American Brain Tumor Association (1992). *About the American Brain Tumor Association*. Chicago, IL: Author.

American Psychiatric Association (1987). *Diagnostic and statistical manual of mental disorders* (3rd ed. – rev.). Washington, DC: Author.

Anderson, T. P., & Feary, M. S. (1989). Legal guardianship in traumatic brain injury rehabilitation: Ethical implications. *Journal of Head Trauma Rehabilitation, 4*, 57–64.

Annis, H. M., & Davis, C. S. (1989). Relapse prevention. In R. K. Hester & W. R. Miller (Eds.), *Handbook of alcoholism treatment approaches* (pp. 170–182). New York: Pergamon.

Annis, H. M., Davis, C. S., Graham, M., & Levinson, T. (1987). A controlled trial of relapse prevention procedures based on self-efficacy theory. Unpublished manuscript.

Aurich, L. (1990). The neuropsychologist as expert witness: Stepping into the adversarial arena. *Cognitive Rehabilitation, 8*(3), 22–28.

Bakal, D. A. (1982). *The psychobiology of chronic headache.* New York: Springer.

Balla, J. L., & Moraitis, S. (1970). Knights in armour: A follow-up study of injuries after legal settlement. *Medical Journal of Australia, 2,* 355–361.

Bandura, A. (1982). Self-efficacy mechanism in human agency. *American Psychologist, 37,* 122–147.

Bandura, A. (1986). *Social foundations of thought and action: A social cognitive perspective.* Englewood Cliffs, NJ: Prentice-Hall.

Banja, J. D. (1986). Proxy consent to medical treatment implications for rehabilitation. *Archives of Physical Medicine and Rehabilitation, 67,* 790–792.

Baumeister, R. F. (1991). *Meanings of life.* New York: Guilford.

Beck, A. T., Freeman, A., Pretzer, J., Davis, D. D., Flemming, B., Ottaviani, R., Beck, J., Simon, K. M., Padesky, C., Meyer, J., & Trexler, L. (1990). *Cognitive therapy of personality disorders.* New York: Guilford.

Begun, J. H. (1976). The sociopathic or psychopathic personality. *International Journal of Social Psychiatry, 14,* 965–975.

Bellak, L. (1979). Psychiatric aspects of minimal brain dysfunction in adults: Their ego function assessment. In L. Bellak (Ed.), *Psychiatric aspects of minimal brain dysfunction in adults* (pp. 73–102). New York: Grune & Stratton.

Benedict, R. H. B. (1989). The effectiveness of cognitive remediation strategies for victims of traumatic head injury: A review of the literature. *Clinical Psychology Review, 9,* 605–626.

Benjamin, S. (1989). Psychological treatment of chronic pain: A selective review. *Journal of Psychosomatic Research, 33,* 121–131.

Benjamin, S., Barnes, D., Berger, S., Clarke, I., & Jeacock, J. (1988). The relationship of chronic pain, mental illness, and organic disorder. *Pain, 32,* 185–195.

Bennett, T. L. (1987). Neuropsychological counseling of the adult with minor head injury. *Cognitive Rehabilitation, 5*(1), 10–16.

Bennett, T. L. (1988). Post-traumatic headaches: Subtypes and behavioral treatments. *Cognitive Rehabilitation, 6*(2), 34–39.

Bennett, T. L. (1989). Individual psychotherapy and minor head injury. *Cognitive Rehabilitation, 7*(5), 20–25.

Benson, D. F. (1977). Psychiatric problems in aphasia. In Sarno & Hook (Eds.), *Aphasia: Assessment and treatment.* New York: Masson.

Ben-Yishay, Y., & Diller, L. (1983). Cognitive remediation. In E. A. Griffith, M. Bond, & J. Miller (Eds.), *Rehabilitation of the head injured adult.* Philadelphia: F. A. Davis.

Ben-Yishay, Y., Silver, S., Piasetsky, E., & Rattok, J. (1987). Relationship between employability and vocational outcome after intensive holistic cognitive rehabilitation. *Journal of Head Trauma Rehabilitation, 2,* 35–48.

Bergland, M. M., & Thomas, K. R. (1991). Psychosocial issues following severe head injury in adolescence: Individual and family perceptions. *Rehabilitation Counseling Bulletin, 35,* 5–22.

Berglund, M. (1988). Alcoholics committed to treatment: A prospective long-term study of behavioral characteristics, mortality, and social adjustment. *Alcoholism: Clinical and Experimental Research, 12,* 19–24.

Berglund, M., & Leijonquist, H. (1978). Prediction of cerebral function in alcoholics: A study of health insurance records. *Journal of Studies on Alcohol, 39,* 1968–1974.

Berman, A., & Siegal, A. M. (1976). Adaptive and learning skills in juvenile delinquents: A neuropsychological analysis. *Journal of Learning Disabilities, 9,* 583–590.

Berry, G. C. (1990). The legal system and the expert witness. *Cognitive Rehabilitation, 8*(3), 14–16.

Binder, L. M. (1986). Persisting symptoms after mild head injury: A review of the postconcussive syndrome. *Journal of Clinical and Experimental Neuropsychology, 8,* 323–346.

Binder, L. M. (1992). Deception and malingering. In A. Puente & R. McCaffrey (Eds.),

Handbook of neuropsychological assessment: A biopsychosocial perspective (pp. 353–374). New York: Plenum.

Binder, R. L., Trimble, M. R., & McNiel, D. E. (1991). The course of psychological symptoms after resolution of lawsuits. *American Journal of Psychiatry, 148*, 1073–1075.

Black, P., Jeffries, J., Blumer, D., Wellner, A., & Walker, A. E. (1969). The post-traumatic syndrome in children: Characteristics and incidence. In A. E. Walker, W. F. Caveness, & M. Critchley (Eds.), *The late effects of head injury* (pp. 142–149). Springfield, IL: Charles Thomas.

Blanchard, E. B., Hickling, E. J., & Taylor, A. E. (1991). The psychophysiology of motor vehicle accident related posttraumatic stress disorder. *Biofeedback and Self-Regulation, 16*, 449–458.

Blau, T. H. (1984). *The psychologist as expert witness.* New York: Wiley.

Blau, T. H. (1988). *Psychotherapy tradecraft: The technique and style of doing therapy.* New York: Brunner/Mazel.

Blumer, D., & Benson, D. F. (1975). Personality changes with frontal and temporal lobe lesions. In D. F. Benson & D. Blumer (Eds.), *Psychiatric aspects of neurological disease* (pp. 151–170). New York: Grune & Stratton.

Blumer, D., & Heilbronn, M. (1981). The pain-prone disorder: A clinical and psychological profile. *Psychosomatics, 22*, 395–402.

Bond, M. R. (1984). The psychiatry of closed head injury. In N. Brooks (Ed.), *Closed head injury: Psychological, social, and family aspects* (pp. 148–178). New York: Oxford University Press.

Bond, M. R. (1986). Neurobehavioral sequelae of closed head injury. In I. Grant & K. Adams (Eds.), *Neuropsychological assessment of neuropsychiatric disorders* (pp. 347–373). New York: Oxford University Press.

Borland, B. L. (1979). Minimal brain dysfunction in adults: Evidence from studies of psychiatric illness in the families of hyperactive children. In L. Bellak (Ed.), *Psychiatric aspects of minimal brain dysfunction in adults* (pp. 45–60). New York: Grune & Stratton.

Bowler, R. M., Thaler, C. D., & Becker, C. E. (1986). California Neuropsychological Screening Battery (CNS/BI&II). *Journal of Clinical Psychology, 42*, 946–955.

Brayton, R., Stokes, P., Schwartz, M., & Louria, D. (1970). Effect of alcohol and various diseases on leukocyte mobilization, phagocytosis, and intracellular bacterial killing. *New England Journal of Medicine, 282*, 123–128.

Brismar, B., Engstrom, A., & Ryberg, U. (1983). Head injury and intoxication: A diagnostic and therapeutic dilemma. *Acta Chirurgica Scandinavica, 149*, 11–14.

Brooks, N. (1984). Head injury and the family. In N. Brooks (Ed.), *Closed head injury: Psychological, social, and family aspects* (pp. 123–147). New York: Oxford University Press.

Brooks, N. (1991). The head-injured family. *Journal of Clinical and Experimental Neuropsychology, 13*, 155–188.

Brooks, N., Campsie, L., & Symington, C. (1986). The five-year outcome of severe blunt head injury: A relative's view. *Journal of Neurology, Neurosurgery, and Psychiatry, 49*, 764–770.

Brooks, N., Campsie, L., Symington, C., Beattie, A., & McKinlay, W. (1987). The effects of severe head injury on patients and relatives within seven years of injury. *Journal of Head Trauma Rehabilitation, 2*, 1–13.

Brooks, N., McKinlay, W. W., & Symington, C. (1987). Return to work within the first seven years of severe head injury. *Brain Injury, 1*, 5–19.

Brown, G., Chadwick, O., Shaffer, D., Rutter, M., & Traub, M. (1981). A prospective study of children with head injuries: III. Psychiatric sequelae. *Psychological Medicine, 11*, 63–78.

Bryant, E. T., Scott, M. L., Golden, C. J., & Tori, C. D. (1984). Neuropsychological deficits, learning disability, and violent behavior. *Journal of Consulting and Clinical Psychology, 52*, 323–324.

Bucher, J., Smith, E., & Gillespie, C. (1984). Short-term group therapy for stroke patients in a rehabilitative centre. *British Journal of Medical Psychology, 57*, 283–290.

Burke, W. H., & Wesolowski, M. D. (1988). Applied behavior analysis in head injury rehabilitation. *Rehabilitation Nursing, 13*, 186–188.

Burling, T. A., Reilly, P. M., Moltzen, J. O., & Ziff, D. C. (1989). Self-efficacy and relapse among inpatient drug and alcohol abusers: A predictor of outcome. *Journal of Studies on Alcohol, 50*, 354–360.

Buskirk, J. R. (1992). Headlock: Psychotherapy of a patient with multiple neurological and psychiatric problems. *Bulletin of the Menninger Clinic, 56*, 361–378.

Butler, N. R., & Golding, J. (1986). *From birth to five: A study of the health and behavior of Britain's 5-year-olds*. New York: Pergamon.

Cantwell, D. P. (1979). Minimal brain dysfunction in adults: Evidence from studies of psychiatric illness in the families of hyperactive children. In L. Bellak (Ed.), *Psychiatric aspects of minimal brain dysfunction in adults* (pp. 37–44). New York: Grune & Stratton.

Carberry, H. (1983). Psychological methods for helping the angry, resistant, and negative patient. *Cognitive Rehabilitation, 1*(4), 4–5.

Carberry, H., & Burd, B. (1985). The use of psychological theory and content as a media in the cognitive and social training of head-injured patients. *Cognitive Rehabilitation, 3*(4), 8–10.

Carberry, H., & Burd, B. (1986). Individual psychotherapy with the brain-injured adult. *Cognitive Rehabilitation, 4*, 22–24.

Cartlidge, N. E. F., & Shaw, D. A. (1981). Head injury. *Major Problems in Neurology, 10*, 1–5.

Casson, I. R., Siegel, O., Sham, R., Campbell, E. A., Tarlau, M., & DiDomenico, A. (1984). Brain damage in modern boxers. *Journal of the American Medical Association, 251*, 2663–2667.

Chandra, V., Kokmen, E., Schoenberg, B. S., & Beard, M. P. H. (1989). Head trauma with loss of consciousness as a risk factor for Alzheimer's disease. *Neurology, 39*, 1576–1578.

Chandra, V., Philipose, V., Bell, P. A., Lazaroff, A., & Schoenberg, B. S. (1987). Case-control study of late-onset "probably Alzheimer's disease." *Neurology, 37*, 1295–1300.

Chastian, R. L., Lehman, W. E. K., & Joe, G. W. (1986). Estimated intelligence and long-term outcomes of opioid addicts. *American Journal of Drug and Alcohol Abuse, 12*, 331–340.

Cicerone, K. D. (1989). Psychotherapeutic interventions with traumatically brain-injured patients. *Rehabilitation Psychology, 34*, 105–114.

Cicerone, K. D., & Tupper, D. E. (1991). Neuropsychological rehabilitation: Treatment of errors in everyday functioning. In D. E. Tupper & K. D. Cicerone (Eds.), *The neuropsychology of everyday life: Issues in development and rehabilitation* (pp. 271–292). Boston: Kluwer.

Clark, M., Hager, M., & Witherspoon, D. H. (1985). Living with strokes: The prospects of coping have improved dramatically. *Newsweek, 83*, 86.

Clarke, J. C., & Saunders, J. B. (1988). *Alcoholism and problem drinking: Theories and treatment*. New York: Pergamon.

Cleckley, H. (1976). *The mask of sanity* (5th ed.). St. Louis, MO: Mosby.

Cloninger, C. R. (1987). Neurogenetic adaptive mechanisms in alcoholism. *Science, 236*, 410–416.

Cloninger, C. R., Christiansen, K. O., Reich, T., & Gottesman, I. I. (1978). Implications of sex differences in prevalences of antisocial personality, alcoholism, and criminality for familial transmission. *Archives of General Psychiatry, 35*, 941–951.

Coen, S. J., & Sarno, J. E. (1989). Psychosomatic avoidance of conflict in back pain. *Journal of the American Academy of Psychoanalysis, 17*, 359–376.

Corsellis, J. A. N. (1978). Posttraumatic dementia. In R. D. Katzman & K. L. Terry (Eds.), *Alzheimer's disease: Senile dementia and related disorders*. New York: Raven.

Craig, R. J. (1982). Personality characteristics of heroin addicts: Empirical research 1976–1979. *International Journal of the Addictions, 17*, 227–248.

Craig, R. J., Olson, R., & Shalton, G. (1990). Improvement in psychological functioning among drug abusers: Inpatient treatment compared to outpatient methadone maintenance. *Journal of Substance Abuse Treatment, 7*, 11–19.

Crook, J., Tunks, E., Rideout, E., & Browne, G. (1986). Epidemiologic comparison of persistent pain sufferers in a specialty pain clinic and in the community. *Archives of Physical Medicine and Rehabilitation, 67*, 451–455.

Cullum, C. M., & Bigler, E. D. (1986). Ventricle size, cortical atrophy, and the relationship with neuropsychological status in closed head injury: A quantitative analysis. *Journal of Clinical and Experimental Neuropsychology, 8*, 437–452.

Cullum, C. M., Heaton, R. K., & Grant, I. (1991). Psychogenic factors influencing neuropsychological performance: Somatoform disorders, factitious disorders, and malingering. In H. O. Doerr & A. S. Carlin (Eds.), *Forensic neuropsychology: Legal and scientific cases* (pp. 141–171). New York: Guilford.

Dalby, P. R., & Obrzut, J. E. (1991). Epidemiologic characteristics and sequelae of closed head-injured children and adolescents: A review. *Developmental Neuropsychology, 7*, 35–68.

Davidoff, D. A., Kessler, H. R., Laibstain, D. F., & Mark, V. R. (1988). Neurobehavioral sequelae of minor head injury: A consideration of plot-concussive syndrome versus post-traumatic stress disorder. *Cognitive Rehabilitation, 6*(2), 8–13.

Davis, D. L., & Boster, L. (1988). Multifaceted therapeutic interventions with the violent psychiatric inpatient. *Hospital and Community Psychiatry, 39*, 867–869.

Deitz, J. (1992). Self-psychological approach to posttraumatic stress disorder: Neurobiological aspects of transmuting internalization. *Journal of the American Academy of Psychoanalysis, 20*, 277–293.

Delapaine, R., Ifabamuyi, O. L., Merskey, H., & Zarfas, J. (1978). Significance of pain in psychiatric hospital patients. *Pain, 4*, 361–366.

Denker, P. G., & Perry, G. F. (1954). Postconcussion syndrome in compensation and litigation. *Neurology, 4*, 912–918.

Dimond, S. J. (1980). *Neuropsychology: A textbook of systems and psychological functions of the human brain*. London: Butterworths.

Doerr, H. O., & Carlin, A. S. (Eds.) (1991). *Forensic neuropsychology: Legal and scientific cases*. New York: Guilford.

Donders, J. (1992). Premorbid behavioral and psychosocial adjustment of children with traumatic brain injury. *Journal of Abnormal Child Psychology, 20*, 233–246.

Donovan, D. M., Kivlahan, D. R., & Walker, R. D. (1984). Clinical limitations of neuropsychological testing in predicting treatment outcome among alcoholics. *Alcoholism: Clinical and Experimental Research, 8*, 470–475.

Donovan, D. M., Marlatt, G. A., & Salzberg, P. M. (1983). Drinking behavior, personality factors, and high-risk driving: A review and theoretical formulation. *Journal of Studies on Alcohol, 44*, 395–428.

Dorsel, T. N. (1989). Chronic pain behavior pattern: A simple theoretical framework for healthcare providers. *Psychological Reports, 65*, 783–786.

Dougherty, C. J. (1991). Values in rehabilitation: Happiness, freedom, and fairness. *Journal of Rehabilitation*, January/February/March, 7–12.

Drew, R. H., Templer, D. I., & Schuyler, B. A. (1986). Neuropsychological deficits in active licensed professional boxers. *Journal of Clinical Psychology, 42*, 520–525.

Dywan, J., Kaplan, R. D., & Pirozzolo, F. J. (Eds.) (1991). *Neuropsychology and the law*. New York: Springer-Verlag.

Eames, P. (1988). Behavior disorders after severe head injury: Their nature and causes and strategies for management. *Journal of Head Trauma Rehabilitation, 3*, 1–6.

Edna, T. (1982). Alcohol influence and head injury. *Acta Chirurgica Scandinavica, 148*, 209–212.

Edwards, G. (1986). The alcohol dependence syndrome: A concept as stimulus to inquiry. *British Journal of Addiction, 81*, 171–183.

Edwards, G., Arif, A., & Hodgeson, R. (1981). Nomenclature and classification of drug and alcohol related problems. *Bulletin of the World Health Organization, 59*, 225–242.

Elliott, F. A. (1982). Neurological findings in adult minimal brain dysfunction and the dyscontrol syndrome. *Journal of Nervous and Mental Disease, 170*, 680–687.

Elliott, F. A. (1984). The episodic dyscontrol syndrome and aggression. *Neurologic Clinics of North America, 2*, 113–125.

Elmer, O., Gustafsson, L. C., Goransson, G., & Thomson, D. (1983). Acute alcohol intoxication and traumatic shock: An experimental study on circulating nonaggregates and survival. *European Surgical Research, 15*, 268-275.

Elmer, O., & Lim, R. (1985). Influence of acute alcohol intoxication on the outcome of severe nonneurologic trauma. *Acta Chirurgica Scandinavica, 151*, 305-308.

Encel, S., & Johnson, C. E. (1978). *Compensation and Rehabilitation.* Kensington: New South Wales University Press.

Erickson, R., & Burton, M. (1986). Working with psychiatric patients with cognitive deficits. *Cognitive Rehabilitation, 4*(4), 26-31.

Eslinger, P. J., & Damasio, A. R. (1985). Severe disturbance of higher cognition after bilateral frontal lobe ablation: Patient EVR. *Neurology, 35*, 1731-1741.

Fahy, T. J., Irving, M. H., & Millac, P. (1967). Severe head injuries: A six-year followup. *Lancet, ii*, 475-479.

Fantie, B. D., & Kolb, B. (1991). The problems of prognosis. In J. Dywan, R. D. Kaplan, & F. J. Pirozzolo (Eds.), *Neuropsychology and the law* (pp. 186-238). New York: Springer-Verlag.

Field, J. H. (1976). *Epidemiology of head injuries in England and Wales.* London: HMSO.

Filley, C. M., Cranberg, M. D., Alexander, M. P., & Hart, E. J. (1987). Neurobehavioral outcome after closed head injury in childhood and adolescence. *Archives of Neurology, 44*, 194-198.

Finkle, B. (1982). Alcohol and traffic safety. *American Journal of Forensic Medical Pathology, 3*, 273-276.

Fishbain, D., Goldberg, M., Meagher, B. R., Steele, R., & Rosomoff, H. (1986). Male and female chronic pain patients categorized by DMS-III psychiatric criteria. *Pain, 26*, 181-197.

Fisher, C. M. (1966). Concussion amnesia. *Neurology, 16*, 826-830.

Fisher, C. M. (1982). Whiplash amnesia. *Neurology, 32*, 667-668.

Flor-Henry, P. (1983). Neuropsychological studies in patients with psychiatric disorders. In K. M. Heilman & P. Satz (Eds.), *Neuropsychology of human emotion* (pp. 193-220). New York: Guilford.

Fordyce, W. E., Fowler, R. S., Lehman, J. F., Delateur, B. J., Sand, P. L., & Trieschmann, R. B. (1973). Operant conditioning in the treatment of chronic pain. *Archives of Physical Medicine and Rehabilitation, 54*, 399-408.

Fordyce, W. E., Roberts, A. H., & Sternbach, R. A. (1985). The behavioral management of chronic pain: A response to critics. *Pain, 22*, 113-125.

Forrest, D. V. (1987). Psychosocial treatment in neuropsychiatry. In R. E. Hales & S. C. Yudofsky (Eds.), *American Psychiatric Press textbook of neuropsychiatry* (pp. 387-409). Washington, DC: American Psychiatric Press.

Franceschi, M., Truci, G., Comi, G., Lozza, L., Marchettini, P., Galardi, G., & Smirne, S. (1984). Cognitive deficits and their relationship to other neurological complications in chronic alcoholic patients. *Journal of Neurology, Neurosurgery, and Psychiatry, 47*, 1134-1137.

Freud, S. (1915/1957). The unconscious. In J. Strachey (Trans. & Ed.), *The standard edition of the complete psychological works of Sigmund Freud* (Vol. 14, pp. 161-215). New York: W. W. Norton.

Freud, S. (1923/1957). The ego and the id. In J. Strachey (Trans. & Ed.), *The standard edition of the complete psychological works of Sigmund Freud* (Vol. 19, pp. 12-60). New York: W. W. Norton.

Friedman, W. A. (1983). *Head injuries.* Summit, NJ: CIBA.

Fry, W. F., & Salameh, W. A. (Eds.) (1987). *Handbook of humor and psychotherapy: Advances in the clinical use of humor.* Sarasota, FL: Professional Resource Exchange.

Funch, D. P., & Gale, E. N. (1986). Predicting treatment completion in a behavioral therapy program for chronic temporomandibular pain. *Journal of Psychosomatic Research, 30*, 57-62.

Galasko, C. S. B., & Edwards, D. H. (1974). The causes of injuries requiring admission to hospital in the 1970s. *Injury, 6*, 107-112.

Galbraith, S., Murray, W. R., Patel, A. R., & Knill-Jones, R. (1976). The relationship between alcohol and head injury and its effects on the conscious level. *British Journal of Surgery, 63*, 128–130.

Gallagher, E. B. (1976). Lines of extension and reconstruction in the Parsonian sociology of illness. *Social Science and Medicine, 10*, 207–218.

Gardner, R. W., Holzman, P. S., Klein, G. S., Linton, H. B., & Spence, D. P. (1959). Cognitive control: A study of individual consistencies in cognitive behavior. *Psychological Issues, 1*, 1–185.

Gennarelli, T. (1986). Mechanisms and pathophysiology of cerebral concussion. *Journal of Head Trauma Rehabilitation, 1*, 23–29.

George, W. H. (1989). Marlatt & Gordon's relapse prevention model: A cognitive-behavioral approach to understanding and preventing relapse. *Journal of Chemical Dependency Treatment, 2*, 125–152.

Gill, T., Calev, A., Greenberg, D., Kugelmass, S., & Lerer, B. (1990). Cognitive functioning in post-traumatic stress disorder. *Journal of Traumatic Stress, 3*, 29–45.

Golden, C. J. (1986). Forensic neuropsychology: Introduction and overview. In C. J. Golden & M. A. Strider (Eds.), *Forensic neuropsychology* (pp. 1–47). New York: Plenum.

Golden, C. J., & Strider, M. A. (Eds.) (1986). *Forensic neuropsychology.* New York: Plenum.

Goldstein, F. C., & Levin, H. S. (1987). Disorders of reasoning and problem-solving ability. In M. Meier, A. Benton, & L. Diller (Eds.), *Neuropsychological rehabilitation.* New York: Guilford.

Goldstein, K. (1952). The effect of brain damage on the personality. *Psychiatry, 15*, 245–260.

Goldstein, K., & Scheerer, M. (1941). Abstract and concrete behavior: An experiential study with special tests. *Psychological Monographs, 43*, 1–151.

Goodwin, D. W. (1979). Alcoholism and heredity: A review and hypothesis. *Archives of General Psychiatry, 36*, 57–61.

Gordon, S. M., Kennedy, B. P., & McPeake, J. D. (1988). Neuropsychologically impaired alcoholics: Assessment, treatment considerations, and rehabilitation. *Journal of Substance Abuse Treatment, 5*, 99–104.

Gorenstein, E. E. (1982). Frontal lobe function in psychopaths. *Journal of Abnormal Psychology, 91*, 368–379.

Gotten, N. (1956). Survey of one hundred cases of whiplash injury after settlement of litigation. *Journal of the American Medical Association, 162*, 865–867.

Gouvier, W. D., Cubic, B., Jones, G., Brantly, P., & Cutlip, Q. (1992). Postconcussion symptoms and daily stress in normal and head-injured college populations. *Archives of Clinical Neuropsychology, 7*, 193–211.

Grande, T. P., Wolf, A. W., Schubert, D. S. P., Patterson, M. B., & Brocco, K. (1984). Associations among alcoholism, drug abuse, and antisocial personality: A review of the literature. *Psychological Reports, 55*, 455–474.

Grant, I., Adams, K. M., & Reed, R. (1984). Aging, abstinence, and medical risk factors in the prediction of neuropsychologic deficit among long-term alcoholics. *Archives of General Psychiatry, 41*, 710–718.

Grattan, L. M., & Eslinger, P. J. (1989). Higher cognition and social behavior: Changes in cognitive flexibility and empathy after cerebral lesions. *Neuropsychology, 3*, 175–185.

Grattan, L. M., & Eslinger, P. J. (1991). Frontal lobe damage in children and adults: A comparative review. *Developmental Neuropsychology, 7*, 283–326.

Greenblatt, S. H. (1973). Posttraumatic transient cerebral blindness. *Journal of the American Medical Association, 225*, 1073–1076.

Greer, B. G. (1986). Substance abuse among people with disabilities: A problem of too much accessibility. *Journal of Rehabilitation*, January/February, 34–38.

Greer, B. G., Roberts, R., May, G., & Jenkins, W. M. (1988). Identification of substance abuse in a vocational evaluation setting. *Journal of Rehabilitation*, July/August/September, 27–30.

Gregson, R. A. M., & Taylor, G. M. (1977). Prediction of relapse in men alcoholics. *Journal of Studies on Alcohol, 38*, 1749–1760.

Grubb, R. L., & Coxe, W. S. (1978). Central nervous system trauma: Cranial. In S. G.

Eliasson, A. L. Prensky, & W. B. Hardin (Eds.), *Neurological pathophysiology* (pp. 329–347). New York: Oxford University Press.

Guttman, E. (1946). Late effects of closed head injuries; Psychiatric observations. *Journal of Mental Science, 92*, 1–18.

Guze, S. B. (1988). Psychotherapy and the etiology of psychiatric disorders. *Psychiatric Developments, 3*, 183–193.

Haas, D. C., & Sovner, R. D. (1969). Migraine attacks triggered by mild head trauma and their relation to certain posttraumatic disorders of childhood. *Journal of Neurology, Neurosurgery, and Psychiatry, 32*, 548–554.

Hanson, R. W., & Gerber, K. E. (1990). *Coping with chronic pain: A guide to patient self-management*. New York: Guilford.

Harder, D. W., Strauss, J. S., Greenwald, D. F., Kokes, R. F., Rotzler, B. A., & Gift, T. E. (1990). Predictors of outcome among adult psychiatric first-admissions. *Journal of Clinical Psychology, 46*, 119–128.

Harrell, M., Parente, F., Bellingrath, E. G., & Lisicia, K. A. (1992). *Cognitive rehabilitation of memory*. Gaithersburg, MD: Aspen.

Hartlage, L. C. (1991). Major legal implications of minor head injuries. *Journal of Head Injury, 2*(3), 8–11.

Hartmann, H. (1939/1958). *Ego psychology and the problem of adaptation*. New York: International Universities Press.

Heath, D. H., & Heath, H. E. (1991). *Fulfilling lives: Paths to maturity and success*. San Francisco: Jossey-Bass.

Heather, N., Rollnick, S., & Winston, M. (1983). A comparison of objective and subjective measures of alcohol dependence as predictors of relapse following treatment. *British Journal of Clinical Psychology, 22*, 11–17.

Hecaen, H., & Albert, M. L. (1978). *Human neuropsychology*. New York: Wiley.

Heilman, K. M., Bowers, D., Valenstein, E., & Watson, R. T. (1986). The right hemisphere: Neuropsychological functions. *Journal of Neurosurgery, 64*, 693–704.

Heilman, K. M., & Valenstein, E. (Eds.) (1985). *Clinical neuropsychology* (2nd ed.). New York: Oxford University Press.

Hendler, N. (1982). The anatomy and psychopharmacology of chronic pain. *Journal of Clinical Psychiatry, 43*, 15–20.

Hesselbrock, M. N., Meyer, R. E., & Keener, J. J. (1985). Psychopathology in hospitalized alcoholics. *Archives of General Psychiatry, 42*, 1050–1055.

Heyman, A., Wilkinson, W. E., Stafford, J. A., Helms, M. J., Sigmon, A. H., & Weinberg, T. (1984). Alzheimer's disease: A study of epidemiological aspects. *Annals of Neurology, 15*, 335–341.

Hillbom, M., & Holm, L. (1986). Contribution of traumatic head injury to neuropsychological deficits in alcoholism. *Journal of Neurology, Neurosurgery, and Psychiatry, 49*, 1348–1353.

Hodgeson, R., Stockwell, T., Rankin, H., & Edwards, G. (1978). Alcohol dependence: The concept, its utility, and measurement. *British Journal of Addiction, 73*, 339–342.

Hogan, R. T. (1988). Behavior management for community reintegration. *Journal of Head Trauma Rehabilitation, 3*, 62–71.

Hohl, M. (1974). Soft-tissue injuries of the neck in automobile accidents. *Journal of Bone and Joint Surgery, 56A*, 1575–1682.

Horowitz, M. J. (1986). *Stress response syndromes* (2nd ed.). Northvale, NJ: Jason Aronson.

House, A., Dennis, M., Mogridge, L., Hawton, K., & Warlow, C. (1990). Life events and difficulties preceding stroke. *Journal of Neurology, Neurosurgery, and Psychiatry, 53*, 1024–1028.

Huessy, H. R., Cohen, S. M., Blair, C. L., & Rood, P. (1979). Clinical explorations in adult minimal brain dysfunction. In L. Bellak (Ed.), *Psychiatric aspects of minimal brain dysfunction in adults* (pp. 19–36). New York: Grune & Stratton.

Hughes, A. M., Medley, I., Turner, G. N., & Bond, M. R. (1987). Psychogenic pain: A study in marital adjustment. *Acta Psychiatrica Scandinavica, 75*, 166–170.

Jacobson, S. A. (1969). Mechanisms of the sequelae of minor craniocervical trauma. In A. E. Walker, W. F. Caveness, & M. Critchley (Eds.), *The late effects of head injury* (pp. 35–45). Springfield, IL: Charles Thomas.

Jamieson, K. G. (1971). Prevention of head injury. In *Head injuries: Proceedings of an international symposium* (pp. 12–15). Edinburgh, Scotland: Churchill Livingstone.

Jamieson, K. G., & Kelly, D. (1973). Crash helmets reduce head injuries. *Medical Journal of Australia, ii,* 806.

Jenkins, A., Teasdale, G., Hadley, M. D. M., MacPherson, P., & Rowan, J. O. (1986). Brain lesions detected by magnetic resonance imaging in mild and severe head injuries. *Lancet, 2,* 445–446.

Jernigan, D. H. (1991). Alcohol and head trauma: Strategies for prevention. *Journal of Head Trauma Rehabilitation, 6,* 48–59.

Jeste, D. V., Lohr, J. B., & Goodwin, F. K. (1988). Neuroanatomical studies of major affective disorders: A review and suggestions for further research. *British Journal of Psychiatry, 153,* 444–459.

Johnson, P., Armor, D., Polich, S., & Stambol, H. (1977). *US adult drinking practices: Time, trends, social correlates, and sex roles.* Santa Monica, CA: Rand Corp.

Johnson, W., Stokes, P., & Kaye, D. (1969). The effect of intravenous ethanol on the bactericidal activity of human serum. *Yale Journal of Biology and Medicine, 42,* 71–85.

Joseph, R. (1982). The neuropsychology of development: Hemispheric laterality, limbic language, and the origin of thought. *Journal of Clinical Psychology, 38,* 4–33.

Joseph, R. (1990). *Neuropsychology, neuropsychiatry, and behavioral neurology.* New York: Plenum.

Kahn, E. M. (1992). Imaging of brain electrophysiologic activity: Applications in psychiatry. *General Hospital Psychiatry, 14,* 99–106.

Kaiser, J., & Brown, J. (1988). The ethical dilemmas in private rehabilitation. *Journal of Rehabilitation,* October/November/December, 27–32.

Kay, T., & Silver, S. M. (1988). The contribution of the neuropsychological evaluation to the vocational rehabilitation of the head-injured adult. *Journal of Head Trauma Rehabilitation, 3,* 65–76.

Keefe, F. J., & Williams, D. A. (1989). New directions in pain assessment and treatment. *Clinical Psychology Review, 9,* 549–568.

Kellner, R. (1986). *Somatization and hypochondriasis.* New York: Praeger.

Kelly, J. P., Nichols, J. S., Filley, C. M., Lillehei, K. O., Rubenstein, D., & Kleinschmidt-DeMasters, B. K. (1991). Concussion in sports: Guidelines for the prevention of catastrophic outcome. *Journal of the American Medical Association, 266,* 2867–2869.

Kelly, R. (1975). The posttraumatic syndrome: An iatrogenic disease. *Forensic Science, 6,* 17–24.

Kerr, T., Kay, D., & Lasman, L. (1971). Characteristics of patients, type of accident, and mortality in a consecutive series of head injuries admitted to a neurosurgical unit. *British Journal of Preventive and Social Medicine, 25,* 179–185.

Klein, G. S. (1954). Need and regulation. In M. R. Jones (Ed.), *Nebraska symposium on motivation.* Lincoln: University of Nebraska Press.

Klein, G. S. (1958). Cognitive control and motivation. In G. Lindzey (Ed.), *Assessment of human motives.* New York: Rinehart.

Kleinknecht, R. A., Mahoney, E. R., & ALexander, L. D. (1987). Psychosocial and demographic correlates of temporomandibular disorders and related symptoms: An assessment of community and clinical findings. *Pain, 29,* 313–324.

Klonoff, H. (1971). Head injuries in children: Predisposing factors, accident conditions, accident proneness, and sequelae. *American Journal of Public Health, 61,* 2405–2417.

Klonoff, H., Crockett, D. D., & Clark, C. (1984). Head injuries in children: A model for predicting course of recovery and prognosis. In R. E. Tarter & G. Goldstein (Eds.), *Advances in clinical neuropsychology* (vol. 2). New York: Plenum.

Klonoff, P. S., Costa, L. D., & Snow, W. G. (1986). Predictors and indicators of quality of life in patients with closed head injury. *Journal of Clinical and Experimental Neuropsychology, 8,* 469–485.

Kolb, B., & Whishaw, I. Q. (1985). *Fundamentals of human neuropsychology* (2nd ed.). New York: Freeman.

Kolb, L. C. (1987). A neuropsychological hypothesis explaining posttraumatic stress disorders. *American Journal of Psychiatry, 144*, 989–995.

Kosten, T. A., Kosten, T. R., & Rounsaville, B. J. (1989). Personality disorders in opiate addicts show prognostic specificity. *Journal of Substance Abuse Treatment, 6*, 163–168.

Kottler, J. A. (1991). *The compleat therapist*. San Francisco: Jossey-Bass.

Kottler, J. A. (1992). *Compassionate therapy: Working with difficult clients*. San Francisco: Jossey-Bass.

Kramlinger, K. G., Swanson, D. W., & Maruta, T. (1983). Are patients with chronic pain depressed? *American Journal of Psychiatry, 140*, 747–749.

Krapnick, J. L., & Horowitz, M. J. (1981). Stress response syndromes. *Archives of General Psychiatry, 38*, 428–435.

Kreutzer, J. S., Doberty, K. R., Harris, J. A., & Zasler, N. D. (1990). Alcohol use among persons with traumatic brain injury. *Journal of Head Trauma Rehabilitation, 5*, 9–20.

Kreutzer, J. S., Marwitz, J. H., & Wehman, P. H. (1991). Substance abuse assessment and treatment in vocational rehabilitation for persons with brain injury. *Journal of Head Trauma Rehabilitation, 6*, 12–23.

Kreutzer, J. S., Wehman, P. H., Harris, J. A., Burns, C. T., & Young, H. F. (1991). Substance abuse and crime patterns among persons with traumatic brain injury referred for supported employment. *Brain Injury, 5*, 177–187.

Krishnan, R. R. K., France, R. D., Pelton, S., McCann, U. D., Davidson, J., & Urban, B. J. (1985). Chronic pain and depression: I. Classification of depression in chronic low back pain patients. *Pain, 22*, 279–287.

Krynicki, V. E. (1978). Cerebral dysfunction in repetitively assaultive adolescents. *Journal of Nervous and Mental Disease, 166*, 59–67.

Kupke, T., & O'Brien, W. (1985). Neuropsychological impairment and behavioral limitations exhibited within an alcohol treatment program. *Journal of Clinical and Experimental Neuropsychology, 7*, 292–304.

Kurtzke, J. F., & Kurland, L. T. (1985). The epidemiology of neurologic disease. In A. B. Baker & L. H. Baker (Eds.), *Clinical neurology* (vol. 4, pp. 1–143). New York: Harper & Row.

Kwentus, J., Hart, R., Peck, E., & Kornstein, S. (1985). Psychiatric complications of closed head trauma. *Psychosomatics, 26*, 8–17.

Lam, C. S., Priddy, D. A., & Johnson, P. (1991). Neuropsychological indicators of employability following traumatic brain injury. *Rehabilitation Counseling Bulletin, 31*, 68–74.

Landrum, J. W., & Windham, G. O. (1981). A comparison of DWI repeaters and nonrepeaters in a level I rehabilitation program. *Journal of Alcohol and Drug Education, 26*, 11–23.

Langley, M. J., Lindsay, W. P., Lam, C. S., & Priddy, D. A. (1990). A comprehensive alcohol abuse treatment programme for persons with traumatic brain injury. *Brain Injury, 4*, 77–86.

Leber, W. R., Parsons, O. A., & Nichols, N. (1985). Neuropsychological test results are related to ratings of men alcoholics' therapeutic progress: A replicated study. *Journal of Studies on Alcohol, 46*, 116–121.

Lees-Haley, P. (1987). Mild head injury. *Trial*, November, 83–86.

Leestma, J. E. (1991). Neuropathology and pathophysiology of trauma and toxicity. In H. O. Doerr & A. S. Carlin (Eds.), *Forensic neuropsychology* (pp. 45–69). New York: Guilford.

Leftoff, S. (1983). Psychopathology in light of brain injury: A case study. *Journal of Clinical Neuropsychology, 5*, 51–63.

Lehr, E. (1990). *Psychological management of traumatic brain injuries in children and adolescents*. Rockville, MD: Aspen.

Leichtman, M. (1992a). Psychotherapeutic interventions with brain-injured children and their families: I. Diagnosis and treatment planning. *Bulletin of the Menninger Clinic, 56*, 321–337.

Leichtman, M. (1992b). Psychotherapeutic interventions with brain-injured children and their families: II. Psychotherapy. *Bulletin of the Menninger Clinic, 56*, 338–360.

Leininger, B. E., Gramling, S. E., Farrell, A. D., Kreutzer, J. S., & Peck, E. A. (1990). Neuropsychological deficits in symptomatic minor head injury patients after concussion and mild concussion. *Journal of Neurology, Neurosurgery, and Psychiatry, 53*, 293–296.

Levin, H. S. (1990). Pioneers in research on the behavioral sequelae of head injury. *Journal of Clinical and Experimental Neuropsychology, 13*, 1–22.

Levin, H. S., Benton, A. L., & Grossman, R. G. (Eds.) (1982). *Neurobehavioral consequences of closed head injury*. New York: Oxford University Press.

Levin, H. S., & Grossman, R. G. (1978). Behavioral sequelae of closed head injury. *Archives of Neurology, 35*, 720–727.

Levin, H. S., Mattis, S., Ruff, R., Eisenberg, H., Marshall, L., Tabaddor, K., High, W., & Frankowski, R. (1987). Neurobehavioral outcome following minor head injury: A three-center study. *Journal of Neurosurgery, 66*, 324–343.

Levine, M. J. (1988). Issues in neurobehavioral assessment of mild head injury. *Cognitive Rehabilitation, 6*(2), 14–20.

Lewis, F. D., Nelson, J., Nelson, C., & Reusink, P. (1988). Effects of three feedback contingencies on the socially inappropriate talk of a brain-injured adult. *Behavior Therapy, 19*, 203–211.

Lewis, L., Allen, J. G., & Frieswyk, S. (1983). The assessment of interacting organic and functional factors in a psychiatric population. *Clinical Neuropsychology, 5*, 65–68.

Lewis, L., & Rosenberg, S. J. (1990). Psychoanalytic psychotherapy with brain-injured adult psychiatric patients. *Journal of Nervous and Mental Disease, 178*, 69–77.

Lezak, M. D. (1978). Living with the characterologically altered brain injured patient. *Journal of Clinical Psychiatry, 39*, 592–598.

Lezak, M. D. (1983). *Neuropsychological assessment* (2nd ed.). New York: Oxford University Press.

Lezak, M. D. (1988). Brain damage is a family affair. *Journal of Clinical and Experimental Neuropsychology, 10*, 111–123.

Lishman, W. A. (1973). The psychiatric sequelae of head injury: A review. *Psychological Medicine, 3*, 304–318.

Lishman, W. A. (1978). *Organic psychiatry: The psychological consequences of cerebral disorder*. London: Blackwell.

Lishman, W. A. (1988). Physiogenesis and psychogenesis in the "post-concussional syndrome." *British Journal of Psychiatry, 153*, 460–469.

Livingston, M. G. (1987). Head injury: The relatives' response. *Brain Injury, 1*, 33–39.

Livingston, M. G., & Brooks, N. (1988). The burden on families of the brain-injured: A review. *Journal of Head Trauma Rehabilitation, 3*(4), 6–15.

Livingston, M. G., Brooks, N., & Bond, M. R. (1985a). Three months after severe head injury: Psychiatric and social impact on relatives. *Journal of Neurology, Neurosurgery, and Psychiatry, 48*, 870–875.

Livingston, M. G., Brooks, N., & Bond, M. R. (1985b). Patient outcome in the year following severe head injury, and relatives' psychiatric and social functioning. *Journal of Neurology, Neurosurgery, and Psychiatry, 48*, 876–881.

London, P. S. (1967). Some observations on the course of events after severe injury of the head. *Annals of the Royal College of Surgeons, 41*, 460–479.

Ludwig, A. M. (1985). Cognitive processes associated with "spontaneous" recovery from alcoholism. *Journal of Studies on Alcohol, 46*, 53–58.

Luria, A. R. (1973). *The working brain: An introduction to neuropsychology*. New York: Basic Books.

Luria, A. R. (1980). *Higher cortical functions in man* (2nd ed.). New York: Basic Books.

Macciocchi, S. N., Ranseen, J. D., & Schmitt, F. A. (1989). The relationship between neuropsychological impairment in alcoholics and treatment outcome at one year. *Archives of Clinical Neuropsychology, 4*, 365–370.

Mandelberg, I. A., & Brooks, D. N. (1975). Cognitive recovery after severe head injury: I. Serial testing on the Wechsler Adult Intelligence Scale. *Journal of Neurology, Neurosurgery, and Psychiatry, 38*, 1121–1126.

Mark, V. H., & Ervin, F. R. (1970). *Violence and the brain*. New York: Harper & Row.

Markwalder, T. (1981). Chronic subdural hematomas: A review. *Journal of Neurosurgery, 54*, 637–645.

Marlatt, G. A., & Gordon, J. R. (1980). Determinants of relapse: Implications for the maintenance of behavior change. In P. O. Davidson & S. M. Davidson (Eds.), *Behavioral medicine: Changing health lifestyles* (pp. 410–452). New York: Brunner/Mazel.

Marlatt, G. A., & Gordon, J. R. (Eds.) (1985). *Relapse prevention: Maintenance strategies in the treatment of addictive behaviors*. New York: Guilford.

Marsh, N. V., & Knight, R. G. (1991). Behavioral assessment of social competence following severe head injury. *Journal of Clinical and Experimental Neuropsychology, 13*, 729–740.

Martland, H. S. (1928). Punch drunk. *Journal of the American Medical Association, 91*, 1103–1107.

Masterson, J. F. (1988). *The search for the real self: Unmasking the personality disorders of our age*. New York: Free Press.

Mattson, A. J., & Levin, H. S. (1990). Frontal lobe dysfunction following closed head injury. *Journal of Nervous and Mental Disease, 178*, 282–291.

McClellan, A. T. (1986). "Psychiatric severity" as a predictor of outcome from substance abuse treatments. In R. E. Meyer (Ed.), *Psychopathology and addictive disorders* (pp. 97–139). New York: Guilford.

McFie, J. (1975). *Assessment of organic intellectual impairment*. New York: Academic Press.

McKinlay, W. W., Brooks, D. V., & Bond, M. R. (1983). Post-concussional symptoms, financial compensation, and outcome of severe blunt head injury. *Journal of Neurology, Neurosurgery, and Psychiatry, 46*, 1084–1091.

McKinlay, W. W., Brooks, N., Bond, M., Martinage, D. P., & Marshall, M. M. (1981). The short-term outcome of severe head injury as reported by relatives of the injured persons. *Journal of Neurology, Neurosurgery, and Psychiatry, 44*, 527–533.

McKinlay, W. W., & Hickox, A. (1988). How can families help in the rehabilitation of the head injured? *Journal of Head Trauma Rehabilitation, 3*(4), 64–72.

McLaughlin, A. M., & Schaffer, V. (1985). Rehabilitate or remold? Family involvement in head trauma recovery. *Cognitive Rehabilitation, 3*(1), 14–17.

McMordie, W. R. (1988). Twenty-year follow-up of the prevailing opinion on the posttraumatic or postconcussional syndrome. *The Clinical Neuropsychologist, 2*, 198–212.

McNab, I. (1964). Acceleration injuries of the cervical spine. *Journal of Joint and Bone Surgery, 46A*, 1797–1799.

McQueen, J., & Posey, J. (1975). Changes in intracranial pressure and brain hydration during acute ethanolism. *Surgical Neurology, 4*, 375–379.

Mechanic, D., & Angel, R. I. (1987). Some factors associated with the report and evaluation of back pain. *Journal of Health and Social Behavior, 28*, 131–139.

Meier, M., Benton, A., & Diller, L. (Eds.) (1987). *Neuropsychological rehabilitation*. New York: Guilford.

Mendelson, G. (1982). Not "cured by a verdict." Effect of legal settlement on compensation claimants. *Medical Journal of Australia, 2*, 132–134.

Merskey, H. (1980). The role of the psychiatrist in the investigation and treatment of pain. *Pain, 8*, 249–260.

Merskey, H., & Trimble, M. (1979). Personality, sexual adjustment, and brain lesions, in patients with conversion symptoms. *American Journal of Psychiatry, 136*, 179–182.

Merskey, H., & Woodforde, J. M. (1972). Psychiatric sequelae of minor head injury. *Brain, 95*, 521–528.

Miller, H. (1961). Accident neurosis. *British Medical Journal, 1*, 919–925, 992–998.

Miller, L. (1984a). Neuropsychological concepts of somatoform disorders. *International Journal of Psychiatry in Medicine, 14*, 31–46.

Miller, L. (1984b). Hemispheric asymmetry of cognitive processing in schizophrenics. *Psychological Reports, 55*, 932–934.

Miller, L. (1985). Neuropsychological assessment of substance abusers: Review and recommendations. *Journal of Substance Abuse Treatment, 2,* 5–17.

Miller, L. (1986a). Some comments on cerebral hemispheric models of consciousness. *Psychoanalytic Review, 73,* 129–144.

Miller, L. (1986b). The subcortex, frontal lobes, and psychosis. *Schizophrenia Bulletin, 12,* 340–341.

Miller, L. (1986c). "Narrow localizationism" in psychiatric neuropsychology. *Psychological Medicine, 16,* 729–734.

Miller, L. (1986–87). Is alexithymia a disconnection syndrome? A neuropsychological perspective. *International Journal of Psychiatry in Medicine, 16,* 199–209.

Miller, L. (1987). Neuropsychology of the aggressive psychopath: An integrative review. *Aggressive Behavior, 13,* 119–140.

Miller, L. (1988a). Neurocognitive aspects of remorse: Impulsivity-compulsivity-reflectivity. In E. M. Stern (Ed.), *Psychotherapy of the remorseful patient* (pp. 63–76). New York: Haworth.

Miller, L. (1988b). Neuropsychological perspectives on delinquency. *Behavioral Sciences and the Law, 6,* 409–428.

Miller, L. (1988c). Ego autonomy, creativity, and cognitive style: A neuropsychodynamic approach. *Psychiatric Clinics of North America, 11,* 383–387.

Miller, L. (1989a). On the neuropsychology of dreams. *Psychoanalytic Review, 76,* 375–401.

Miller, L. (1989b). Neuropsychology, personality, and substance abuse: Implications for head injury rehabilitation. *Cognitive Rehabilitation, 7*(5), 26–31.

Miller, L. (1990a). Neuropsychodynamics of alcoholism and addiction: Personality, psychopathology, and cognitive style. *Journal of Substance Abuse Treatment, 7,* 31–49.

Miller, L. (1990b). Litigating the head trauma case: Issues and answers for attorneys and their clients. *Cognitive Rehabilitation, 8*(3), 8–12.

Miller, L. (1990c). Chronic pain complicating head injury: Recommendations for clinicians. *Cognitive Rehabilitation, 8*(5), 12–19.

Miller, L. (1990d). Neurobehavioral syndromes and the private practitioner: An introduction to evaluation and treatment. *Psychotherapy in Private Practice, 8*(3), 1–12.

Miller, L. (1990e). Major syndromes of aggressive behavior following head injury: An introduction to evaluation and treatment. *Cognitive Rehabilitation, 8*(6), 14–19.

Miller, L. (1990f). *Inner natures: Brain, self, and personality.* New York: St. Martin's Press.

Miller, L. (1991a). Psychotherapy of the brain-injured patient: Principles and practice. *Journal of Cognitive Rehabilitation, 9*(2), 24–30.

Miller, L. (1991b). Significant others: Treating brain injury in the family context. *Journal of Cognitive Rehabilitation, 9*(3), 16–25.

Miller, L. (1991c). Brain and self: Toward a neuropsychodynamic model of ego autonomy and personality. *Journal of the American Academy of Psychoanalysis, 19,* 213–234.

Miller, L. (1991d). The "other" brain injuries: Psychotherapeutic issues with stroke and brain tumor survivors. *Journal of Cognitive Rehabilitation, 9*(5), 10–16.

Miller, L. (1991e). Predicting relapse and recovery in alcoholism and addiction: Neuropsychology, personality, and cognitive style. *Journal of Substance Abuse Treatment, 8,* 277–291.

Miller, L. (1991f). *Freud's brain: Neuropsychodynamic foundations of psychoanalysis.* New York: Guilford.

Miller, L. (1992a). The primitive personality and the organic personality: A neuropsychodynamic model for evaluation and treatment. *Psychoanalytic Psychology, 9,* 93–109.

Miller, L. (1992b). Cognitive rehabilitation, cognitive therapy, and cognitive style: Toward an integrative model of personality and psychotherapy. *Journal of Cognitive Rehabilitation, 10*(1), 18–29.

Miller, L. (1992c). Back to the future: Legal, vocational, and quality-of-life issues in the long-term adjustment of the brain-injured patient. *Journal of Cognitive Rehabilitation, 10*(5), 14–20.

Miller, L. (1992d). When the best help is self-help, or, Everything you always wanted to know about brain injury support groups. *Journal of Cognitive Rehabilitation, 10*(6), 14–17.

Miller, L. (1992e). Neuropsychology, personality, and substance abuse in the head injury case: Clinical and forensic issues. *International Journal of Law and Psychiatry, 15*, 303–316.

Miller, L. (1993a). Toxic torts: Clinical, neuropsychological and forensic aspects of chemical and electrical injuries. *Journal of Cognitive Rehabilitation, 11*(1).

Miller, L. (1993b). The "trauma" of head trauma: Clinical, neuropsychological, and forensic aspects of posttraumatic stress disorder in brain injury. *Journal of Cognitive Rehabilitation, 11*(2).

Miller, L. (in press a). Psychotherapy of the chronic pain patient: I. Clinical syndromes and sources. *Psychotherapy In Private Practice*.

Miller, L. (in press b). Psychotherapy of the chronic pain patient: II. Treatment principles and practices. *Psychotherapy In Private Practice*.

Miller, L. (in press c). Psychotherapeutic approaches to chronic pain. *Psychotherapy*.

Miller, L. (in press d). Who are the best psychotherapists? Qualities of the effective practitioner. *Psychotherapy in Private Practice*.

Miller, T. W., & Kraus, R. F. (1990). An overview of chronic pain. *Hospital and Community Psychiatry, 41*, 433–440.

Miller, W. (1983). Motivational interviewing with problem drinkers. *Behavioural Psychotherapy, 11*, 147–172.

Miller, W. (1988). Motivational interviewing with problem drinkers: II. The Drinker's Checkup as a preventive intervention. *Behavioural Psychotherapy, 16*, 251–268.

Miller, W. (1989). Increasing motivation for change. In R. K. Hester & W. R. Miller (Eds.), *Handbook of alcoholism treatment approaches: Effective alternatives* (pp. 67–80). New York: Pergamon.

Millon, T. (1981). *Disorders of personality: DSM-III, Axis II*. New York: Wiley.

Millon, T. (1990). *Toward a new personology: An evolutionary model*. New York: Wiley.

Millspaugh, J. A. (1937). Dementia pugilistica. *US Naval Medical Bulletin, 35*, 297–303.

Monroe, R. R. (1982). Limbic ictus and atypical psychoses. *Journal of Nervous and Mental Disease, 170*, 711–716.

Montgomery, E. A., Fenton, G. W., McClelland, R. J., MacFlynn, G., & Rutherford, W. H. (1991). The psychobiology of minor head injury. *Psychological Medicine, 21*, 375–384.

Monti, P. M., Abrams, D. B., Kadden, R. M., & Cooney, N. L. (1989). *Treating alcohol dependence: A coping skills training guide*. New York: Guilford.

Mortimer, J. A., French, L. R., Hutton, J. T., & Schuman, L. M. (1985). Head injury as a risk factor for Alzheimer's disease. *Neurology, 35*, 264–267.

Motet-Grigoras, C., & Schuckit, M. A. (1986). Depression and substance abuse in handicapped young men. *Journal of Clinical Psychiatry, 47*, 234–237.

Nadell, J. (1991). Towards an existential psychotherapy with the traumatically brain-injured patient. *Journal of Cognitive Rehabilitation, 9*(6), 8–13.

Najeson, T., Mendelson, L., Schecter, I., David, C., Mintz, N., & Grosswater, Z. (1974). Rehabilitation after severe head injury. *Scandinavian Journal of Rehabilitation Medicine, 6*, 5–14.

Naliboff, B. D., Cohen, M. J., & Yellen, A. N. (1983). Frequency of MMPI profile types in three chronic illness populations. *Journal of Clinical Psychology, 39*, 843–847.

Nathan, W. A. (1992). Integrated multimodal therapy of children with attention deficit hyperactivity disorder. *Bulletin of the Menninger Clinic, 56*, 283–312.

National Head Injury Foundation (1988). *National Head Injury Foundation-Professional Council Substance Abuse Task Force white paper*. Southborough, MA: Author.

Nauta, W. J. (1971). The problem of the frontal lobe: A reinterpretation. *Journal of Psychiatric Research, 8*, 167–187.

Newton, M. R., Greenwood, R. J., Britton, K. E., Charlesworth, M., Nimmon, C. C., Carroll, M. J., & Dolke, G. (1992). A study comparing SPECT with CT and MRI after closed head injury. *Journal of Neurology, Neurosurgery, and Psychiatry, 55*, 92–94.

Novack, T. A., Roth, D. L., & Boll, T. J. (1988). Treatment alternatives following mild head injury. *Rehabilitation Counseling Bulletin, 31*, 313–324.

Oddy, M. (1984). Head injury and social adjustment. In N. Brooks (Ed.), *Closed head injury: Psychological, social, and family consequences* (pp. 108–122). New York: Oxford University Press.

Oddy, M., & Humphrey, M. (1980). Social recovery during the year following severe head injury. *Journal of Neurology, Neurosurgery, and Psychiatry, 43*, 798–802.

O'Hara, C. (1988). Emotional adjustment following minor head injury. *Cognitive Rehabilitation, 6*(2), 26–33.

Olsnes, B. T. (1989). Neurobehavioral findings in whiplash patients with long-lasting symptoms. *Acta Neurologica Scandinavica, 80*, 584–588.

Oradei, D. M., & Waite, N. S. (1974). Group psychotherapy with stroke patients during the immediate recovery phase. *American Journal of Orthopsychiatry, 44*, 386–395.

Osterweis, M., Kleinman, A., & Mechanic, D. (1987). *Pain and disability: Clinical, behavioral, and public policy perspectives.* Washington, DC: National Academy Press.

Packard, R. (1979). What does the headache patient want? *Headache, 19*, 370–374.

Panting, A., & Merry, P. (1972). The long-term rehabilitation of severe head injuries with particular reference to the need for social and medical support for the patient's family. *Rehabilitation, 38*, 33–37.

Parker, N. (1979). Malingering: A dangerous diagnosis. *Medical Journal of Australia, 1*, 568–569.

Parker, R. S. (1987). Recognizing employees who have suffered brain damage. *EAP Digest*, March/April, 55–59.

Parker, R. S. (1988). Brain-damaged victims: They may not be the best witnesses for themselves. *Trial*, February, 68–73.

Parker, R. S. (1990). *Traumatic brain injury and neuropsychological impairment: Sensorimotor, cognitive, emotional, and adaptive problems of children and adults.* New York: Springer-Verlag.

Parsons, O. A. (1987a). Neuropsychological consequences of alcohol abuse: Many questions — some answers. In O. A. Parsons, N. Butters, & P. E. Nathan (Eds.), *Neuropsychology of alcoholism: Implications for diagnosis and treatment* (pp. 153–175). New York: Guilford.

Parsons, O. A. (1987b). Do neuropsychological deficits predict alcoholics' treatment course and recovery? In O. A. Parsons, N. Butters, & P. E. Nathan (Eds.), *Neuropsychology of alcoholism: Implications for diagnosis and treatment* (pp. 273–290). New York: Guilford.

Pasnau, R. O., Fawzy, F. I., & Lansky, M. R. (1981). Organic brain syndrome and the family. In M. R. Lansky (Ed.), *Family therapy and major psychopathology* (pp. 301–324). New York: Grune & Stratton.

Pavlov, I. (1927). *Conditioned reflexes.* New York: Oxford University Press.

Peele, S. (1989). *Diseasing of America: Addiction treatment out of control.* Lexington, MA: Lexington Books.

Perrott, S., Taylor, H. G., & Montes, J. L. (1991). Neuropsychological sequelae, familial stress, and environmental adaptation following pediatric head injury. *Developmental Neuropsychology, 7*, 69–86.

Peters, L. C., Stambrook, M., & Moore, A. D. (1990). Psychosocial sequelae of closed head injury: Effects on marital relationship. *Brain Injury, 4*, 39–47.

Philips, H. C. (1988). *The psychological management of chronic pain: A treatment manual.* New York: Springer.

Pilowsky, I. (1985). Cryptotrauma and "accident neurosis." *British Journal of Psychiatry, 147*, 310–311.

Pilowsky, I. (1992). Minor accidents and major psychological trauma: A clinical perspective. *Stress Medicine, 8*, 77–78.

Pilowsky, I., Chapman, C. R., & Bonica, J. J. (1977). Pain, depression, and illness behavior in a pain clinic population. *Pain, 4*, 183–192.

Pincus, J. H., & Tucker, G. J. (1978). *Behavioral neurology.* New York: Oxford University Press.

Pine, F. (1985). *Developmental theory and clinical process*. New Haven, CT: Yale University Press.

Pine, F. (1990). *Drive, ego, object, and self: A synthesis for clinical work*. New York: Basic Books.

Pipitone, P. (1992). Computers in cognitive rehabilitation today. *Headlines*, May/June, p. 26.

Pollens, R. D., McBratnie, B. P., & Burton, P. L. (1988). Beyond cognition: Executive functions in closed head injury. *Cognitive Rehabilitation, 6*(5), 26–32.

Post, R. M. (1980). Intermittent versus continuous stimulation: Effect of time interval on the development of sensitization or tolerance. *Life Sciences, 26*, 1275–1282.

Posthuma, A., & Wild, U. (1988). Use of neuropsychological testing in mild traumatic head injuries. *Cognitive Rehabilitation, 6*(2), 22–24.

Potter, J. M. (1967). Head injuries today. *Postgraduate Medical Journal, 43*, 574–581.

Potter-Efron, R. T., & Potter-Efron, P. S. (1991). *Anger, alcoholism, and addiction: Treating individuals, couples, and families*. New York: W. W. Norton.

Povlishock, J. T. (1992). Traumatically induced axonal injury: Pathogenesis and pathobiological implications. *Brain Pathology, 2*, 1–12.

Powell, B. J., Penick, E. C., Othmer, E., Bingham, S. F., & Rice, A. F. (1982). Prevalence of additional psychiatric syndromes among male alcoholics. *Journal of Clinical Psychiatry, 43*, 404–407.

Prigatano, G. P., Altman, I. M., & O'Brien, K. P. (1990). Behavioral limitations that traumatic brain-injured patients tend to underestimate. *The Clinical Neuropsychologist, 4*, 163–176.

Prigatano, G. P., Fordyce, D. J., Zeiner, H. K., Roueche, J. R., Pepping, M., & Wood, B. C. (1984). Neuropsychological remediation after closed head injury in young adults. *Journal of Neurology, Neurosurgery, and Psychiatry, 47*, 505–513.

Prigatano, G. P., Fordyce, D. J., Zeiner, H. K., Roueche, J. R., Pepping, M., & Wood, B. C. (1986). *Neuropsychological rehabilitation after brain injury*. Baltimore, MD: Johns Hopkins.

Prigatano, G. P., & Klonoff, P. S. (1988). Psychotherapy and neuropsychological assessment after brain injury. *Journal of Head Trauma Rehabilitation, 3*, 45–56.

Prigatano, G. P., Klonoff, P. S., & Bailey, I. (1987). Psychosocial adjustment associated with brain injury: Statistics BNI rehabilitation must beat. *BNI Quarterly, 3*, 10–17.

Prigatano, G. P., O'Brien, K. P., & Klonoff, P. S. (1988). The clinical management of paranoid delusions in postacute traumatic brain-injured patients. *Journal of Head Trauma Rehabilitation, 3*, 23–32.

Racine, R. (1978). Kindling: The first decade. *Neurosurgery, 3*, 234–252.

Rambo, K. C., & Cohen, M. (1990). The legal field and the health care professional: Weathering involvement with a patient's lawsuit. *Cognitive Rehabilitation, 8*(3), 18–21.

Ranseen, J. D. (1990). Positive personality change following traumatic head injury: Four case studies. *Cognitive Rehabilitation, 8*(2), 8–12.

Rao, N., Jellink, H. M., Harvey, R. F., & Flynn, M. M. (1984). Computerized tomography head scans as predictors of rehabilitation outcome. *Archives of Physical Medicine and Rehabilitation, 65*, 18–20.

Raskin, N. H., & Appenzeller, O. (1980). *Headache*. Philadelphia: Saunders.

Reich, J., Tupin, J. P., & Abramowitz, S. I. (1983). Psychiatric diagnosis of chronic pain patients. *American Journal of Psychiatry, 140*, 1495–1498.

Resnick, P. J. (1988). Malingering of post-traumatic disorders. In R. Rogers (Ed.), *Clinical assessment of malingering and deception* (pp. 84–103). New York: Guilford.

Richman, A. (1985). Human risk factors in alcohol-related crashes. *Journal of Studies on Alcohol, 10*, 21–31.

Rimel, R. W., Giordani, B., Barth, J. T., Boll, T. J., & Jane, J. A. (1981). Disability caused by minor head injury. *Neurosurgery, 9*, 221–228.

Robbins, M. (1989). Primitive personality organization as an interpersonally adaptive modification of cognition and affect. *International Journal of Psycho-Analysis, 70*, 443–459.

Robins, L. N., Helzer, J. E., Weissman, M. M., Orvaschel, H., Gruenberg, E., Burke, J. D.,

& Regier, D. A. (1984). Lifetime prevalence of specific psychiatric disorders in three sites. *Archives of Clinical Psychiatry, 41*, 949–958.

Robinson, R. G. (1986). Post-stroke mood disorders. *Hospital Practice, 21*, 83–89.

Robinson, R. G., Kubos, K. L., Starr, L. B., Rao, K., & Price, T. R. (1984). Mood disorders in stroke patients: Importance of location of lesion. *Brain, 107*, 81–93.

Robinson, R. G., Lipsey, J. R., & Price, T. R. (1985). Diagnosis and clinical management of post-stroke depression. *Psychosomatics, 26*, 769–778.

Romano, M. D. (1974). Family response to traumatic head injury. *Scandinavian Journal of Rehabilitation Medicine, 4*, 1–5.

Ron, M. A., Acker, W., Shaw, G. K., & Lishman, W. A. (1982). Computerized tomography of the brain in chronic alcoholism: A survey and followup study. *Brain, 105*, 497–514.

Rosenbaum, A., & Hoge, S. K. (1989). Head injury and marital agression. *American Journal of Psychiatry, 146*, 1048–1051.

Rosenbaum, M., & Najeson, T. (1976). Changes in life pattern and symptoms of low mood as reported by wives of severely brain-injured soldiers. *Journal of Consulting and Clinical Psychology, 44*, 881–886.

Rosenthal, M. (1987). Trauamtic head injury: Neurobehavioral consequences. In B. Caplan (Ed.), *Rehabilitation psychology desk reference* (pp. 37–64). Rockville, MD: Aspen.

Rosenthal, M., & Kaplan, K. I. (1986). Head injury rehabilitation: Psycholegal issues and roles for the rehabilitation psychologist. *Rehabilitation Psychology, 31*, 37–46.

Rosenthal, M., & Young, T. (1988). Effective family intervention after traumatic brain injury: Theory and practice. *Journal of Head Trauma Rehabilitation, 3*(4), 42–50.

Ross, E. D. (1981). The aprosodias: Functional-anatomic organization of language in the right hemisphere. *Archives of Neurology, 38*, 561–569.

Ross, E. D., Harvey, J. H., deLacoste-Utamsing, C., & Purdy, P. D. (1981). How the brain integrates affective and propositional language into a unified behavioral function: Hypothesis based on clinico-anatomical evidence. *Archives of Neurology, 38*, 745–748.

Ross, E. D., & Rush, A. J. (1981). Diagnosis and neuroanatomical correlates of depression in brain-damaged patients: Implications for a neurology of depression. *Archives of General Psychiatry, 38*, 1344–1354.

Ross, E. D., & Stewart, R. S. (1987). Pathological display of affect in patients with depression and right frontal brain damage: An alternative mechanism. *Journal of Nervous and Mental Disease, 175*, 165–172.

Ross, R. J., Cole, M., Thompson, J. S., & Kim, K. H. (1983). Boxers—computed tomography, EEG, and neurological evaluation. *Journal of the American Medical Association, 249*, 211–213.

Rounsaville, B. J., Dolinsky, Z. S., Babor, T. F., & Meyer, R. E. (1987). Psychopathology as a predictor of treatment outcome in alcoholics. *Archives of General Psychiatry, 44*, 505–513.

Rounsaville, B. J., & Kleber, H. D. (1986). Psychiatric disorders in opiate addicts: Preliminary findings on the course and interaction with program type. In R. E. Meyer (Ed.), *Psychopathology and addictive disorders* (pp. 140–168). New York: Guilford.

Roy, R. (1985). Family treatment for chronic pain: State of the art. *International Journal of Family Therapy, 7*, 297–309.

Rutter, M. (1980). Raised lead levels and impaired cognitive/behavioral functioning: A review of the evidence. *Developmental Medicine and Child Neurology, 22* (Suppl. 21).

Rutter, M., Chadwick, O., & Shaffer, D. (1983). Head injury. In M. Rutter (Ed.), *Developmental neuropsychiatry*. New York: Guilford.

Rutter, M., Chadwick, O., Shaffer, D., & Brown, G. (1980). A prospective study of children with head injuries: I. Design and methods. *Psychological Medicine, 10*, 633–645.

Ryan, C. M., Morrow, L. A., Bromet, E. J., Parkinson, D. K. (1987). Assessment of neuropsychological dysfunction in the workplace: Normative data from the Pittsburgh Occupational Exposures Test Battery. *Journal of Clinical and Experimental Neuropsychology, 9*, 665–679.

Sackheim, H. A., Greenberg, M. S., Weiman, A. L., Gur, R. C., Hungerbuhler, J. P., &

Geschwind, N. (1982). Hemispheric asymmetry in the expression of positive and negative emotions: Neurologic evidence. *Archives of Neurology, 39*, 210–218.

Salcman, M., & Kaplan, R. S. (1986). Intracranial tumors in adults. In A. R. Moossa, M. C. Robson, & S. C. Schimpff (Eds.), *Oncology.* Los Angeles: Williams & Wilkins.

Schuckit, M. A. (1972). The alcoholic woman: A literature review. *Psychiatry in Medicine, 3*, 37–43.

Schuckit, M. A. (1985). The clinical implications of primary diagnostic groups among alcoholics. *Archives of General Psychiatry, 42*, 1043–1049.

Schuckit, M. A. (1986). Genetic and clinical implications of alcoholism and affective disorder. *American Journal of Psychiatry, 143*, 140–147.

Schuckit, M. A., & Morrissey, E. R. (1976). Alcoholism in women: Some clinical and social perspectives with an emphasis on possible subtypes. In M. Greenblatt & M. A. Schuckit (Eds.), *Alcoholism problems in women and children* (pp. 5–35). New York: Grune & Stratton.

Schuckit, M. A., Pitts, F. N., Reich, T., King, L. J., & Winokur, G. (1969). Alcoholism: Two types of alcoholism in women. *Archives of General Psychiatry, 20*, 301–306.

Schutt, C. H., & Dohan, F. C. (1968). Neck injury to women in auto accidents. *Journal of the American Medical Association, 206*, 2689–2692.

Segalowitz, S. J., & Brown, D. (1991). Mild head injury as a source of developmental disabilities. *Journal of Learning Disabilities, 24*, 551–559.

Selzer, M. L., & Barton, E. (1977). The drunken driver: A psychosocial study. *Drug and Alcohol Dependence, 2*, 239–253.

Shapiro, D. (1965). *Neurotic styles.* New York: Basic Books.

Shapiro, D. (1989). *Psychotherapy of neurotic character.* New York: Basic Books.

Slagle, D. A. (1990). Psychiatric disorders following closed head injury: An overview of biopsychosocial factors in their etiology and management. *International Journal of Psychiatry in Medicine, 20*, 1–35.

Small, L. (1980). *Neuropsychodiagnosis in psychotherapy* (rev. ed.). New York: Brunner/ Mazel.

Soderstrom, C. A., & Cowley, R. A. (1987). A national alcohol and trauma center survey: Missed opportunities, failures of responsibility. *Archives of Surgery, 122*, 1067–1071.

Sparadeo, F. R., & Gill, D. (1989). Effects of prior alcohol use on head injury recovery. *Journal of Head Trauma Rehabilitation, 4*, 75–82.

Spellacy, F. (1978). Neuropsychological discrimination between violent and nonviolent men. *Journal of Clinical Psychiatry, 34*, 49–52.

Stambrook, M., Moore, A. D., Peters, L. C., Zubek, E., McBeath, S., & Friesen, I. C. (1991). Head injury and spinal cord injury: Differential effects on psychosocial functioning. *Journal of Clinical and Experimental Neuropsychology, 13*, 521–530.

Steinbok, P., & Thompson, G. (1978). Metabolic disturbances after head injury: Abnormalities of sodium and water balance with special reference to the effects of alcohol intoxication. *Neurosurgery, 3*, 9–15.

Sternbach, R. A. (1974). *Pain patients.* New York: Academic Press.

Sternbach, R. A. (1986). Pain and "hassles" in the United States: Findings of the Nuprin Pain Report. *Pain, 27*, 69–80.

Strauss, I., & Savitsky, N. (1934). Head injury: Neurologic and psychiatric aspects. *Archives of Neurology and Psychiatry, 31*, 893–954.

Strub, D. T., & Black, F. W. (1981). *Organic brain syndromes: An introduction to neurobehavioral disorders.* Philadelphia: F. A. Davis.

Strupp, H. H. (1989). Psychotherapy: Can the practitioner learn form the researcher? *American Psychologist, 44*, 717–724.

Stuss, D. T., & Benson, D. F. (1984). Neuropsychological studies of the frontal lobes. *Psychological Bulletin, 95*, 3–28.

Stuss, D. T., Gow, C. A., & Hetherington, C. R. (1992). "No longer Gage": Frontal lobe dysfunction and emotional changes. *Journal of Consulting and Clinical Psychology, 60*, 349–359.

Sulkava, R., Erkinluntti, T., & Palo, J. (1985). Head injuries in Alzheimer's disease and vascular dementia. *Neurology, 35*, 922–931.

Sutker, P. B., & Allain, A. N. (1987). Cognitive abstraction, shifting, and control: Clinical sample comparisons of psychopaths and nonpsychopaths. *Journal of Abnormal Psychology, 96*, 73–75.

Sweet, J. J., Newman, P., & Bell, B. (1992). Significance of depression in clinical neuropsychological assessment. *Clinical Psychology Review, 12*, 21–45.

Tankle, R. S. (1988). Application of neuropsychological test results to interdisciplinary cognitive rehabilitation with head injured adults. *Journal of Head Trauma Rehabilitation, 3*, 34–42.

Taphoorn, M. J. B., Heimans, J. J., Snoek, F. J., Lindeboom, J., Oosterink, B., Wolbers, J. G., & Karim, A. B. M. F. (1992). Assessment of quality of life in patients treated for low-grade glioma: A preliminary report. *Journal of Neurology, Neurosurgery, and Psychiatry, 55*, 372–376.

Tarsh, M. J., & Royston, C. (1985). A follow-up study of accident neurosis. *British Journal of Psychiatry, 146*, 18–25.

Tarter, R., & Edwards, K. (1985). Neuropsychology of alcoholism. In R. Tarter & D. Van Theil (Eds.), *Alcohol and the brain: Chronic effects*. New York: Plenum.

Tarter, R. E., Hegedus, A., & Gavaler, J. (1985). Hyperactivity in sons of alcoholics. *Journal of Studies on Alcohol, 46*, 259–261.

Tarter, R. E., Hegedus, A. M., Goldstein, G., Shelly, C., & Alterman, A. I. (1984). Adolescent sons of alcoholics: Neuropsychological and personality characteristics. *Alcoholism: Clinical and Experimental Research, 8*, 216–222.

Taylor, H., & Curran, N. M. (1985). *The Nuprin Pain Report*. New York: Louis Harris.

Teasdale, G., & Mendelow, D. (1984). Pathophysiology of head injuries. In N. Brooks (Ed.), *Closed head injury: Psychological, social, and family consequences* (pp. 4–36). New York: Oxford University Press.

Teuber, H. L., & Rudel, R. G. (1962). Behavior after cerebral lesions in children and adults. *Developmental Medicine and Child Neurology, 4*, 3–20.

Thomsen, I. V. (1974). The patient with severe head injury and his family. *Scandinavian Journal of Rehabilitation Medicine, 6*, 180–183.

Tobis, J. S., Puri, K. B., & Sheridan, J. (1982). Rehabilitation of the severely brain-injured patient. *Scandinavian Journal of Rehabilitation Medicine, 14*, 655–667.

Toglia, J. V., Rosenberg, P. E., & Ronis, M. L. (1970). Posttraumatic dizziness. *Archives of Otolaryngology, 92*, 485–492.

Trieschmann, R. G. (1984). The psychological aspects of spinal cord injury. In C. J. Golden (Ed.), *Current topics in rehabilitation psychology* (pp. 125–137). Orlando, FL: Grune & Stratton.

Tuchfield, B. S. (1981). Spontaneous remission in alcoholics: Empirical observations and theoretical implications. *Journal of Studies on Alcohol, 42*, 626–641.

Tunks, I. (1990). Is there a chronic pain syndrome? In S. Lipton (Ed.), *Advances in pain research and therapy*. New York: Raven Press.

Tuohima, P. (1978). Vestibular disturbances after acute mild head injury. *Acta Otolaryngologica* (Suppl. 359).

Turk, D. C., Meichenbaum, D., & Genest, M. (1983). *Pain and behavioral medicine: A cognitive-behavioral perspective*. New York: Guilford.

Turner, J. A., & Chapman, C. R. (1982). Psychological intervention for chronic pain: A critical review. II. Operant conditioning, hypnosis, and cognitive-behavioral therapy. *Pain, 12*, 23–46.

Urbach, J. R., & Culbert, J. P. (1991). Head injured patients and their children: Psychosocial consequences of a traumatic syndrome. *Psychosomatics, 32*, 24–33.

U.S. Bureau of the Census (1986). *Statistical abstract of the United States* (107th ed.). Washington, DC: U.S. Government Printing Office.

van der Kolk, C. J., & van der Kolk, J. K. (1990). Follow-up of persons with litigation-related injuries. *Journal of Rehabilitation*, October/November/December, 36–40.

van der Kolk, C. J., & Stewart, W. W. (1988). Characteristics of injured persons involved in litigation. *Vocational Evaluation and Work Adjustment Bulletin, 21*, 103–106.

Varney, N. R. (1990). Litigation concerning mild head injury. *Cognitive Rehabilitation, 8*(3), 30–33.

Vygotsky, L. (1962). *Thought and language.* Cambridge, MA: MIT Press.

Walsh, K. W. (1978). *Neuropsychology: A clinical approach.* London: Churchill Livingstone.

Ward, N. G., Bloom, V. L., & Friedel, R. O. (1979). The effectiveness of tricyclic antidepressants in the treatment of coexisting pain and depression. *Pain, 7*, 331–341.

Watzlawick, P., & Coyne, J. C. (1980). Depression following stroke: Brief problem-focused family treatment. *Family Process, 19*, 13–18.

Weddell, R., Oddy, M., & Jenkins, D. (1980). Social adjustment after rehabilitation: A two-year follow-up. *Psychological Medicine, 10*, 257–263.

Weiner, H. (1992). *Perturbing the organism: The biology of stressful experience.* Chicago, IL: University of Chicago Press.

Weisman, M. M., Meyers, J. K., & Harding, P. S. (1980). Prevalence of psychiatric heterogeneity of alcoholism in a United States urban community. *Journal of Studies on Alcohol, 41*, 672–681.

Wender, P. H. (1979). The concept of minimal brain dysfunction. In L. Bellak (Ed.), *Psychiatric aspects of minimal brain dysfunction in adults* (pp. 1–13). New York: Grune & Stratton.

Werman, D. S. (1984). *The practice of supportive psychotherapy.* New York: Brunner/Mazel.

Whitehouse, A. M., & Carey, J. L. (1991). Composition and concerns of a support group for families of individuals with brain injury. *Journal of Cognitive Rehabilitation, 9*(6), 26–29.

Wilkinson, D. A. (1987). CT scan and neuropsychological assessments of alcoholism. In O. A. Parsons, N. Butters, & P. E. Nathan (Eds.), *Neuropsychology of alcoholism: Implications for diagnosis and treatment* (pp. 76–102). New York: Guilford.

Williams, D. (1969). Neural factors related to habitual aggression: Consideration of the differences between those habitual aggressives and others who have committed crimes of violence. *Brain, 92*, 503–520.

Wilson, B. A. (1987). *Rehabilitation of memory.* New York: Guilford.

Wilson, J. T. L., Wiedmann, K. D., Hadley, D. M., Condon, B., Teasdale, G., & Brooks, D. N. (1988). Early and late magnetic resonance imaging and neuropsychological outcome after head injury. *Journal of Neurology, Neurosurgery, and Psychiatry, 51*, 391–396.

Winokur, G., Rimmer, J., & Reich, T. (1971). Alcoholism: IV. Is there more than one type of alcoholism? *British Journal of Psychiatry, 118*, 525–531.

Wood, R. L. (1984). Behavior disorders following severe brain injury: Their presentation and psychosocial management. In N. Brooks (Ed.), *Closed head injury: Psychological, social, and family consequences* (pp. 195–219). New York: Oxford University Press.

Wood, R. L. (1987). *Brain injury rehabilitation: A neurobehavioral approach.* Rockville, MD: Aspen.

Wood, R. L. (1988). Management of behavior disorders in a day treatment setting. *Journal of Head Trauma Rehabilitation, 3*, 53–61.

Woodward, J. E. (1982). Diagnosis and prognosis in compensation claims. *Annals of the Royal College of Surgery, 64*, 192–194.

Yalom, I. (1980). *Existential psychotherapy.* New York: Basic Books.

Yarnell, P. R., & Lynch, S. (1973). The "ding." Amnesic states in football trauma. *Neurology, 23*, 196–197.

Yeudall, L. T., Fromm-Auch, D., & Davies, P. (1982). Neuropsychological impairment in persistent delinquency. *Journal of Nervous and Mental Disease, 170*, 257–265.

Zastrow, C. (1988). What really causes psychotherapy change? *Journal of Independent Social Work*, Spring, 5–16.

Zelhart, P. F. (1972). Types of alcoholics and their relationship to traffic violations. *Quarterly Journal of Studies on Alcohol, 33*, 811–813.

Zelhart, P. F., & Schurr, B. C. (1977). People who drink while impaired: Issues in treating the drinking driver. In N. J. Estes & M. E. Heinemann (Eds.), *Alcoholism: Development, consequences, and intervention.* St. Louis, MO: Mosby.

Index

251